I am a lineaged Witch.

I'm proud of my choice of religion. Every day I thank Spirit for allowing me to participate in the divine dance of Earth.

Through the religion of WitchCraft I have brought about many of my greatest desires: Mick and I have managed to stay happily married for eighteen years; we have raised four healthy, well-adjusted children; I have enjoyed life to the fullest; and I have found myself.

I have discovered my strength. I have learned to use my talents. I have danced under the full moon. I have enjoyed the power of Spirit. I have become one with the universe.

Am I perfect? Absolutely not, but through the advantages of my Craft training I have always been able to find a solution to my problems. Rather than a passive bystander, I am an active participant in my life.

How do you feel right now—are you happy? Have you met many of your goals? Are you in a good relationship? Are you proud of your accomplishments?

If you answer "no" to any of these questions, then perhaps the religion of WitchCraft is for you, too . . . .

—The author

About the Author

Born in the heart of Pennsylvania, Silver has been interested in the magickal arts since childhood. "York, Cumberland, and Lancaster counties are alive with magick," she says.

"The best way for a magickal person to be accepted is to let people know you firsthand," explains Silver. "Once they get to know you and understand your personal values and principles, their attitudes on your alternative religious interests take a back seat. Let them know you—for you inside and the works that you do. It should be that way for everybody."

Born on September 11, 1956, Silver is a true Virgo: she adores making lists and arranging things. Definitely a lady of the 90s, she's hard to pin down. "I spend a great deal of my time with my four children," she says. "They come first in my life—everybody else, take a number!"

Silver teaches several magickal sciences as she tours the United States. She has attained Wiccan Priesthood, and is the Tradition Head of the Black Forest Clan, covering eight states, and an Elder of Family of Serphant Stone. She is the Director of the International Wiccan/Pagan Press Alliance. Be sure to visit her website at **http:www.silverravenwolf.com**.

To Write to the Author

If you wish to contact the author or would like more information about this book, please write to the author in care of Llewellyn Worldwide and we will forward your request. Both the author and publisher appreciate hearing from you and learning of your enjoyment of this book and how it has helped you. Llewellyn Worldwide cannot guarantee that every letter written to the author can be answered, but all will be forwarded. Please write to:

Silver RavenWolf
⁒ Llewellyn Worldwide
P.O. Box 64383, Dept. K721-8
St. Paul, MN 55164-0383, U.S.A.

Please enclose a self-addressed, stamped envelope for reply, or $1.00 to cover costs.
Silver cannot get back to you if you don't, so always include a SASE!
If outside U.S.A., enclose international postal reply coupon.

TO LIGHT A
SACRED FLAME

Practical WitchCraft for the Millennium

Silver RavenWolf

1999
Llewellyn Publications
St. Paul, Minnesota 55164-0383, U.S.A.

FIRST EDITION
Third printing, 1999

Cover art by Lisa Iris
Cover design by Michael David Matheny
Editing and book design by Rebecca Zins

Library of Congress Cataloging-in-Publication Data
RavenWolf, Silver, 1956–
    To light a sacred flame: practical witchcraft for the millennium / Silver Raven-Wolf.—1st ed.
          p.   cm.
    Includes bibliographical references and index.
    ISBN 1-56718-721-8 (trade paper)
    1. Witchcraft.   2. Neopaganism.   3. Magic.   I. Title.
BF1571.R37   1999
133.4'3—dc21   98-45978
                                                                                    CIP

Llewellyn Publications
A Division of Llewellyn Worldwide, Ltd.
P.O. Box 64383, Dept. K721-8
St. Paul, MN 55164-0383

Printed in the United States of America

This book is dedicated to Lord Serphant
(deceased 21 September 1996)
and the Family of Serpent Stone
(. . . and the Coven grows)

Ever changing, ever coiling
Ever circling, ever opening
Serpentine, your mystic coursing,
Take us to the center.
Down into the very core
Back around and down once more
Serpent changing back again
Three times three we dost descend.
Shed our skins of other days
shed our fears and other ways
Spiral spin the dance around
Draw the magick fire down.

—"THE SERPENT SPIRAL"
©1997 BY DAVID NORRIS

Other Books by Silver RavenWolf

To Stir A Magick Cauldron
To Ride A Silver Broomstick
American Folk Magick—Charms, Spells & Herbals
Angels—Companions in Magick
Beneath A Mountain Moon (fiction)
Witches Runes (formerly *The Rune Oracle)* (with Nigel Jackson)
Teen Witch

Forthcoming

Silver's Spells for Prosperity
Halloween—Customs, Recipes & Spells

Contents

Introduction:
Blazing the Path

Magick rituals are concerned with the basics of our existence.
Success, health, luck, money and love—the numerous problems in life
which can affect one's equilibrium.

—HERMAN SLATER, THE MAGICKAL FORMULARY

Did you know that you can practice successful, positive magick in minutes? Here, I'll prove it to you. Angelique, my oldest daughter, will time me. The very first thing I want you to do, before you read past the second paragraph, is to put this book down and go find a white candle. (Twenty-two seconds for me, how about you?) Hold it tightly in your hands and envision positive success and power coming into your life. (Thirteen seconds for me.) Ground and center: you know, take a deep breath, feel yourself relax, and feel your inner self stabilize. As you light the candle, say the following:

> *Great Mother, help me to open the pathways to my success.*
> *Great Father, assist me to remove any blocks that stand between*
> *myself and my goals. Thank you for my protection and the gift of*
> *focus. Thank you for the successes I have had before, and the successes*
> *that I know I am going to achieve. Thank you both for my success.*
> *With harm to none. So mote it be!*

(Another thirteen seconds on this end, but that's because I know this spell by heart. It's okay if it takes you longer to say the spell.) Stand back from the candle, then stretch your arms out in front of you, a little above your head, palms facing outward. Envision abundance and white light surrounding you. (Angelique says, "Twelve seconds this time!") Ground and center if you feel jumpy. My total act of positive magick and spiritual prayer amounted to sixty seconds out of my day.

Introduction

Whoa! Angelique also thinks I'm crazy because I asked her to follow me around and count. Eye roll. Sigh. Back to trimming the Yule tree for her.

Did you do the candle thing? No cheating! Tap. Tap. Tap. (I'm tapping my foot on the floor.) Now have you done it? *Well?* If you haven't done the candle thing, shame on you. How can I help you be the Little Witch That Could if you don't do the work? If you have, then I'm awfully proud of you, and you are ready to dive into my wonderful world of magick!

Welcome to *To Light A Sacred Flame: Practical WitchCraft for the Millennium*. Throughout you will find little sections entitled Magickal Minutes and Spiritual Seconds. These are ideas for practical magick and spirituality that you can add to your growing compendium of "material for my enlightenment." You might want to share many of these ideas with magickal and non-magickal friends and family, because you know as soon as someone finds out you're into magick, you get snagged into functioning as a magickal request line. Magickal Minutes and Spiritual Seconds might be a welcome relief to you, since all of us realize that none of us function as the great and powerful Oz. Well, at least not full time. Just kidding.

Included also are longer applications that you can modify and practice at will. My main goal in magickal writing is to create books that let you step into the mind of a practicing Witch with enough years of magick under her garter to give you the bare bones of how the metaphysical world works without filling your head with mumbo-jumbo or sidetracking your brain with promises that can't be kept.

Each day you spend as a magickal person can manifest into a bonanza of excellent karma. Just think of it. Every hour of every day, you have the power to pull the loving energy of the universe toward you. Not only can you create the spiritual light needed to uplift our planet, but you can infuse that light with your love and enhance your personal life in the process. By learning to manifest practical, magickal living, you can fulfill your most ardent desires as well as learn to help your fellow human beings in a quiet, meaningful manner.

Blazing the Path

Are you ready? You and I will blaze a path together along your road of harmony and enlightenment. Not all magickal practices bring a wonderful smack on the head (normally called an epiphany)—sometimes divine intervention moves into our lives like a sluggish river in the Georgia summertime. That's okay. If we got everything we wanted, and discovered everything we needed to know about ourselves right away, we might not be particularly happy. If we all sipped mint juleps on the porch of our estate in that Georgia heat, nothing important in life would ever get done. There are people to be healed, the environment to protect, children to be guided . . . well, you get the picture.

Every magickal application in this book went through rigorous testing by the members of the Black Forest Clan and myself. If something didn't work, fit, or whatever, I threw it out. I work divine magick all the time—I don't wait for things in my life to get so uncomfortable that I've got to magick my brains out at the last minute. (Though I must tell you, that's happened, believe me. We all get lazy.) You will find a great deal of preventative magick in these pages, but you'll find last-minute tricks too. If you want things to move smoothly in your life, you've got to get into the habit of planning and work on the ability to think fast on your magickal toes when the situation arises.

One of the compliments I have received from hundreds of readers is that I don't hide anything from you. No sugar-coated promises. No beguiling statements of what I can do for you. This book is about what *you* can do for yourself. If you've read my previous books, then you know what you are in for—basically, a lot of work. That's right. You don't think you're just going to snap your fingers and the boo-boo will be all better, do you? Nope. We're going to do it the hard way. I'm going to give you the same training I received. We're going to get right in there and we are going to pitch our magickal backs to the wall and start moving those nasty blocks in our lives. We're going to stomp that mountain down to the size of a molehill. And we're gonna succeed. For every problem, there is a solution. You can bet on it. The trick is finding that elusive answer.

Oh, yes, the Magickal Minute application I gave you on the first page. If your candle still burns, you may allow it to continue until finished; or, you can light the candle each day, say the words given, then put the candle out. When the candle can't be lit again, bury the candle end in your backyard. Some candles, I realize, burn the whole way with nothing left—that's fine too.

So, hitch up your magickal buggy. We're going to take a fantastic ride into the realms of the Mother and her consort, where we'll ford the streams of emotion, climb the heights of all we can be, and spread universal love under our feet. Come on, people, let's rock and roll. Time's a' wasting!

Are you an ember
Are you a flame?
Do you stand strong
Or melt in the rain?
Are you a weak link
or part of the chain?
Are you the solution
Or part of the blame?
For we are the People
and we are the change.

Who should be watching
Protecting the earth?
Is the land sacred
Or just so much dirt?
Your sisters and brothers,
Who helps with their pain?
Are you part of the filling
Or part of the drain?
For we are the Power
and we are the change.

When modern-day Witches
Are put to the flame
Do you go for more kindling
Or shout down in shame?
Do you just hang out
When others are hanged?
Do you make a difference
Or just stay the same?
Are you part of the problem
Or part of the change?

For we are the People
We are the Power
We are the Change.

—"EMBER OR FLAME"
©1997 BY DAVID NORRIS

1

As the World Coven Grows

The future of the world lies in your hands. By living a practical magickal life, you can empower yourself and others every single day. Humans need to actively participate in the world, helping ourselves and others as much as we can. This participation makes us feel wanted, loved, and in balance with all things. If we bury our minds, we deaden our souls and remove the opportunities presented to us at the hour of our birth.

I am a lineaged Witch. I'm proud of my choice of religion. Every day I thank Spirit for allowing me to participate in the divine dance of Earth. Through the religion of WitchCraft I have brought about many of my greatest desires: Mick and I have managed to stay happily married for eighteen years; we have raised four healthy, well-adjusted children; I have enjoyed life to the fullest; and I have found myself. I have discovered my strength. I have learned to use my talents. I have danced under the full moon. I have enjoyed the power of Spirit. I have become one with the universe. Am I perfect? Absolutely not, but through the advantages of my Craft training I have always been able to find a solution to my problems. Rather than a passive bystander, I am an active participant in my life.

How do you feel right now—are you happy? Have you met many of your goals? Are you in a good relationship? Are you proud of your accomplishments? If you answer "no" to any of these questions, then perhaps the religion of WitchCraft is for you, too. Perhaps not. Religion, after all, is a choice—not a demand.

WitchCraft, like any other religion, embodies a path to the divine. Many paths exist for you. Please don't think that there can be only one way to God, because this thinking actually limits the divine as

1

much as it limits you. Wicca (or WitchCraft) represents one shining thread among thousands of religions, across thousands of years, through thousands of mythos. Should you choose to weave your personal life-tapestry with the thread of Wicca, then understand that you show great courage—because Wiccans (Witches) do not fear the unknown. They embrace it. Once you realize you no longer fear, then the panorama of religious experience blossoms before you like a flower opening to the gentle touch of the sun.

Your Mission in Life

I think we all want to know our primary mission in life. Have you ever sat alone late on a temperate, summer night, staring at a star-studded sky, wishing you knew the answers to all those age-old questions? Have you rested your chin on your knees, willing your mind to touch the power of the universe? Have you asked Spirit, "Why am I here? What am I supposed to be doing? Where should I be?" Let me assure you that no one's life has popped off the assembly line in perfect working order. We've all been through many experiences that can either help us fine-tune our mission mechanism or throw sludge into the works. I can't promise you that living a practical, magickal life will dissolve the goo or turn you into a high-performance engine with a full understanding of your personal mission, but I can tell you that this is precisely what the religion of the Craft has done for me.

I have learned that to know your mission, you must search for it. Granted, you may have several, even hundreds of missions to accomplish throughout your lifetime. Life, as they say, is a fleeting proposition, and you must make the most of every second, every minute, every opportunity that you can. I tell my four children:

Never limit yourself.

Never say the word "can't."

Never turn your back on what may be the perfect opportunity to complete one of your missions.

Over the past four years, I have toured all over the United States doing book signings, seminars, and tarot card readings. The question most asked by those I meet is: "Where do I go from here?" As we reach the year 2000, I've noticed that more and more individuals ask this question. Out of every fifty card and psychic readings I do, over half of the individuals want to know where they are heading and what they should be doing. Let's work on discovering your mission for the moment.

Spell of Wisdom and Strategy

1. You will need a two-inch wide by six-inch piece of yellow ribbon and three candles, two white and one yellow. Cleanse, consecrate, dress, and empower them with your favorite oil. Place the candles on your altar or table in a triangle shape. Place the yellow candle at the apex, with the two white candles forming the bottom of the triangle.

2. Cast a magick circle by using your finger (pointing down) and walking in a clockwise circle, and say:

> *I cast the circle-hedge between the worlds. Be thou the girdle of the Goddess and a protection against all negative energies. I call upon the positive spirits of the North, the East, the South, and the West, to aid me in this consecration. I weave the hedge. I create a tapestry of power. I call forth my birthright. So mote it be!*

Tap the floor with your hand or foot, and say:

> *This circle is sealed.*

3. Open the South Quarter by saying:

> *Hail guardians of the South, element of fire. I (your name) do call you forth to assist in this rite and guard this sacred space. So mote it be.*[1]

4. On a piece of yellow ribbon, write:

> *Wisdom to know my mission in life at this time.* (Sign your name.)

5. Light the three candles, beginning with the yellow candle. Say:

> *I light these candles in honor of Lady Brigid, bringer of wisdom, who carries the passion of creativity in her breast and the energy of healing in her hands.*

---

1. For more complicated uses of Quarter calls and circle castings, please see my book *To Stir A Magick Cauldron* (Llewellyn, 1995).

6. Turn to the South and say:

> *Winds of the South, carry the wisdom I desire to my ears. I call the spirits of the South who may serve my need, that they may heed the power of the angels of light and perform the magick I seek. Salamanders and all spirits of fire, lend your power, wisdom, and strength to my request. Spirits of Jupiter, in all your forms and shapes, gather now with thunder and lightning to serve my purpose. Lady Brigid, guide the winds of the South, the spirits of Jupiter, and the might of the element of fire to bring me the wisdom I seek.*[2]

7. Hold up the yellow ribbon, and say:

> *This is what I seek: wisdom to know my mission in life at this time, and a strategy to fulfill my purpose.*

8. With the ribbon in both hands, close your eyes and see yourself before you came into this incarnation. Imagine you are talking to the guide of souls or the guardian angel assigned to you. The guide of souls or guardian angel is the friendly type, and you know he or she has your best interest at heart. What is the game plan for your life right now? Ask the guide of souls to talk to you in a manner you will understand.

9. When you have finished, place the ribbon in the middle of the table, surrounded by the three candles. Thank the South Quarter, then close that Quarter. Thank Brigid for her assistance. Take up the magick circle. Allow the candles to burn until they are gone.

Suggested Enhancements for This Spell

Day of the Week: Thursday

Moon Phase: Full, new, or waxing

Angel of the Day: Sachiel

Totem Animal: Bear (self-knowledge); crow (wisdom)

You may receive your answer in a variety of ways. During the operation, the guide of souls (or your guardian angel) may have spoken to you, or you may receive

---

2. Spell adapted from a magickal operation in *The Solomon Manual of Divination and Ritual Spells* by Priscilla Schwei (Llewellyn, 1988).

your answer in a dream, through conversation with a friend, or by reading an article or book. Try not to limit how your answer will come to you. Simply be ready to receive it.

How did the conversation go with your guide of souls? If you didn't get very far, don't worry about it at the moment. Our subconscious desires often outmaneuver our conscious will. That's how mental blocks form. Have you ever thought to yourself, *I'm going to sit down and think about this problem* and then, when you do, you think about everything else? Happens to me. This occurs because, for some reason—either sane or unreasonable—we fear the future, which includes the emotions that may go along with that future.

When one partakes of the initiation through group ceremony or self-dedication into the mysteries of WitchCraft, a transformation takes place in every level of the seeker's being. We begin to lose the fear of the unknown. Perhaps you have already experienced this type of divine and mystical transformation. In this manifestation, the mysteries of the Witch tradition surround you, encompassing your life, allowing you to aspire to spiritual heights. Your oath, whether taken within a group ceremony or in a ritual written privately by yourself, represents your first step in learning the secrets of invoking your own power through the loss of subconscious fears, which opens the mind, body, and Spirit to the greater things in life. Elder Witches will tell you that if you don't learn to let go of those subconscious fears fast enough and move in the direction that Spirit wants you to go, then Spirit steps in and moves things *for* you. Equate this to a divine smack upside the head.

A woman in New York City once related that she was planning to take a cross-country trip. The windshield of her car had a small hole, and a crack decided to begin sneaking over the surface of the glass. She kept telling herself that, before she went on her trip, she needed to fix that windshield. Like most of us, she put off the repair. *I'll do it tomorrow. I'll get the car fixed next week.* Over a month went by; still, she did not get the windshield repaired and the crack merrily marched, inch by inch, across the glass. One rainy evening a branch from the tree outside of her house plunged into the windshield, forcing her to take the vehicle in for repair. Of course, she had to take the train to work and back again for a few days, which presented a definite inconvenience and added expense. Had she made her appointment earlier, she would have expended about an hour of her time. Instead, she was forced into inconvenience by her own inaction. This is the way Spirit works if you don't listen the first time a message is sent to you. Many times we cause the complications in our lives because we simply haven't been observant.

Mysteries, Secrets, Power

Mysteries. Secrets. Power. These three words sell more advertising copy than you could ever imagine. Divine magick does not work with negatives. When Witches work with divine magick, they do indeed ride the mysterious current of treasured secrets while wielding the enchantments of enormous power. These secrets, enchantments, and powers raise the spiritual vibrations of the Witch, pulling him or her toward the white light of universal love. Far from New Age belief, this has always been the way of the Hidden Children. That's what we Witches are called—the divine issue of Herself; we are Her shining ones. We carry Her secrets and Her magick in our soul bodies.

With the belief of the God and the Goddess as our spiritual foundation, Witches no longer need fear the divine cycle of birth and death, whether we are talking about the death of a job or a person. To be afraid is the most human of all emotions. Fear stops us from becoming all we can be. Fear drags us down, binds our intuition, robs us of our power, damns the magickal secrets, and pushes us blindly into the rocky paths of the unknown. Every one of us has struggled with secret, nameless fears, never knowing where reality ends and illusion takes over. New Witches struggle with logic, fearing they tread the path of illusion, worrying that since the rest of the world does not believe in divine magick, such magick therefore may not exist. Experienced Witches may understand the art or science of magick but fail to employ their training, whimpering over mindless fears fashioned by years of negative programming from parents, peers, other religions, and other cultures, integrating that same negative programming into funky magickal rules they follow meticulously. From these struggles, strange creatures of thought form, shackling our abilities, taunting our greatness, driving us further from our spirituality. Whether we have been in the Craft two years or twenty years, we all battle the same enemy—that of our self-manufactured fears. We must learn to turn to the mysteries of the Spirit to help us eliminate these fears. It is my belief that no matter what religious rail system we plan to use, Spirit will always be at the end of the line.

Magickal Minutes

The Fear Disposal Can

Supplies: One cleaned, empty coffee can with lid. One piece of black
construction paper, felt, or leather cut to fit outside of can. Glue.

Seven or nine small stones. Black acrylic paint. Flat egg noodles (at least an inch wide) from the grocery store. Black marker. A lock of your hair. Choose a Dark Goddess, or the one provided in the example.

Timing: Best done on Saturday in the hour of Saturn; during the dark of the moon; during the waning moon; or during a full moon (depending on your magickal training).

Quarters to Open: All

Element: Air

Planetary Ruler: Saturn

Planetary Hour: 1st (sunrise or sunset)

Angel of the Day: Cassiel

Candle Color: Black

Archetypes: Goddess—Hecate, Dame Holda, Lillith, or the Morrigan

Totem Animal: Rabbit (conquering fear)

1. Cover outside of can with black paper, felt, or leather. Glue in place. Let dry thoroughly. Cut out a picture of a rabbit and paste it on the can, or draw your own rabbit, or—if you can't draw—write the word "rabbit" on the can.

2. Consecrate the can in the name of the chosen Dark Goddess. In this example, we used Hecate, as she is familiar to most magickal practitioners.

3. Paint the seven small stones with black paint, or you could use seven black glass marbles. (Allow stones to dry thoroughly.)

4. With the black marker, write a fear that you have on a noodle. (You might want to make a list before you begin.) Keep writing your fears on the noodles. It doesn't matter how many fears you may have. They can be big fears or little fears.

5. Drop all the noodles in the can.

6. Drop the stones on top.

7. Add the lock of your hair.

8. Close the lid and say:

> *I seal my fears inside this can,*
> *where they will be pulverized.*

9. Ground and center.

10. At the prescribed time, draw a pentacle on the floor with your finger (or cast a magick circle, if you so desire). Stand within the pentacle (or within the magick circle).

11. Open all Quarters (if you have cast a magick circle). Say:

> *Hecate, Queen of the UnderWorld, Mother of the Dark Night,*
> *behold my fears.*

Hold the can out and away from you. Say:

> *Dark Goddess, take these fears away from me.*
> *Smash them, trash them, banish them.*

12. Begin to shake the can softly, repeating the "Smash them, trash them, banish them" line. Raise energy by shaking the can louder and louder, increasing the tone of your voice with the shaking noise of the can. Don't stop until:

    a) You know all the noodles are broken into little bitty pieces.

    b) You are sure you have raised a sufficient amount of energy to combat those fears.

Then bang the can on the floor to finish the spell and say:

> *May this spell not reverse, or place upon me any curse.*
> *With harm to none. So mote it be!*

13. Thank Hecate.

14. Close the Quarters and take down your magick circle, or remove the pentacle.

15. Take the can outside to a place where the four roads meet.

16. Dump the noodles at the crossroads, and say:

> *I dump the contents of this can and, with them,*
> *the last vestige of my fear. So mote it be!*

17. Clean out the can and save to use again another time.

If you do not like the words I have written, please feel free to design your own; but please remember to keep your words positive. This book is about spinning negative experiences into positive ones, rolling bad thoughts into ideas of greatness, and whirling rotten luck into planned success—all through the practice of a religion known distinctively as WitchCraft.

WitchCraft Laws

When people come to the Black Forest Clan for training, the first lesson they dig into after their dedication ceremony consists of the wealth of laws designed for practical WitchCraft. Of the thirteen standard lessons I've written for the tradition, this first lesson is the most important, most thought-provoking, and most difficult of the training process. If the student manages to get through this lesson, then I know there's a good chance he or she may last until the end of the training program. I used to present the laws later in the program, but found that without this important base to consider and work from, the student doesn't grasp the full impact of the religion. After much consideration, I moved the information about the laws to the beginning of the training course. When writing this book, I thought about placing the details of Craft law near the end of the book, but changed my mind. The reader, to me, is no different from my students at home. Although some might feel that this information falls into the snooze category, I really feel that you need this information to build on, too.

There are lots of laws that Witches may (or may not) choose to follow. Collectively, these laws fall under the heading of **the Ordains.** Most of these laws stem from the Craft practices of Gerald Gardner, Alex Saunders, Sybil Leek, and Charles Quatrain. (According to my information, Quatrain committed suicide, which is why you don't hear much about him.) Although many Crafters think that the laws are older than the 1950s, no one has any definitive proof either of their validity or their age. We can trace undercurrents to Greek Mystery Traditions and, in some cases, Gnostic texts. I believe it was Doreen Valiente, who worked with Gardner, who said Gerald trotted out many of these rules only when his students had the unmitigated gall to break them. Regardless of the historical accuracy or inaccuracies surrounding the origin of the Laws of the Craft, many of these rules continue to serve us well today.

The Ordains fall into three basic categories: Spiritual Laws, Practical Laws, and Mundane Laws. The **Spiritual Laws** exist as a code of ethics or morals giving the Crafter a guideline for spiritual living, whether you choose to practice as a solitary (a Witch alone) or within a group structure. These Spiritual Laws apply to all magickal people, and most magickal individuals incorporate these laws into their group workings as well as their solitary practices.

Consider **Practical Laws** as the blossoms of experience from those who have practiced magick before you. Therefore, not all of the Practical Laws will apply to every person. Think of these laws as guidelines for creating your own set of Practical Laws.

The third type of Craft law, **Mundane Law**, belongs to group hierarchy, and most of these laws do not apply to the Witch practicing alone. This doesn't mean that solitary Witches should ignore these laws entirely, as many in their community may follow some sort of coven or group government and practice their type of WitchCraft within the confines of these laws. Although many of the Mundane Laws fall under the "archaic" category, they do serve a purpose and can be used as a guideline for the solitary when certain questions arise. Many Crafters have difficulty understanding the Ordains because they don't know what applies to their brand of Craft and what does not. They also don't understand them because of the author's attempt at archaic sentence structure and wording. There are no Cliff's Notes or cheat sheets for the Ordains. Many Crafters don't even know that the Ordains exist. Well . . . now you do.

Aw, come on, Silver, this is boring stuff. I want to cast spells, put the world at my feet, you know . . . more power! I want riches! Fame! Fortune! I do not want to talk about laws!

Primarily, the Craft is a religion. True, it is a religion of self-empowerment and fulfillment , but it is a religion, after all. Why am I talking about laws? Isn't the Craft based on freedom, the use of my will to create my future, and the idea that the world is an abundant place and I can access that abundance in my own good time? Isn't the Craft a religious philosophy where I can do what I want to do as long as I don't hurt anybody? *Well?*

Whether you like it or not, any type of religion needs a structure to survive, including Wicca.

The Spiritual Laws of WitchCraft

Life isn't perfect, and our paths will always have potholes, big boulders, and slippery-when-wet areas. By contemplating the Spiritual Laws, and then (hopefully) enacting them of our own desire, we can raise our spiritual as well as mundane circumstances. The Spiritual Laws listed below aren't the only ones I've found, but they appear to be the most forthright.

1. Witches know that no truths are absolute. Indeed, the downfall of humanity relies on the belief that there is an absolute truth for everything. There is no one absolute way to interpret reality, to behave, or to live. Therefore, there is no single correct way to practice magick, pray, celebrate the seasons, or reach our peak of spirituality. The idea that there is only one truth to any question leads to fanaticism, compulsion, and persecution.

2. Witches understand that the universe consists of perfect balance; therefore, everything has an opposite (not necessarily equated to a negative). For example, male and female—the two complement each other in balance, but one is not better than the other. Easy opposites that come to mind are light and dark, right and left, up and down, forward and backward, et cetera.

3. Witches realize that for every action there is a reaction. Most of us see this as the law of karma. Witches use the poem *Ever mind the rule of three, what you manifest comes back to thee.* Therefore, if you create evil, then you will receive evil back. If you create harmony, then you will experience harmony in kind.

4. Witches know that we are all one. We are all connected. Everything you do influences yourself as well as someone else. We are not as separated from humanity as we perceive ourselves to be; therefore, when we make decisions for one, we invariably make decisions for others.

5. The Witch understands that the ultimate act of spirituality is the act of positive creation through love. Positive creations manifest harmony; negative formulations create chaos. As much as possible, we should attempt to concentrate our energies on positive creativity. In essence, all humans were born to create through love; this is our primary mission statement.

6. Witches realize that the energy created through worship and ritual manifests as a circular stream of positive energy. What we give to Spirit will return to us.

7. A Witch should never close his or her mind to knowledge, because it is through the continuous process of learning that we raise our personal vibrations.

8. A Witch uses the magick circle as a physical/non-physical representation of a church or temple on the earth plane. Witches purify themselves mentally, physically, and spiritually before entering or casting a magick circle. When you are in circle, you are in a holy place. Arguments, hatreds, or evil of any kind is not permitted within the magick circle.

9. Witches use the energies around them to assist in raising power. These energies manifest as the elements (earth, air, fire, and water) and Spirit. Witches also raise their own energies to Spirit. In this way, the Witch's body becomes a conduit for divine and earthly energies now used to manifest their needs and desires. Witches know that the greatest energy manifests as love.

10. Witches use common sense and do not share their mysteries with fools. Good energy was never meant to be wasted on idiocy.

11. Witches do not point out the identity of other Witches to the general public, as discrimination still haunts many of our brothers and sisters. If one Witch brings discrimination on the head of another Witch, then he or she is directly responsible for the harm and will reap the karmic consequences. It is also said that if a Witch knowingly breaks the Laws or Ordains, then he or she will not be permitted to incarnate on Earth again and will instead be delegated to the mythical hell that the standard religions have created. It is their thought form, after all.

Magickal Minutes

Chain of Harmony

Supplies: One box of paper clips

Day of the Week to Begin: Friday

Planetary Hour to Begin: 8th

Angel of the Day: Anael

Planetary Ruler: Venus

Element: Water (or air)

Candle Color: Light blue

Totem Animal: Dolphin (harmony); pelican (abundance)

At the eighth planetary hour,[3] or at the end of each day, before you go to bed, hook one paper clip to another. Each paper clip symbolizes a harmonious thing that you did for someone that day. If you have done six things, then hook six paper clips together; if ten things, then hook ten paper clips together. After a month or so of doing this every night, you will have a huge (hopefully) string of paper clips hooked together. Whenever you feel depressed, sad, or unhappy, hold your chain of paper clips and know that you do make a difference in the world. These clips prove it!

---

3. If you do not understand how to calculate planetary hours, please refer to Appendix V.

The Practical Laws of the Craft

As I explained earlier, the Practical Laws of the Craft grew out of the experiences of other Witches and magickal individuals. Indeed, Witches are very good at taking concepts developed by others and improving on them—such is the way with the magickal applications of the Witch. We can see this in ritual, where many Witches (including Gerald Gardner) moved information from ceremonial practices of those he befriended at the time into the shamanistic methods of the Witch. Indeed, the concept of the pentacle (five-pointed star representing earth, air, water, fire, and the Spirit of Man encompassed by the positive circle of the universe) was originally a ceremonial concept. Some say that the pentacle grew from astrological movements of the planet Venus, others indicate that the Knights Templar were responsible for its inception into the world of the mystical monks. Today, the pentacle has been adapted, of course, to the point where most Witches don't know that their primary symbol digs its roots deep within ceremonial magick. You see, Witches don't believe in reinventing the magickal wheel, and have a habit of changing circumstances and objects to suit their needs. Clever, aren't we?

Let's go over some of those Practical Laws. Oh, stop groaning. After you are finished, you may want to begin a Practical Laws section in your Book of Shadows (BOS). As you read further, you'll discover that most of the Practical Laws encompass matters of common sense and sage advice. Perhaps there are laws here that don't apply to you, or perhaps you have some laws of your own that you wish to follow but are not listed below. That's okay. Here we go.

1. Never practice a magickal application or system that you don't fully understand. Which is why you are reading these laws, right? An adept practitioner is an informed practitioner. This goes for the use of any magickal symbol, too. If you don't know the full gambit of what it can invoke, then don't mess with it.

2. Do not set a price on magickal work. To link money to magick influences the outcome of the working. It is acceptable to ask for reimbursement of supplies or set a fair fee for your time (as in tarot readings). Along with this issue also comes an addendum—do not accept money (any money for anything) that you know came to you through illegal means. Today's slang calls money gained from illegal enterprises "dirty money." The psychic slime on this money goes deeper than a mere cleansing and consecration to exorcise. Better not to accept this type of money at all.

3. Never use your magickal skills to show off. Most likely, you will fall flat on your face. Spirit has a habit of pulling the proverbial rug out from underneath us if we get too big for our magickal britches. You will experience the equivalent of a flying carpet with a bad case of the hiccups. That carpet will take to the sky while you find yourself with your face in the dirt.

4. Magickal bindings may be foolish—learn to banish negativity instead. If you bind something, then you will have to deal with it later, and you risk being bound yourself.

5. Know that thoughts are things, and what you create in thought may manifest in reality.

6. Never lie to yourself, for this is the epitome of deceit.

7. Injuries, accidents, sickness, or poverty often manifest as a result of low self-esteem or negative programming, not bad mo-jo.

8. A Witch's power grows in direct relation to his or her level of wisdom. Therefore, if someone is threatening you with magick, know that they are without wisdom and an idiot, and that their power comes only from your fear.

9. You should in no way use your personal power or honed abilities for malefic purposes; however, you may defend if attacked, and you may ask the universe to formulate justice in the manner most befitting the attack. Indeed, it is your responsibility to defend yourself and others, not stick your head in the cauldron and hope that the bad people go away.

10. Always do the best that you can, which does not mean you must fulfill the role of Super Witch. If you have done the best of your ability on anything, then you shouldn't worry about the outcome.

11. As long as you are acting in accordance with a positive belief system, don't worry about what others think of you, or what they are saying. Comments against you show poor self-esteem or fear of the owner of the comment. Don't waste your time or energy on such a person.

12. Don't lend your Book of Shadows to anyone. You may permit others to copy your information under your guidance, but never let the book out of your sight, because pentacles to broomsticks, one of these days the book won't come back. Someone's well-meaning relative might take it upon themselves to destroy your work.

13. Property owned by Crafters should be guarded both mundanely and spiritually by the Witch.

14. Now here's one I've seen broken quite a few times in the last few years, and I've taken the exact wording out of Lady Galadrial's modernized version of The Laws and Ordains because I think this law is exceedingly important. Law #27 says:

    > Do nothing that will endanger anyone in the Craft, or which will bring them into conflict with the law of the land, or any of our persecutors. In this regard, it is NEVER permissible, in any dispute involving the Craft, to invoke any laws other than those of the Craft, nor may any tribunals be held other than one consisting of the High Priestess, the High Priest, and the elders.

    In other words, it is dirty pool to call child services on the Witch across the street because she practices differently than you do, and it is inconceivably ignorant to stop another Witch in your town from practicing with his or her group by using the city ordinances against them. To me, the rats who turned these people in are just that—rats, not Witches at all, just humans who have shapeshifted beneath themselves. Now, this doesn't mean that you can't call the cops on a wife-beater just because he is Wiccan. No, no, no. As with all laws, use this one wisely and with common sense.

15. Although magick can be considered a science, its use should be viewed as sacred. Magick represents the greatest gift given to us by Spirit. When first learning, one should work all magicks and ritual within the confines of a magick circle, since the beginning student may not understand the nature of the force they are working with. The magick circle, since it represents the Witch's church, teaches students the necessary reverence and focus that will enable them to become an adept practitioner.

16. This one is a law for the nineties not followed during the sixties, seventies, or even eighties: Do not sleep with your students. If your student is your life partner or spouse, of course you are expected to do what comes naturally— but under other circumstances, this has become a very big no-no in the magickal community. Some teachers in the past extorted sex for magickal information. Boo, hiss. This is just not done in the nineties. Witches are proud of their sexuality, but they have matured enough to realize they don't have to prove it.

17. Witches may teach others about the Craft if (and here we refer to Lady
Galadrial again) the place is safe, the teacher is knowledgeable, the student
is willing, and the information taught is available publicly or is not secret
to the organization to which he or she belongs. No one may charge for
teaching, unless it is to cover such expenses as the cost of the room, books or
other printed materials, refreshments, postage, travel, and so forth. This law
is considered a sticky one for some, not for others. To charge someone an
exorbitant fee and promise initiation at the end of a six-week course, in my
mind, borders on irresponsible teaching. My training dictates that if you
initiate someone, then you have bought into the responsibility of his or her
karma, at least in part. To train someone for six weeks, take their money,
initiate them, and then let them go could dip you into some pretty heavy
karma. Not my bowl of Gravy Train.

These are just a few of the Practical Laws I've managed to come across in my
research. I think I've collected over two hundred of these babies. You don't have to
agree with the Practical Laws, but you should consider them. If you don't agree with
one or two of the laws, then you should think carefully about why you do not agree
with them— Law #6 there, to thine own self be true. Never thrust the Practical Laws
at a prospective student with the design of making the student learn them or trot
them out when the student doesn't conform with everyone else in your group
(should you have one). Practical Laws should make you think.

When a Witch takes the oath through a group or has performed a self-dedication,
that Witch acknowledged that he or she will strive to be a better person and will
continue to study the mysteries throughout this lifetime, and beyond. This includes
both the formulation and adherence to the Spiritual and Practical Laws. In taking
the oath, the Witch also agrees that he or she will try to work in harmony and balance in all aspects of his or her life, from mundane to magickal experiences. In that
moment of the Witch's solemn promise to the Lord and Lady, he or she took the
reins of the future and moved forward into harmony and success.

By now, most of you have found that learning the mysteries of the Craft can manifest in a slow and winding process that will grow differently for each individual. No
two people can, or should, mentally process the Wiccan mysteries in the same manner. To demand such is in direct opposition with the mysteries themselves.

The Wiccan Mysteries

The primary root of Wicca is Spirit—peace, trust, beauty, love. No other "mystery" associated with the Craft is more important to understand or to internalize. It is our responsibility as Witches to serve ourselves and others with love, in harmony with Spirit. People outside of our community think that WitchCraft is only hocus-pocus and messing with the supernatural. Tsk-tsk-tsk. Oh, we deal with the supernatural all right—the natural way to be a super person. To us, what the outside world shies away from as supernatural, we welcome, knowing that as long as we rely on Spirit, we will reach new heights, drawing toward us the harmony of the universe.

It is our responsibility as magickal people to do the work. And what, should we be so bold to ask, is the work? What do you think the work is? You think about it for me, and we'll get back to that subject a little later.

Summary

In this chapter we've discussed your mission in life, the mysteries and secrets of the Craft, and the laws that govern our religion. If you plan to use this book as a working guide, you might want to sit down with a notebook and review some of the things you have learned. Even if you have been in the Craft several years, you may wish to refresh your thoughts on the theology of the Craft. If this material is totally new for you, take your time and review our laws carefully. This chapter presents a strong building block for your future endeavors.

For those of you who have a serious urge to delve deeply into the Craft, I have provided a list of questions for you to work through. Remember, there are no wrong answers. I've designed these questions to make you think. The exercise of contemplation will assist you on your spiritual path.

1. Write a book blessing for your study manual.
2. Study the Wiccan Laws presented. Are there any laws you do not agree with? Why?
3. Perform the Magickal Minutes or Spiritual Seconds in this chapter. Keep notes of your experiences.
4. Why did you buy this book?

5. What goals would you like to accomplish in:

   One Week

   One Month

   Six Months

   One Year

   Five Years?

   After each time designation, write a short outline on how you will begin to accomplish these goals.

6. What do you feel constitutes your mission in life?

2

The Mysteries of Self-Empowerment

Before you start reading this chapter on power, I would like you to rumble around your house or apartment and find ten candles. They don't have to be ten BIG candles. Ten small votive candles will do. As you read each secret for invoking your personal power, I would like you to light a candle. By the time you finish, you will have ten candles burning. Yes, you over there in the corner madly waving your hand, you *can* cleanse, consecrate and empower the candle before you begin. Yes? You there in the front? The appropriate candle color? Nah. Not telling you. Use your intuition.

Okay, did you get the ten candles? No, it doesn't matter that the candles are different sizes. Not really. The important part of the exercise here is the act—the tools (in this case, the candles) are just tools. Now, got the ten candles? Good. Here we go!

The First Mystery of Invoking Your Power

The first mystery of invoking your own power revolves around understanding the Wiccan attunement to **self-individuation**. So, light your first candle and say: *"I welcome my self-individuation."* You must strongly visualize yourself as the Little Witch Who Could . . . and Can. What? You've been a Witch for twenty years and you don't need to do this part? Do it anyway. I'm sure there's something in your life right now that you're wrestling to overcome. I think you'll find a pleasant surprise. If you haven't thought about who you are, or what navigational course you've chosen lately, then why not sit down and write out a paragraph about who you want to be? From this time spent in consideration of yourself and how you wish to manifest that-which-is-you in the world, you can target your self-individuation process with better accuracy.

Let's have a bit of fun, shall we? Under the paragraph where you wrote down who you want to be, answer this question: If you could have any career in the world, and the guarantee stands firm for absolute success, what would you choose? Consider your answer carefully, then write yourself a mission statement.

Whether you have been a practicing Witch for six months or thirty years, there's always room for improvement. I don't care if you are an eclectic Witch, a solitary Witch, a Gardnerian, an Alexandrian, Strega, Druid, North Wind, Serpent Stone, Dianic, OTO, Covenant of the Goddess, Aquarian Tabernacle Church, Black Forest, Cabot, Rosarian, Church of All Worlds (the list is endless here in the states), you still are a spirit body underneath whatever religious mantle you choose to wear. Improvement of one's self and one's circumstances begins at home, in your spirit body and in your mind.

Allowing divinity to manifest through self is called self-individuation. When people turn away from the divine spark within—when they stop *experiencing* divinity in their lives—then many rely on an external manifestation or an organization that pales against the true glory of the God/dess. Real WitchCraft is the process of living it—not watching it. There is no such thing as a couch-potato Witch! Our inward knowledge should be rooted in divine experience and not on what someone else tells us is right or wrong in the matters of the God/dess. By beginning within and manifesting outward, it is possible for one individual to impact the entire world in a positive way with his or her actions.

Magickal Minutes ————

For the next thirty days, at least three times a day, go outside alone and watch the world around you. Listen to the world around you. Don't worry if you see only city streets—raise your eyes to the heavens. Rain or shine, sleet or snow, out the door you go. Breathe deeply in through your nose and out through your mouth. Feel yourself relax in the arms of the Mother or the strong embrace of the Father. Just let yourself go. If negative thoughts intrude on your mind, repeat a positive statement over and over again. For example:

My life is filled with positive abundance
and all my needs are met, and more.

Repeat this statement like a mantra until the negative thoughts and worries find themselves obscured by your will. Hopefully, after thirty days, this little jaunt into the outdoors will become a habit you choose to keep.

In your everyday thought, you must learn not to lower yourself to the base emotions of hatred, jealousy, even irritability. These self-manufactured thoughtforms will and do drag you down. You must learn to honor the good in others without the ever-present human emotion of judgment. I'm not talking about judgment for crimes here, that is something else altogether. I'm discussing when that lady in the supermarket line forgets to move her cart up so that you can put your items on the conveyor belt and your brain immediately flies into a litany of condemnation. Perhaps she is absent-minded today, something terrible may have happened in her life and she's just not with it, or you could be right and she has fallen into the habit or was raised to not consider the feelings of others. Whatever the case, your fuming will not correct her personality dysfunction for all time. Indeed, your negative emotions will drag *you* down. Not worth it. Finally, not only will those negative thoughts cause difficulties with you, they have a habit of empowering others in a negative manner.

We must school our minds to create harmony. One way to do this is to constantly jettison negative thoughts in your daily life. If something upsets you, tell yourself it is okay to have those feelings, then let them go. If you have trouble doing this, create a mental mantra that will sufficiently block out those dark, angry feelings. A friend of mine recites *The Witches Rune* by Doreen Valiente when something makes her mad. Another fellow I know recites the Kore chant: "Isis, Astarte, Diana, Hecate, Demetri, Kali, Inanna." Pick some sort of affirmation and stick with it.

Allow the anger of others to travel through you, sort of like a continuous wave, where you do not become part of the negativity that belongs to someone else.

You can also learn to raise your spiritual vibrational rate and practice this elevation of soul any time during the day or night, not just when anger lights your personal fuse. You don't need the correct planetary hour, perfect moon phase, or the right element to work in and with Spirit. You can raise your vibrational rate by blocking out negative thoughts (or dumb thoughts) and replacing them with positive, balance-affirming ones. Although daily devotions, rituals, and acts of honor at your altar will raise your vibrational rate, you can learn to access the divine at any time, in any place. In actuality, devotionals teach you to raise your spiritual self, rituals enhance and draw power to you, and acts of honor affirm your ability to raise and draw power. Petitions and acts of honor at a shrine also assist in raising your vibrational level. Of course devotionals, rituals, petitions, and acts of honor serve many other functions in your religious life as well as your mundane existence.[1] At the moment, we want to concentrate on raising your vibrational spiritual level. You can do this by reciting positive affirmations designed to enhance your life and by actively taking part in the planning of your future.

Magickal Minutes

Every night, before you go to bed, I'd like you to read this statement aloud (and no, this statement can't replace your devotional):

Great Mother. Thank you for everything you have done for my family and me. Thank you for the successes I have had before, and the successes that I know you are going to give to me. Cleanse and bless the hearts of my family and myself. Raise my spiritual vibrations so that I may be useful to you and successful in all my undertakings. Great Father. Thank you for my protection and the gift of focus. Thank you for the successes I have had before, and the successes that I know you are going to give me. Thank you for my success.
So mote it be!

Now I want you to close your eyes and imagine great power coalescing from your ancestors, your many lifetimes, and the ground at your feet flooding from both palms of your hands. Direct that energy outward, visualizing the truth of these words. You needn't stand there for hours on end. A few seconds at first will do nicely. Later on, you will find that you can hold this emanation of power longer. Do *not* use your own energy. That is a no-no, because I am trying to teach you how to draw power from universal sources. Using your own energy depletes you, therefore you should draw from yourself only when the situation dictates. Save that power for more important matters. You can always throw your own energy at something, but learning to draw it from the world around you is a magickal nuance you need to learn. Draw your energy from the world around you, nature, the elements, divinity, and so on, but not other people—another major no-no. Draw your energy through time and space, from the reservoir of those who have gone before and those who will succeed you. Keep track of your progress in your personal journal.

---

1. I cover the nuances of devotionals in my book *To Stir A Magick Cauldron*.

When you succeed in raising your vibrations, several things happen. Sometimes these things happen simultaneously, sometimes they happen one after the other. The important idea to remember lies in the certainty that everyone's path to the divine is different and everyone has special missions in life slated for their accomplishment. No two paths march through life the same. We all step to the beat of a different drummer. These differences in humans meld together to create a divine plan. Therefore, each and every one of us, Witch or no, has important contributions to make in this lifetime. Whether we choose to make those contributions or not is up to us. As we raise our vibrational rate, harmony comes a' knockin' at our soul door. You'll probably notice this in little ways at first. Sometimes harmony mushrooms around us, in other instances the manifestation of balance takes a slower, more sinewy path.

Spiritual Seconds

For the next thirty days, twice a day (more if you like) I want you to visualize yourself drawing in the energy of the moon, stars, and sun. Do this with your eyes closed. See this universal energy in the form of white light that enters the crown of your head and pulsates through your body. Don't think of anything but that white light. Push all other thoughts away. Even if you can only concentrate for a few seconds, that's okay. Eventually those few seconds will lengthen into minutes. Trust me, you just need to practice. Those of you who meditate regularly probably won't have any trouble with this exercise. Those of you who have difficulty meditating will find this exercise helpful—a stepping stone, if you will, to better meditational practices. Once you can hold that white light within yourself, imagine that the light carries great properties of positive change. *Feel* yourself change. *Know* that you are changing. Visualize your third eye (at the center of your forehead) opening and accepting wisdom and knowledge from divinity. No matter what magickal endeavor you practice, this simple little exercise will help you tremendously if you just keep it up.

When you succeed in raising your vibrational rate, you will find yourself with new abilities. These abilities show themselves as psychic occurrences. For example, you may be able to acquire your desires easier, you may become more telepathic, your dreams might be exceedingly vivid and prophetic, you may see energy patterns, auras, spirits, et cetera. Here is where some students of the occult open their little eyeballs very, very wide, and subsequently quit their training. Why? That darned old fear thang again. They think that because harmony manifests, they may be too powerful and hurt someone. A wise consideration, but not necessarily a true one. Each person evolves differently. As his or her vibrational rate increases, each individual has different experiences. Regardless of how your path manifests, you will learn to see the miracles in everyday life. Seeing these miracles becomes a key to raising your personal power.

So how do you do that?

Practice.

What, you mean I actually have to *work* at it?

Yup. I promise this work won't take much time, or require you to spend any money. What more can you ask for?

Spiritual Seconds

Pick a personal mantra and stick with it. Write your mantra down and pin the paper up where you can see the mantra often. Use the mantra to obstruct and block negative thoughts.

Take a deep breath now and look at your burning candle. Visualize yourself as the Witch you want to be.

The Second Mystery of Invoking Your Power

The second mystery of invoking your personal power lies in **your willingness to trust the Mother and the Father.** Light your second candle now, and say:

I trust in the Mother and the Father. I trust in Spirit.

For many people, trusting something you can't see is like walking the plank blindfolded high above shark-invested waters. Of course, these aren't normal sharks. They are big, fat, hungry beasties whose only purpose in life is to swim, make little sharks, and eat you for breakfast. We'd rather trust the things we can see, hear, feel, taste, or touch. Dollars in the bank (though truly mythical in today's paper tiger world) create more security in many of us than looking at the moon and calling on the Mother, the Father, or Spirit for help. I've met Witches who have been in the Craft ten years who would trust their stockbroker more than they would trust the Mother. They may mouth the words of Wiccan beliefs, but they turn around and do the usual dirty tricks that humans are prone to do. In my mind, these people aren't real

Witches. They simply play the part. Eventually the Mother will get tired of their shenanigans and give them the boot, but She only does that after they have learned a hard lesson or two.

Trusting in the Mother may not be as easy as it sounds. Witches must learn to take their problems to Her when the going gets tough. Yes, She expects you to do your best on your own, working your Craft and employing the mysteries, but She is not above assisting you when you truly need it. The God, Her Consort, acts in the same manner. He directs Her power and brings protection and strength. However, a Witch who doesn't ask for help is a dip-Witch who is asking for trouble. The underlying premise of Wicca is kinship, not civilization.

So, what if you just want to talk to the Mother? That's okay. The God won't find your behavior insulting. He's not going to aim thunderbolts at your head. If you want to have a private discussion with the God, our Mother will not have a jealous hissy fit. She won't throw a cauldron, starbursts, or tornadoes at you. If you would like to talk to them together, that's fine and dandy too.

Magickal Minutes

The Mother Candle

Many Witches use a Mother Candle to sanctify and protect the shrine or temple area, whether that area belongs to the group or acts as a personal shrine. In some North American Traditions, the need-fire represents the same function as the Mother Candle; however, most need-fires exist out-of-doors. The Mother Candle allows you to bring the same energies of the need-fire into your home or temple area without having to worry about digging a huge fire pit in your living room floor. Not only would it be difficult to explain your excavation to your spouse or parent, your kids would always be filling it with broken cookies, empty cups, toys, dirt balls, or sports equipment. Not a good idea.

The Mother Candle (or need-fire) becomes a receptacle for a higher power than yourself. When lit, the Mother Candle symbolizes the eternal flame of creation and epitomizes the physical manifestation of the Goddess. This candle is always the first illuminary to dispel the darkness of the area and the last candle to be extinguished in any working, ritual, or meditation. Technically, the candle represents the white light of universal peace. Witches who have worked with the Mother Candle for many years will tell you that, when lit, they can see the face of our Mother in the room or in the candle flame. Her presence manifests in calming, peaceful energy that fills the magickal area with universal love.

The Mother Candle constitutes a "built candle," which is putting one candle on top of another in a continuing process. You will need a short, black pillar candle (no taller than three inches in height), two to three inches in diameter, and a white pillar candle, slightly smaller in diameter. Cleanse, consecrate, and empower both candles, dedicating the candles to the Mother. In a magick circle with closed Quarters, place the black candle on your altar or shrine, and say:

Out of the void, from the depths of chaos, our Mother emerged,
giving birth to the Holy Light. In honor of the Divine Mother,
I bring light to the void, as She brought illumination to the souls
of Her blessed children.

Light the black candle. Sing, drum, chant, or hum as the black candle continues to burn. As the edges of the candle become soft, pull them out gently with your fingers so that they curl slightly downward.

Hold the white candle in your hands, and say:

This white candle represents the embodiment of the Mother in my life
and in my home. Whenever I light this candle, I invite the Mother and
ask Her to let me feel Her presence. As the flame rises, my soul will be
uplifted, my home safe, and my life movement graced with harmony.

Light the white candle from the flame of the black candle. Place the white candle firmly on top of the black candle, which now becomes the base of your Mother Candle. Allow the candle to burn while you welcome the Mother into your ritual area. You can work magick, meditate, or simply enjoy the peace and harmony of the moment.

When you extinguish the candle, say:

Although the flame disappears in the world of form, the eternal flame
of the Mother's love continues to burn within my spirit. Each time I set
flame to wick, I reaffirm my devotion to the Mother and call Her into
my sacred space. So mote it be.

Don't forget to deactivate your circle.

As you continue to use your Mother Candle, keep rolling the warm edges of the white candle down (gently). In this way, you will get longer life from the white candle, and at the same time prepare the current white candle as a base for the next white candle when you need a replacement. (I realize that sentence bordered on cumbersome, but sometimes you've got to be specific to get your point across.) Always light the new white candle from the old flame. Over time, the candle itself will become a valuable working tool.

If you are working with a partner at home, you may wish to build both a Mother Candle and a Father Candle. These candles can serve as the basic illuminaries for any circle or magickal working. Create the Mother Candle first, then, using a red candle as the base for the Father Candle, say the following:

> *Our Holy Mother gave birth to Her Consort and Son, our Father.*
> *May His strength, protection, and wisdom be with me always,*
> *as I walk the path of the Hidden Children.*

Light the red candle from the flame of the white Mother Candle. Allow the red candle to burn (as you did with the black candle) until the edges are soft. Take another white candle (slightly smaller in diameter than the red candle) in your hand, and say:

> *Our Father died to be reborn. This white candle represents the*
> *embodiment of the birth of the Father in my life and in my home.*
> *Whenever I light this candle, I invite the Father, and ask Him to let*
> *me feel His presence. As the flame rises, my soul will be strengthened,*
> *my home protected, and my life movement graced with order and*
> *clarity. As the Oak King gives way to the Holly King, as the Holly King*
> *battles the Oak King, so I witness His rebirth!*

When extinguishing the Father candle, say:

> *Although the flame disappears in the world of form, the eternal flame*
> *of the Father's love continues to burn within my soul. Each time I set*
> *flame to wick, I reaffirm my devotion to the Father and call Him into*
> *my sacred space. So mote it be.*

When using both candles in ceremony, customary procedure instructs the magickal practitioner to light the Mother Candle first, then the Father Candle. When the flames need to be extinguished, put out the Father Candle first, followed by the Mother Candle.

If you plan to use this concept in a coven environment, you can use the Mother Candle at strategic points of the ritual where each Covener lights a candle of their own from the Mother Candle, allowing the group energies to flow into the separate candles, which they may extinguish and take home with them.

Spiritual Seconds

Learn to talk to divinity. Sure, we interact with divinity during spellcasting, devotionals, and rituals, but how about at other times during the day? Did you ever get in a bad patch and mutter to the Goddess under your breath? A silent plea, if you will? One of my standard lines goes like this:

> *Please Goddess, let the right words come out of my mouth.*

Or,

> *Please Goddess, help me get out of this with my face intact.*

If you have, good for you! Keep it up. Do it more often. If you haven't done this, then learn now how to interact with divinity on a daily basis, whenever the need arises. Be sure to write down any significant experiences you have had that relate to this lesson in your personal journal.

Look again at the second candle, which represents the second secret of invoking your power. How do you feel now?

The Third Mystery of Invoking Your Power

The third mystery of your personal power centers on **learning how to call on your ancestors.** Light your third candle and say:

> *Loving ancestors, I connect with your positive energy*
> *to help me in my work and study.*

The Mysteries of Self-Empowerment

I believe most of today's Witches need more training on accessing their personal lineage. Believe it or not, you already possess the ability to move through time. One of the easiest ways to begin moving through time is by learning how to access your ancestors.

Now, what do I mean when I say "ancestors"? I don't mean the mass murderer in your family tree who was hung by his irate neighbors in 1827. Rather, we search to draw forth positive energy patterns from those people linked to us by blood and spirit. The qualities you wish to concentrate on are honor, courage, compassion, determination, strength, wisdom, unconditional love, and so on. There is nothing wrong with calling these energies forward into your time and place.

Okay. I hear someone asking, "How do you do that?" Easy: walk outside, open your mouth, and start talking. You can cast a circle, create sacred space, or just sit on your front porch and look at the full moon dancing over the Carolina mountains— I don't care how you do it—just do it.

When Mick and I went to the French Quarter in New Orleans, we learned how to access the energies of the dead. We hadn't expected this unique gift, but we got it anyway. One technique is to go to the graveyard. Since there may be all sorts of strange things floating around in graveyards (living and non-living), one should pray for protection before you step foot over the line of the living and the abode of the dead. An offering of some type, whether it be rum, smoke, or soda (no kidding) is acceptable.

Once inside the graveyard, approach the tomb, stone, or whatever of the deceased. Give another offering, much like the first, accompanied by a gift such as a flower, beads, a trinket, money, et cetera. Then knock three times on the tombstone. This is the signal to the dead that you wish to speak to them. Take a deep breath and hold your hand on the tombstone (or whatever). You can talk aloud, whisper, or talk in your head if others were with you. Leave your hand on the tombstone the entire time you are communicating. When you've finished, rap once to indicate that you have completed your prayer, then mark the stone with a piece of chalk (don't use a crayon, because laws do exist against defacing the signposts of the dead) three times with an equal armed cross or an "x." Be sure to say "thank you" to the deceased.

You can work with ancestral energies in your sacred space or temple area when you need answers to questions. Different magickal religions and traditions will teach you various ways to contact your ancestors. If you like, you may try the following technique. You will need a white candle, a glass of water, and a bell.

Magickal Minutes

Talking to the Dead

Cast a magick circle by using your power arm finger (pointing down) and walking in a clockwise circle, saying:

> *I cast the circle-hedge between the worlds; be thou the girdle of the Goddess, and a protection against all negative energies. I call upon the positive spirits of the North, the East, the South, and the West to aid me in this consecration. I weave the hedge. I create a tapestry of power. I call forth my birthright. So mote it be!*

Tap the floor with your hand or foot, and say:

> *This circle is sealed.*

You may now call Quarter energies, or not—this is your choice. In circle, empower an "ancestral candle" (any candle color or size will do, though some magickal practitioners prefer to use only white for this purpose) by dressing with oil or holy water from the top to the middle, and from the bottom to the middle, and then holding it tightly in your hands, visualizing a link between yourself and your ancestral energies. Place your candle on your altar (or a table if you don't have one). Light the candle, concentrating on the ancestral energies you wish to contact. Ring the bell nine times,[2] saying:

> *Great ancestors, I invite you into my magick circle.*
> *I ask for your wisdom and guidance.*

Sit quietly and meditate on your question, or you may speak your question or concern aloud. You will mentally "hear" the answers. When you are through, leave the glass of water on your altar (or table) as your gift for the ancestors. If you have called the Quarters, you need to release them. You can take up the circle into your hand by walking counterclockwise and then proclaiming the circle open by saying:

> *This circle is open, but never broken.*

---

2. Historically, ringing a bell nine times within a magick circle equates to the summoning of wisdom.

If you are with others, you may add:

Merry meet and merry part until we merry meet again.

Mick and I do a great deal of traveling by air, which limits my ability to carry loads of magickal tools. Ray Malbrough, author of *Charms, Spells & Formulas,* taught me this neat trick. When we get to the hotel room, I fill a glass halfway with water. I cleanse, consecrate, and empower the water. Then, I hold it out and up, and ask my ancestors to protect our room and belongings during our stay. I change the water each evening for the duration of our visit. Before we check out, I thank the ancestors for their assistance and dump the water.

Spiritual Seconds

For the next thirty days, I'd like you to concentrate on pulling the positive qualities of your ancestors toward you in your present life. Feel these strong, exciting energies floating around you, walking before you, and following behind you. With your mind, touch the loving qualities of those who have gone before. Be sure to write down any unusual occurrences in a personal journal. Oh, and I warn you—once you open your brain to the ancestral dead, you may find them quite the jabberboxes, so be careful if you decide to target a particular ancestor.

The Fourth Mystery of Invoking Your Power

Of all the lessons my students study, the one that focuses on **totem animals** is the lesson that makes the most impact on their training. This lesson, revolving around the five points of the circle and five totem animals of our Clan, brings a magnificent connection from the animal world into the life of the student. Light your fourth candle and say:

Animal spirits, totemic energies, I invite you into my life.

The true shaman has always worked with the natural order of the universe, including the elements and all terrestrial life. The Witch, no matter what path he or she follows, also works with this natural order, and totem animals can figure prominently in the science, art, and religion of one's magickal life.

Today, most of our society believes that the use of totem animals belongs to Native American (or indigenous people's) beliefs. Many people, including Witches, sometimes have difficulty understanding that the indigenous people of this country do not hold sole claim to working with, honoring, and utilizing totemic energies. Since the proto-Celtic peoples emerged in Europe, our Craft shamans have used totemic thoughtforms.

In the Black Forest Clan studies, we link the totem animals with archetypal energies as well as the elements (save for one, there is no deity or element linked to the hearthstone totem). You can use those totemic energies you have already established, or you can devise new ones that suit your personality. Of course, this will require research so that you can gain the most from your associations with the totemic energies you choose. Totemic work falls in the category of primal energies, where you can virtually reach into the soul of the animal-spirit and feel the totality of being.

Here is a general list to assist you in choosing your own totemic energies:

ANIMAL-SPIRIT	ASSOCIATED ENERGIES
Alligator	Survival; Stealth; Power
Ant	Teamwork; Organization; Community; Kinship
Antelope	Speed; Grace
Armadillo	Protection; Safety
Badger	Orderliness; Tenacity
Bat	Insight; Intuition
Bear	Strength; Introspection; Healing; Self-Knowledge
Beaver	Building; Shaping; Beginning New Projects
Bee	Service; Herbalism; Community
Bird	Unity; Freedom; Community
Buffalo	Abundance; Healing; Good Fortune
Butterfly	Transformation; Balance; Grace
Caribou	Travel; Mobility
Cougar	Balance; Leadership
Coyote	Humor; Trickiness; Reversal of Fortune
Crane	Balance; Majesty
Crow	Council; Wisdom; Resourcefulness; Magick
Deer	Gentleness; Sensitivity; Peace; Wisdom
Dog	Loyalty; Companionship
Dolphin	Joy; Harmony; Connection with Self; Communication
Dragonfly	Skill; Refinement; Relentlessness; Creativity
Eagle	Potency; Healing; Power; Illumination

Animal-Spirit	Associated Energies
Elk	Pride; Power; Majesty
Firefly	Communication; Illumination
Fox	Cleverness; Subtlety; Discretion
Frog	Cleansing; Peace; Emotional Healing
Goat	Tenacity; Diligence
Goose	Safe Return; Love of Home
Hawk	Awareness; Truth
Hedgehog	Self-preservation
Horse	Freedom; Power; Safe Movement; Transformation; Shapeshifting
Hummingbird	Beauty; Wonder; Agility
Ladybug	Delight; Trust
Lizard	Letting go; Elusiveness
Loon	Communication; Serenity
Moose	Unpredictability; Spontaneity
Mouse	Illusion; Charm
Otter	Joy; Laughter; Lightness
Owl	Wisdom; Vision; Insight
Peacock	Recognition; Self-Assurance
Pelican	Abundance; Plenty
Pheasant	Warning; Concealment
Porcupine	Innocence; Humility
Quail	Protectiveness; Group Harmony
Rabbit	Conquering Fear; Safety
Raccoon	Curiosity; Inquisitiveness
Ram	Strength; Determination
Raven	Mystery; Exploration of the Unknown
Roadrunner	Speed; Agility
Salmon	Determination; Persistence
Sandpiper	Quickness; Foraging; Scavenging
Scorpion	Defense; Self-Protection
Seagull	Carefree attitude; Versatility; Freedom
Seahorse	Nourishing; Fathering
Seal	Contentment
Skunk	Caution; Warning
Snail	Perseverance; Determination

Animal-Spirit	Associated Energies
Snake	Power; Life force; Sexual Potency
Spider	Interconnectedness; Industry
Squirrel	Trust; Thrift
Swan	Elegance; Nurturing
Turtle	Love; Protection; Healing; Knowledge
Whale	Creativity; Intuition
Wolf	Teaching; Loyalty; Interdependence
Woodpecker	Change; Persistence

When working with totemic energies at the Quarters (North, East, South, West, and center), it is acceptable to place a representation of the animal at the Quarter as well as something that relates to the element of the Quarter. One may leave an offering when closing a Quarter, especially if you have opened only a single Quarter and have relied heavily on the energies you have called. An offering could be something representational of the Quarter or something small, such as a lock of your hair, a piece of bread, a pretty bauble—it doesn't matter what you leave. It's the thought that counts.

Magickal Minutes

Imagine yourself mixing ingredients into a large cauldron. The outcome of your mental potion will be to convert you into the type of person you most want to be. Take a pot of water and heat it on the stove, on an outdoor grill, or in a fire circle. Wait until the pot begins to steam, then boil. As the water boils, imagine those things you desire for yourself coming to pass. Let the pot cool and then, in sacred space or ritual circle, carry the pot to each Quarter, invoking the energies of that Quarter and totem association into the water. Ask politely for the blessings of each. Refrigerate. Every evening, before you go to bed, drink one ounce of the water. As you do so, imagine you are drinking the potion to bring about the person you wish to be. Take daily notes of what is happening in your life. Are the changes you designed for yourself occurring? Drink each day until you empty the pot.

Choose totem animals of your own, and match them with the Quarters and the center. This may take you some time and involve research. You might like to try *Animal Speak* by Ted Andrews (Llewellyn, 1993). Practice working with them whenever you call the Quarters, both in general ritual and spellworking.

The Fifth Mystery of Invoking Your Power

The fifth mystery of accessing your personal power revolves around **the Wiccan mystery of reincarnation**—simply put, your many lifetimes. Light the fifth candle and say:

I access my many lifetimes, both past and future,
to help me in my spiritual growth.

If you have been able to access these memories through hypnosis or meditation, that's wonderful. If you haven't succeeded, don't give up. Everything worthwhile in life takes practice. Although past life memories fill an individual with excitement and wonder, they also perform a specific function. If you recall these memories, then you should be gaining something from them. Even if you cannot come up with anything specific, know that these memories are a part of you, regardless of your present recognition of them.

Every lifetime you have lived (or are slated to live) carries particular skills and talents. Some of these talents travel with us throughout all our lifetimes, while others we cultivate only for a particular lifetime or two. Each successive life builds on our spirit, giving us opportunities to become better physical people and more enlightened souls. Whether we choose to ignore these skills and lessons is entirely up to us. By remembering past (or future) skills or talents, we can meld these energies into our present lifetime when needed. Since we don't necessarily know all our skills or talents, you may think they are now inaccessible. Nope.

I should interject here that the idea of exercising the right to remember should not take up your entire awareness. Meaning—don't get hung up on remembering past lives. That's why they call them *past* lives. They are over. Done with. Finis. The object is not to drag up painful junk but to enhance your growing spirituality now. Trust me, most past life memories are incredibly boring. For example, I went through one long session only to determine that I spent one life as a seamstress. An unappealing, unmarried seamstress who, from dawn to dusk, sewed fine clothes for rich ladies of the day. Exotic, huh? I do call up this skill when making clothing for my children, and you should see the wailing costumes I make for Halloween, but that's as far as I take that skill. I'm not about to spend my life doing it again!

While we're on the topic, you may be one of those people who, no matter what you do, cannot access past life information. Is there something wrong with you? Not at all. It could very well be that you don't need any of that information, therefore you can't tap into past life experiences because you need to be concentrating on this life and what is happening to you now.

Magickal Minutes

For the next six months, on the new moon, sit alone in a favorite place. You could use your ritual room, an outdoor site, or your bedroom. It doesn't matter where you are, what matters revolves around what you plan to do. Be sure that you have at least ten minutes of uninterrupted time. Light a white candle and call on the Mother for assistance, then sit back and close your eyes. To begin, breathe deeply through your nose and exhale through your mouth several times until you feel yourself relax. Allow the tranquillity of the Goddess to move toward and into you. Imagine your body surrounded by a white bubble of light. Relax and let yourself feel at peace with the universe. Once you have pushed the day-to-day garbage out of your mind, imagine you are a giant monolith. In your mind, see the positive lessons, skills, and talents of your past life as glowing light bodies. One by one, move these light bodies into the monolith (yourself), saying to yourself:

I access the skills and talents of past and future lives that best suit my situation right now, and I pull these positive forces into this life. These skills and talents will enhance my life and I will be a better person to myself and to others.

Once you have moved all the light bodies into the monolith, thank divinity for assisting you in this task. Count from one to five in your mind, then open your eyes. If you can, allow the candle to burn throughout the evening as a visual focus and testament to what you have done. If you cannot let the candle burn, snuff out the flame (never blow out a candle, as you are expelling holy breath to kill the element) and save the candle for the next time. If you have part of the candle end remaining, bury the piece in your backyard.

The Sixth Mystery of Invoking Your Power

The sixth mystery of invoking your personal power centers around **your ability to understand the art of manifestation** and how you can apply that art to the totality of your life. Light the sixth candle and say:

I am able to invoke my personal power centers whenever I need to, to manifest whatever I need, without harming anyone, including myself.

An old adage indicates "there is no such thing as a coincidence." Meaningful coincidences show us that a deeper level of order exists and that this hidden organization weaves our universe together, linking all living things (people included). We, as magickal people, must learn to dip into this hidden organization, this underground stream of universal wholeness, and draw out what is needed for ourselves and for the world around us.

So, how do we do this? First, you need to keep your eyes and brain open and school yourself to recognize the synchronicities of life. Have faith that the right thing will happen, even if we don't necessarily understand why events are unfolding as they are. This is not to say that you are helpless in the face of disaster—not at all—but looking at events as integral parts of a whole will assist you in making wiser choices. Learn to tailor your life and your magickal practices by verbally asking that the best for all concerned will manifest. This practice becomes second nature to Witches when they finally understand that there is no such thing as a coincidence, and may then recognize these synchronistic happenings when these events take place. Asking for the best for everyone proves that you have put forth the effort to think of balance and harmony. I believe the words "perfect love and perfect trust" apply here.

Secondly, the magickal practitioner must understand that he or she is what he or she manifests. You are the sum of your mundane life and the magicks you weave in and around that life. When we chant in circle, "We are the flow and we are the ebb, we are the weavers and we are the web," we are talking not only of group magicks but of our individual manifestations as well. If you weave negative magicks, then you have incarnated a negative human persona. If you weave positive magicks, then you have created a glittering tapestry that manifests into a positive person. Indeed, the Witch becomes a life-long manifestation of the magicks they practice as well as what they practice in their mundane lives. To put it bluntly, if you practice positive magicks and positive living, then you will be a holistic person. If you practice negative magicks and a negative lifestyle, then you become a negative person. If you practice positive magicks but a negative lifestyle, you become a confused mud puddle that everyone will try to avoid. If you practice negative magicks and a positive lifestyle, you need a psychiatrist or an exorcist—take your pick.

When the art of manifestation turns from the ability to acquire things to the ability to transform the self in a positive manner, you no longer belong in the Wicca 101 class at your local metaphysical book store. By then, I believe the adage goes, "You've come a long way, baby" and you can take one Witch-step up in the world. Have a cup of herbal tea and pat yourself on the back. You've just skimmed the surface of true WitchCraft. This is not to say that physical manifestation is still not an important part of your being, but it is not the primary reason for functioning or doing magick anymore.

Spiritual Seconds

Learn to spot coincidences as they happen. Keep your eyes and mind open to all possibilities. Remove negative, condescending thoughts from your mind when you do recognize a coincidence.

Magickal Minutes

Don't just work on manifesting money, that car you are itching to put your fingers on, or that new thing-a-ma-jig that everyone else has. Sure, it's fine to work for things, but don't forget to work on yourself. Pick a minor character flaw and practice your magicks on that. Use visualization, affirmations, positive thinking, your favorite tools of the Witch trade, the moon phases, astrological correspondences—whatever. Just *do* it. After you have corrected the minor irritation that your mother is now weeping and clapping hallelujah for, check out how your magicks for other things work out. Better, huh?

Magickal Minutes

Learn to do things with your mind the moment before your hands do the act of movement. For example, if you wish to move a glass, imagine the glass moving by itself to where you want it to go before you actually move the glass with your hand. This technique involves the simple process of "manifest in your head first" before you actively manifest the movement with your motor skills. This is an easy way to work with your visualization techniques without closing your eyes. When you think "I want a drink," it sends an immediate signal to the hand. Your hand moves unconsciously and the act is done before the consciousness recognizes the thought for what it is. Normally, you don't need to go through elongating the thought. In magickal training, however, you should try to slow this thought relay down, which strengthens the visualization process of the mind, which enhances your power in focused prayer or spellcasting techniques. Add the memory of a "feeling" and you're really boom-sailing!

All of the keys to empowerment I've outlined for you so far focus on building your mental agility, teaching you to access your will as well as the will of the divine. After several years of practicing the Craft, mentally, spiritually, and physically I have found that the most invaluable tool to your success in life and harmony with others lies within the workings of your own mind. I can't make you a great Witch or even a decent person. Only you can do that. Only you have the drive and determination to make your life what you want it to be. You cannot count on others to put you where you want to go, nor can you fall back on blaming other people if you don't get to where you'd planned to be. Your personal success lies within your own mind.

The Seventh Mystery of Invoking Your Power

The seventh mystery of personal empowerment can be a toughie, I warn you now. The seventh secret is **learning how to banish stuff from your life**—including people, things, habits, ill health, and general negativity. In essence, anything or anyone that drags you down. So, light that seventh candle and say:

> *Through the guidance of the Lord and Lady, I banish*
> *all things from my life that are not spiritually good for me.*

Sometimes you may simply have to learn the art of delegation, other times you need to let go of a particular person, item, or mode of thought. For example, I received an e-mail from one individual who had started an open circle about six months ago. Most of the members got along, but one fellow began to exhibit bizarre behavior, like walking in the woods at night and screaming strange things, rattling on about how he was a Supreme Being, and so forth—behavior not conducive to spiritual learning, let me tell you. This type of whacked-out behavior doesn't belong in any Wiccan circle I've ever attended.

The person who contacted me wanted to know how the circle could assist this friend. They wanted to bind his behavior. Great, I thought, bind a crazy to you—what a delightful noose around the neck that would be! I suggested moving the person out of the circle environment, and added that they should encourage that person to seek appropriate counseling or therapy. My e-mail person was appalled. This is a *brother*, he said. We *can't* let him alone. He might hurt himself. Then *we* would be responsible.

Horse hockey.

If no one in the group has training in the realms of counseling or therapeutic measures, then none of these people should try to fix the problem by themselves. If they continue to allow this individual to participate with them, then he will bring down the entire group mind, and eventually destroy it. The Goddess and God have little use for that sort of sacrifice. Learn to realize that even Witches can't fix everything. Sometimes, when something looks broken, it is broken. And when things are broken, you don't keep them.

Here's another example. Let's say your friend is an alcoholic. You've done your best to help move him or her through appropriate counseling—alcoholism falls under the category of a diseased condition and needs treatment. Your friend is in denial, which means he or she doesn't think a problem exists. You watch this person exhibit bizarre behavior all the time, to the point where this behavior affects your life in a negative manner. What should you do? Stay with that friend until you are more miserable than everyone else on the planet, or become detached, realizing that your mental health is just as important as your friend's?

When you accept the concept of banishment, then you take the pressure off of yourself to bring forced solutions to form, which may not be good for you or others. This gives you the freedom to be the Witch that you want to be, not the Witch who is painfully constructed by the actions, opinions, and mistakes of others. I'm not saying that you should ignore those in need or not share your wisdom with those who could benefit from this offering of self. What I *am* saying is "Don't teach the mysteries to fools" because, truly, it will be a waste of your breath. When you accept this banishment/detachment energy into your life, you leave the portal open for spontaneous and stable solutions to the different problems you need to work through—problems that belong to you, and not someone else.

I'm not suggesting that you start running around banishing everything in your life right this second. Be realistic. Learn to move negative things out of your life that impair your spiritual progress. If you sit down and pay close attention to what energies ebb and flow in your life, you will instinctively know what energies are good for you and what energies are not. All Witches should honor their common sense and, if you don't have any, find it!

Your Environment and Your Vibrational Rate

Notice that the First Mystery and the Seventh Mystery work together, as all the secrets of personal power will flow through your life once you begin concentrating on them; however, these two are particularly compatible, especially when we are talking about your personal vibrational rate and the act of banishing unwanted negative energies from your life, which affects your rate of vibration.

The people you spend your time with also become part of your energy frequency. For example, if you constantly surround yourself with negative people, then you may find yourself thinking and speaking in a negative manner without meaning to. There is more to peer pressure than meets the eye, especially when you are succeeding in raising your vibrational rate and the rest of the world trails far behind you. I know there will be times in your life when you will find it necessary to move out of those types of relationships entirely, even though this will create a big change for you and will affect many areas of your being. Spiritual maturation is a moving bus. You may have a few layovers but, if you work seriously on manifesting your inner light, onward you will go. We might be talking about a circle of friends or compromised energies with parents, siblings, or even a spouse. Your job and the people working with you bleed energy all around you; sometimes this energy can get mighty unpleasant. If you have exhausted all other avenues, it will take a firm decision and courage to move on. Sometimes a friend or family member can talk turkey to us and help us; other times, we may not be so fortunate. Sometimes we have to learn to do the moving ourselves.

Your environment, whether we're talking about at home or at work, says a lot about you, including what you think, how you react to certain situations, and what kinds of benefits you are (or are not) receiving. Sometimes, changing these two areas of our lives—our home or our jobs—can be the hardest of all. The spiritual bus will wait for you, just don't keep the motor idling too long.

Spiritual Seconds

Make a list of those things you wish to banish from your life. Begin by asking Spirit for assistance, then work toward removing dead issues, uncomfortable relationships, and bad habits from your essence.

The Eighth Mystery of Invoking Your Power

The eighth mystery of your personal power lies in your ability to **understand the cycles of the seasons** and how those cycles relate to your personal life. Yes, I realize you understand the basic concepts of spring, summer, winter, and fall. I, too, remember sitting in grade school and dressing the Colorform Kids (remember those?) with appropriate seasonal clothing. I think I fully realized the impact of

Craft in my life when I discovered that the events in my life closely paralleled the changes of the seasons. Light candle number eight now, and say:

I will move in harmony with the seasons.

Okay, so what does this mean? If you take careful note, you will see that all of humankind moves within the cycle of the seasons, whether they realize it or not. Around Beltaine (May Day), new things abound. Sometimes these new experiences come as a result of sudden change, an exciting insight, an offer from another individual, or they could manifest as the result of careful planning, and now the new experience readies itself for launching. Conversely, the opposite of Beltaine is Samhain, the season of death and transformation. As the year winds down, many old things pass away—experiences severed from our lives by the giant karma combine—and the good things in life give us a bountiful harvest as a time for circumspection approaches.

Your job, as a magickal practitioner, is to learn to take advantage of what this season offers. Learn to work your magick with the provided energy pattern, rather than against it. One way to learn to move with the seasons is to take eight three-by-five-inch cards and label each one with a Pagan holiday. On the front of the card, write what the holiday means to you and what kinds (or kind) of energy you think moves within that season. Here is a guide for you to use:

Spring:	Candlemas
	Spring Equinox
	Beltaine
Summer:	Summer Solstice
Autumn:	Lammas
	Fall Equinox
	Samhain
Winter:	Yule

Notice that the seasons often attributed to the Goddess (spring and fall) contain more Pagan holidays than those attributed to the God (summer and winter). It isn't that we like one deity better than the other. Spring and fall move slowly, with gentle energies, one toward birth, one toward death, where the seasons of the God contain strong, vibrant, robust energies. Spring and fall are soft preludes to summer and winter, giving balance to our year. Now, before someone starts saying that this isn't how their coven or tradition views the seasons—yes, I understand that. This is the way we work with the seasons here at Black Forest, and I'm using our theology as an example, nothing more.

Use the back of the three-by-five-inch card to write what kinds of magick you can work during the season and holiday listed on the front, tailoring the seasons to your specific needs. Put the card on your shrine or altar, and refer back to it occasionally during the season. Check off what magicks you have performed. At the end of the season, write down the salient points of what happened in your life during that holiday on a separate card, and staple that card to the first. File these cards away to look at next year.

Spiritual Seconds

Attune yourself with the seasons by practicing meditational exercises focused on the season, as well as the energy that revolves around that season. One of the best books on the market today for this purpose is the *Celtic Devotional— Daily Prayers & Blessings* by Caitlin Matthews (Harmony Books, 1996).

Other Things to Do

Practice the seasonal exercise given previously. Record your results. Save your cards for next year. The following year, look over the work of the previous year and take note of how wonderfully far you have come!

The Ninth Mystery of Invoking Your Power

The ninth mystery of personal empowerment encompasses **your attitude toward others**. Light the ninth candle now, and say:

> *I will strive to fulfill the needs of others,*
> *without harming myself in the process.*

Just as your behavior affects the lives of others, so the behavior of others influences your life, either in a positive or negative manner. You can learn to control or enhance your responses to others, as well as their responses to you.

I learned two very important lessons last year. Both experiences left considerable marks on my psyche that now, after every third degree initiation or eldering I attend, I pass these lessons on. After much thought, I think that you all need to hear of my experiences also.

A few summers ago, I was eldered by Lord Serphant of the Serpent Stone Family. Serphant was, and still is, in my mind, one of the most interesting Craft elders I've ever met. Tall, with long flowing hair both on his head and from his chin, he truly did remind one of a stately wizard. This is not to say he wasn't human or didn't make mistakes. He would be the first to admit that we are all fallible. He loved dirty jokes, drank black coffee, and smoked cigarettes; however, when he had a mind to, he could look right through your soul in half a second and there was nothing, and I mean absolutely nothing, you could do about it. And then . . . then . . . he would tell you what you needed to hear.

In the fall, I received an invitation to visit another prominent Craft elder. By this time, Mick and I had been on tour for several months. We debated for over a week whether or not we should drive the long distance required. Things at home were hectic, our tour wasn't over, and we hesitated, knowing that what we really needed involved rest, not another trek somewhere. To make the journey, I had to swap the day hours at my job for a long night stint. Since I couldn't seem to make up my own mind on the issue, I asked Spirit to clear the way if Mick and I should make the trip. Spirit opened the pathway, so we decided to go.

The whole way there I was very, very nervous. What would this person think of me? Could this individual help me spiritually? I thought that was a possibility . . . indeed, this person was an elder. By the time we got there, my emotions had reached crispy on the outside, mushy on the inside. I imagined myself walking away from this person's home with a whole new outlook. My spirit would fly, my power would increase exponentially, and my energy would truly encompass the word "elder."

Well, that didn't happen.

In fact, nothing happened. Absolutely nothing at all.

On the way home we stopped at a restaurant. I went into the ladies' room. You know, interesting thoughts have a habit of coming to us in the most unspiritual places. I realized that Spirit did, indeed, gift me as I visited that Craft elder. I learned that no one walks on water, not even a Craft elder; but more importantly, I realized that, as an elder myself, I should try to never, ever let someone walk away from me without gaining "something." I learned that all Witches should carry grace in their hearts, in their minds, and in their words. To act less than that is to act in dishonor toward our Lady and Lord.

I don't need to give you exercises for this one. I think you are capable of understanding this lesson. Look at that ninth candle you lit, and think about what a real Craft elder should be like, then attempt to live up to that thoughtform.

The Tenth Mystery of Invoking Your Power

The tenth mystery of utilizing your personal power takes a lot more work than those listed before. This secret requires you to **learn the art of self-hypnosis.** Light your tenth candle now, and say:

I will train my mind to enhance my spirituality.

Self-hypnosis and the hypnotizing of others (magickally called the "art of fascination") has been around in the magickal community for eons. You want to be adept, don't you? How do you think our ancestors did it?

What about the practical magick I promised you? We've got to light your sacred flame first. Remember that candle in the first Magickal Minute exercise you supposedly did? The one where Angelique timed me? Well, that represents your flight from self-imposed darkness into the spiritual light. The ten candles in the Personal Power exercise that you began at the beginning of this chapter symbolize your willingness to work for what you need. As the candles burn, the flames draw power to your desires. You may keep those candles burning until they burn no more; or, you may put them out now, and re-light them every evening for a short period of time until the candles are "all" (in Pennsylvania Dutch-speak). Bury the candle ends (if there are any) in your backyard.

Now. It's time to turn *your* pilot light on, and keep it burning.

3

The Solution
Lies in You

What would you say is the Witch's most valuable tool? The athame? Perhaps the cauldron? Maybe the rituals practiced? Or how about the book of shadows? Although all these things fall under the definition of a *tool* and all can assist the Witch in their magickal practices, the most powerful tool the Witch possesses is his or her own self. This tool—body, mind, and Spirit—becomes a powerhouse triad if you learn to use what you have. Lord Serphant walked empty-handed out of a ritual circle of over three hundred people one night, took a sly look at me, and said, "Silver! Guess what? I forgot my tools!" To cook any spell, you must learn to fire up your most important tool—yourself. *You* are the greatest gift to the community.

Several years ago I found myself filled with a burning desire to learn hypnotherapy. At the time, I didn't realize that the techniques used in hypnotherapy today consist of the same techniques used in basic spellwork by our magickal ancestors. Witches before us called this very important building block **magickal fascination**. Under this heading, Witches employed self-hypnosis techniques even before hypnosis got its name. So whether you think of your mind as wild-thang or a state-of-the-art computer, the techniques of mental fascination will work for you. For the former you have to train the mind, for the latter you must program the mind—same difference. Many of today's Witches use the word "focus" to describe the practice.

The Enchanted Slinky

When I was a kid, my two favorite toys were the Jingle-Jump (which I don't think they sell anymore) and the Slinky. I spent hours of enjoyment with these two toys. My husband can always find me at a festival because I still wear bells (must be left over from my Jingle-Jump days). Anyway, one afternoon my oldest daughter went shopping at the mall with her friends. She came home with a multi-colored Slinky in the shape of a moon. As soon as she set the toy on the table I snapped it up and started playing with it. (Hey, so we're all kids at heart, what can I say?) As she chatted merrily along about her fascinating excursion, who said what to whom, what cute guys there were (or weren't), I happily played with the Slinky. After awhile she said, "You haven't been listening to a word I said. What *are* you doing?" I snapped out of it and merely replied, "Oh, playing." It became a standard joke in our house to keep Mom away from the Slinky.

Several months later I had a Craft friend over for dinner. Our after-dinner discussion got fairly deep and the next thing I knew, my daughter brought down the Slinky and plopped the toy in front of me. I unconsciously began playing with the toy. Not only did I fascinate myself, I fascinated my guest. Although we both laughed about it, I had two realizations: one, the Slinky has stayed on the market because it puts children into the alpha state, thereby relaxing them (and what Mother doesn't want a few moments of peace and quiet?); and two, you can use the Slinky both in magick and as a hypnotic mechanism.

That night, after my guest left, I sat down with the Slinky, picked a goal I wished to work on, and began playing with the Slinky, focusing only on that goal. The next day, much to my happiness, my goal manifested.

The Art of Mental Fascination

Mental fascination comprises the foundation for the ten paths of power. These paths are:

Meditation

Aspecting (a form of possession) and Invocations

Trance and Astral Projection

Potions (including herbals, incense, and wines)

Dancing and/or Drumming (rattles included in this category as well)

Blood Control (as in bio-feedback techniques)

Working with Stellar, Earth, Sun, Astrological Energies

Chants and Sacred Breath

Spells

Sex

These ten paths of power can overlap. For example, you can meditate on a candle flame, then drum, shake your rattle, chant and consume a potion, all in the focused effort of one particular desire. Conversely, you could use only one path to reach a desired end; for example, meditating every day on enhancing a personal talent. Regardless of which combination or singular path of power you choose to manifest your desires, the main foundation of such work begins with the art of fascination. Likewise, any spell, devotion, ritual, petition, or solution rests on your ability to adequately employ this same technique.

What does the word "fascination" mean? To fascinate your mind basically means to put your mind in the alpha state. In Laurie Cabot's book *Power of the Witch*, there is a good discussion of the alpha state, how to get there, and how to use this state for healing.

To fascinate someone else runs along a different plot line in the fascination story. Let's talk about self-fascination first; to do that, we need to educate you on the levels of the mind. Alpha is a scientific word for a specific number of brain waves per minute. Basically, alpha constitutes a relaxed state of mind. No, you don't have to stumble around with a dazed look in your eye to be in the alpha state. Your mind often experiences alpha when you watch television, eat, drive, read, are under stress, are performing a monotonous task, before you go to sleep, or when you daydream. Ongoing studies of the mind show that the simple act of closing your eyes can put you into a light alpha state. Therefore, attaining alpha is not difficult and represents a normal, natural state of mind. Everyone, everywhere, goes into alpha. All you need to do is train your mind to go into the level of alpha you desire when you want it to and for as long as you want it to. A fascination, then, is the attained skill of focusing your mind while you are in the alpha state for a period of time that you determine. When we meditate, we produce a self-induced alpha or theta state.

To put the alpha state into perspective, let's briefly talk about the other types of brain waves you manufacture. We have beta, the general waking state. Then we move into alpha, which I have already described to you. From there, your mind dips to theta. In theta, many people experience divine revelations, see divinity and angels, and experience astral protection. From theta, your mind moves to delta, which manifests as deep sleep. Each type of brain wave (beta, alpha, theta, delta) has many levels, meaning at any specific point in time you're not in alpha, rather you are in *a level of* alpha; you are not in beta, you are in *a level of* beta. For most purposes, any level of alpha will be of assistance in your magickal and religious work, though the deeper you can train yourself to go, the better. You don't need to be a walking zombie to practice the art of fascination.

This brings us to the most bogus misinterpretation of the art of fascination. No person exists on the planet who cannot move his or her mind into the alpha state. That means that people who claim they can't be hypnotized, or are not capable of practicing fascinations, are full of it. Especially practicing Witches! After all, fascination is the foundation of all of your magick. What they really mean is that they do not desire to relinquish control to another person, and therefore will be too stubborn to move into the alpha state when requested to do so by a hypnotherapist. Standard hypnosis tests, such as the eye-roll, hand tests, hypnosis wheel, fogging numbers, and simple inductions serve two functions: To monitor an individual's behavior and how that behavior works in conjunction with the technique of the hypnotherapist, and whether or not the subject trusts the facilitator. These tests do not judge the subject, they simply monitor whether or not the subject and the hypnotherapist are compatible.

By learning the art of self-hypnosis, or self-fascination, we've cut out the middle person and are relying on ourselves instead. Uh-oh, I hear squeals of indignation from some certified hypnotherapists out there, so I'll add this statement: Not all problems in your life can be dealt with alone. Sometimes it is best to seek out qualified medical care (of course) or a trained hypnotherapist. If you are failing on your own, don't roll yourself into a ball and give up. Seek out the help you need. Back to the subject at hand. The alpha state, then, is an easily obtainable state of mind. Your mind goes into alpha several times during the day naturally. What you need to do now is train your mind to go into alpha when you want it to, as deep as you want it to.

Certain magickal groups exist, as well as a few standard religious groups, that deny the usefulness of working with mind arts such as hypnotherapy and self-hypnosis. This, to be quite frank, revolves around an issue of control. We now know that the use of self-fascinations and hypnotherapy enables the individual to revive approximately ninety-two percent of the unused mind of the average person. We also know that most maladaptive human behavior results from inappropriate self or societal programming and that approximately eighty percent of all illnesses stem from psychosomatic issues, all of which react well to hypnotherapy techniques. I have always believed that if we linked fascination techniques with magickal practices, the possibility of success in any given working rises exponentially.

The Solution Lies in You

Whether using magick or hypnotherapy techniques, the practitioner must have a strong, motivating desire to change. If this strength wanes, or doesn't exist, then the fascination technique will not work. Fascinations bypass the critical, conscious mind and focus on the emotional, subconscious mind. Everything a subject hears, sees, smells, reads, touches, tastes, or experiences (such as a horrendous blind date or a rousing sports competition) remains stored in the mind. Therefore, any memory you desire will surface through self-fascination, and these memories (such as studying for a test or healing a back injury) can function in a positive manner for healing or goal programming, providing you can unlock the door of self-imposed mental blocks.

Neither Witches nor hypnotherapists have the legal ability to diagnose illness, nor can they prescribe medical treatment, nor can they offer drugs or herbs for ingestion. I do have some warnings for you. Medically speaking, if you have a heart condition, use psychotropic drugs through prescriptive method, or have experienced a severe head injury in the past, you should ask your physician if you may practice the meditative and fascination arts safely. You need to make sure that you do not heedlessly throw yourself into the mental arts if it would be unsafe for you to do so. Your physician will advise you on what techniques would be safe for you to practice. Many psychotropic drugs will fight against the benefits of hypnosis and self-hypnosis.

If you have been working magick, you've already gone into the alpha state naturally. The alpha state consists of the following: Relaxation of the body and mind; narrowed focus of attention; reduced awareness of external environment and everyday concerns; and greater internal awareness of sensations. That's why when Witches train their students, they request that the student learn to set aside undisturbed time to work a spell or ritual, and often insist on a series of meditational exercises. You can't be in the alpha state with the phone ringing, kids running in and out of the room, your cat using your nose as a pull toy, or your significant other bugging you to come downstairs and watch television because he or she is lonely (well, you could after you get good at it, but not when you begin to learn the technique). Granted, once you practice sufficiently, you can go into the alpha state at almost any time, but trying to focus and prolong that state for a decent spell or ritual with the world jumping around you can upset you, blowing alpha right out the proverbial window. Into beta you will go, simply because the world got your dander up. Better to firmly set aside the time you need to train yourself, rather than hate the world for stopping you from doing something you truly want to accomplish. Let's face it, the world isn't blocking you; your irritation limits you. So, before we play with spells and numerous solutions to your problems, we are going to teach you how to become an expert at fascination.

Magickal Minutes ———————————————————

Removing Mental Blocks

Supplies: Gather nine sugar cubes; one cup spring water; one white candle; a small, clear bowl; a piece of white parchment; and a red marker.

Timing: Full moon, waning moon, or dark moon

Planetary Hour: Saturn

Planet: Saturn

Day: Saturday

Rune Symbol: Cen

Archetype: Hecate

Totem: Bird or horse (both stand for freedom)

1. Cleanse, consecrate, and empower all supplies with the goal of banishing obstacles in your path to a specific goal, known and unknown.

2. State the goal.

3. Fill the bowl with water. Draw the Cen rune symbol on the parchment. Cen magickally opens the pathways before us and illuminates the darkness. Put the symbol under the bowl so that you can see it through the water.

4. Line the sugar cubes up in a row. Count down from nine to one, touching each sugar cube, then begin the following:

5. One at a time, drop the sugar cubes into the bowl of water, saying:

> *Nine sugar cubes, all in a row I cast a spell, my magick grows.*
> *By drop of nine, the goal is mine!* (Stir the water nine times widdershins while repeating the word "nine" over and over again.)

> *By drop of eight, I weave my fate.* (Stir the water nine times widdershins while repeating the word "eight" over and over again.)

> *By drop of seven, come Queen of Heaven.* (Stir the water nine times widdershins while repeating the word "seven" over and over again.)

> *By drop of six, my goal is fixed.* (Stir the water nine times widdershins while repeating the word "six" over and over again.)

By drop of five, my goal's alive. (Stir the water nine times widdershins while repeating the word "five" over and over again.)

By drop of four, I open the door. (Stir the water nine times widdershins while repeating the word "four" over and over again.)

By drop of three, obstacles dissolve away from me. (Stir the water nine times widdershins while repeating the word "three" over and over again.)

By drop of two, my wish comes true. (Stir the water nine times widdershins while repeating the word "two" over and over again.)

By drop of one, this spell is done. (Stir the water nine times widdershins while repeating the word "one" over and over again.)

6. Hold the bowl up, and say:

Spirits of Saturn, in all your forms and shapes, gather now to serve my magickal purpose. Angel of this day, element of water, lend the power to accomplish my purpose. Hecate, Great Mother of Birth and Death, guide my thoughts, my magick, and my words to accomplish my desire. Give me the power to achieve my magickal purpose.

7. Put the bowl down, hold your hands over the water, and say:

May this spell not reverse, or place upon me any curse. With harm to none. My will be done. May all astrological correspondences be correct for this working.

8. Once all the sugar cubes have dissolved, throw the water at a crossroads in the dead of night or into a living body of water. Remember to thank the archetype you called for assistance.

Number spells, such as the one given above, exemplify the use of magickal fascination. By employing the numbers and rhyme, you fascinate your mind into a level of alpha, which clears the way for the thought to reach out into the universe, take shape, and fulfill your desires. By counting down twice from nine to one (first when you set out the sugar cubes, and again when you intoned the rhyme) you allowed your mind to work in compliance with your will in a focused manner.

I'm sure many of you have seen the knot and cord spells that have won Witches throughout the centuries either fame or flame. These simple yet powerful spells are practices in magickal fascination.

Signposts of Alpha

As I mentioned earlier, all inductions into a fascination must bring about the following results: Relaxation of body and mind; narrowed focus of attention; reduced awareness of external environment and everyday concerns; and a greater awareness of internal sensations. We want to learn the mechanics of inductions so that eventually we can cast better spells. Let's take the results of a fascination one by one to make sure you fully understand.

Relaxation of body and mind means that your body and mind experiences total relaxation. The best place to do this, of course, would be in a chair, on a sofa, on a mat on the floor, et cetera. The seating arrangement must be comfortable. *You* must be comfortable. Your mind should not furiously churn like the parting of the Red Sea. Peaceful and calm, feeling good, no stress, and so on—that's relaxation of mind and body. Breaths per minute slow down and blood pressure lowers. Although you may not think so, you can experience relaxation in body and mind while you are standing. This takes practice, but you can do it! When practicing self-fascinations for complete goal programming, where I am sitting down and taping myself for a full session, I have my blankie. When I practice self-hypnosis, I get cold because my blood pressure lowers. If you experience bodily discomfort, then you won't pay attention to business. My blankie provides the solution. Many individuals do not lie completely down when working through an entire session, because this constitutes a signal to the subconscious that you wish to sleep. We don't want to go to delta in self-fascination techniques.

Narrowed focus of attention means your mind is not playing a full game of tackle football with people, events, feelings, or emotions. Your attention focuses on one thing and one thing only, or a sequence of ideas, such as in a vision quest, or a sequence of mental events as presented on a meditation tape.

Reduced awareness of external environment and everyday concerns: Even though you hear the phone ring in the other room, you don't pay a whit of attention to it. You could care less. The deeper the level of alpha, the less you are likely to even hear the ringing of the phone, the traffic outside your window, or the television set your spouse refuses to turn down in the other room. Somewhere your mind registers the sound but you simply don't worry about that sound and therefore it blends into the background.

Greater awareness of internal sensations: Rather than concentrating on the world around you and being on guard for whatever lies behind any face or around any corner, you are aware of yourself, your needs, and how you are feeling. Eyes closed, you can concentrate on what will work best for you and not entertain worries of your environment, which is why you need to find a place where you know the curiosity seekers of the house won't find you when you practice meditation, spellcasting, or ritual. In order to connect with your internal self, you need peace and quiet.

Do other techniques exist other than counting down from nine to one to help fascinate your mind? Yes indeed! A constant sound, such as the ticking of a clock, the whining blades of a fan, or the monotonous movement of a metronome, will assist in boring the mind (just don't pick a cuckoo clock). Simple drum trancing can assist in putting you into the appropriate zone. You don't have to perform like an expert. A simple, repetitive beat will do. You can use a rattle in the same way.

How Fascinations Relate to Your Magickal Applications

A few years ago, two friends of mine and I went to a local college psych lab to determine how quickly we could go into the lower levels of the alpha state and the subsequent theta state. Because we'd been practicing meditation techniques for several years, we all went into the lower levels of alpha in less than half a minute. We found that you can move your body quickly or slowly in the alpha state, but sudden jerks, such as flailing an arm, will put you back in beta.

Scientifically, your magick works faster and better when you can move your mind into the alpha state while manipulating outside energies or raising your own energy. We also found that a person who relaxes in the alpha state will heal faster when magick enters the equation than when the patient remains in normal beta state and accepts magickal applications. Finally, we discovered that most religious experiences, colorful visions, or an epiphany occur while the individual is in the theta state. By training your mind to enter the alpha state when practicing spellwork, you have a better chance of success than if you don't bother with meditation or other mental exercises.

Adept Witches have always known about fascinations, both for themselves and for others. Mental magicks should be a very important part of your magickal compendium, which is why I'm emphasizing the subject. Once you have achieved control over your own mind and can focus your thoughts in a specific direction for an extended length of time, you will discover that your magickal applications work better and faster than ever before. Fascinations, then, are the first step in honing your spellcasting abilities.

Magickal Minutes ———————————————————

Magickal Fruit Garland:
Spell to Increase the Realm of Possibilities and Abundance

Days: Sunday or Thursday

Planetary Hours: Sun or Jupiter

Planetary Spirits: Sun or Jupiter

Moon Phase: Full or waxing

Element: Fire or Earth

Rune: Feoh (wealth)

Archetype: Rosemerta

Totem Animal: Pelican

Magick Circle: Not needed

Quarter Call: Not needed

1. Go shopping at the grocery store in the produce section. Look for a selection of small fruits such as strawberries, blueberries, mini-bananas, cherry tomatoes, grapes, and so on. As you shop, keep in mind that you are browsing through the possibilities of life.

2. At home, carefully wash the fruit with consecrated water. You may also wish to empower the water for the goal of abundance.

3. Using heavy waxed thread, begin to make a garland, slowly threading the fruit together. Don't jerk your hands, scream at the kids, or get up and down from your chair. Stay put and work through the spell slowly. As you thread the fruit, count down from fifty to one. Each time you thread a piece of fruit, say something like:

> *As this garland grows, so does abundance and*
> *prosperity grow within my life.*

4. When you finish, ask the Goddess Rosemerta to send her blessings into the fruit and fill your life with prosperity and abundance. Tie the garland together so that it forms a circle. Set the garland on a large plate. Pour a small amount of sugar on the plate in the middle of the garland. With your finger, draw the rune Feoh in the sugar. Set in the refrigerator to chill. Serve to your family for supper. As each person partakes of the garland fruit, they bring abundance into their lives.

Simple magickal fascinations are not the same thing as ritual, though you can use fascinations in spells, rites, and rituals. The first two exercises in this chapter focus on simple spellwork without the use of a magick circle or ritual outline.

Techniques for Inducing the Alpha State

You can use several types of inductions to bring your mind into the alpha/theta state. Not all of these techniques relate to solitary use, but I feel you should have this information so that you can understand the full scope of the art of fascination. Remember, we naturally go into the alpha state during normal, daily activity. By using the techniques for inducing the alpha state, we bring something that already constitutes a natural body function into the realm of conscious control, rather than relying on our subconscious to kick-start this state of being.

The Fixation Induction

This induction draws your attention to a very narrow point of interest, such as a candle flame, a swinging pendulum, a metronome, and so on. The object draws our attention away from the room, other people, and our environment in general, allowing us to focus on a single, repetitive movement. As I mentioned earlier, drum trancing would fall into this category, as well as chanting, because you are fixating yourself through sound. The more you work with the fixation induction, the faster your ability to move into the alpha (and subsequently theta) state. For example, the first time you try the fixation procedure it may take you thirty minutes to even slightly bore your brain; however, with successive tries, you may factor this time frame down to less than thirty seconds, as in my example of the Witches in the college psych lab. One of the biggest complaints I hear from readers and students centers on their impatience with themselves. Truly, it takes time and practice to attain focused alpha.

Don't be so hard on yourself. Just relax and let it happen. It may take you one week or it may take you thirty weeks to reap success.

How do you "know" when you have reached the point where the magick begins? The best way I can explain it is a feeling of slight separation from reality accompanied by a pleasant, harmonious feeling with a sense of universal connection. Some Witches call this the "still point."

Hocus Focus (Exercise One):
A Fixation Spell

This exercise involves candle magick. I'm sure you've seen the technique before, but we will treat this magick a bit differently here, as you will work magick while you learn a few fascination techniques.

First, you need a white candle, any size will do; a piece of paper (some magickal individuals like to use virgin parchment); and a skin-safe oil that relates to the goal you choose. If you don't have money for a specific oil, use a bit of perfume, aftershave, or your favorite body splash. Pick something in your life that you would like to manifest. Write down your specific need on an index card or a slip of paper. No, you cannot choose more than one need. If you feel you qualify as an advanced student who has learned a magickal alphabet, by all means go ahead and write your need in the alphabet. Choose one mental picture (and one mental picture only) that you would associate with the fulfillment of this need. The mental picture should revolve around a positive manifestation. Dress the candle in your favorite oil or an oil you have chosen specifically for this goal. Remember: dress from the middle of the candle away from you to push things away from you, and dress from the middle of the candle toward yourself if you wish to draw something into your life. Hold the candle in the direction of compass north for physical manifestations and remember to ask for the blessings of the North in this magickal application. Be sure to keep the mental picture you have chosen in your mind. If you wish to cultivate a transformation in yourself, hold the candle to the West and ask for the blessings of the West in your magickal working. Don't forget the mental picture. If you wish to harvest something or move an issue along that's been dragging and you want this issue over and done with, then ask for the blessings of the South. Finally, if your work centers on mental issues, such as psychic power, mental acuity, or the like, then ask for the blessings of the

East. If you desire to banish something, then hold the candle up above you and ask for Spirit to lend blessings to your working.

Hold the candle in your hands. Close your eyes and take three deep, even breaths. Take your time. Relax and let yourself move into that candle—shut out the world around you and think about holding the candle and what this candle represents. Open your eyes and bring up the mental picture to your conscious mind that you have associated with your need (remember to keep the visualization positive). Connect that picture to the candle and move the picture into the candle flame. Herman Slater once wrote in his book of magick formularies (see bibliography) that while the first half of the candle burns, the wish resounds in heaven; the judgment on earth manifests while the second half burns.

Put the candle in the holder, close your eyes, and breathe in the scent of the oil off your hands. Keep that same picture of your goal in your mind as you breathe in the scent of the oil. Now you are connecting your goal with the scent of the oil. Open your eyes and put the paper listing your need under the candle. Light the candle, then hold it aloft, saying:

> *Element of fire, work my will by my desire. Holy Mother* (or the particular name of a God or Goddess), *work your will with spiritual fire. Bless this moment in time and the magick I am about to do. I thank you for the successes you have given me and the successes that will come to me. My specific desire is* _____ (name your desire). *With harm to none. So mote it be.*

Project that one mental picture into the flame as you hold it aloft. Then put the candle down.

Relax and watch the candle flame. Don't sit there squinting at the candle and don't try to make the candle flame dance, spit, gyrate, or anything else. Don't worry about any messages the candle may be trying to send you at first. That comes later. Just take deep, even breaths and relax, watching the flame of the candle do its thing. Think only of the candle. Think only of the flame. If your eyelids drift shut, that's fine. Think of your connection to the candle, what the candle stands for, and that mental picture of your need. Don't get excited, upset, or worried that you might be doing something wrong. Don't let doubts intercede on your behalf; who's running this show, anyway? Just think of the candle, your need, and your mental picture. If your thoughts drift, don't have heart failure, just bring them gently back into focus by smelling your hands, which carry the scent of the oil that you mentally connected to your goal. Now, add the feeling of your accomplishment that will accompany the attainment of your goal.

See the flame. Concentrate on your need. Put your mental picture into the flame. Most importantly, don't end this exercise with a negative feeling. You have to learn to turn the negatives into positives, right? If you are in doubt, ask the Mother for renewed energy and assistance. When finished, put out the candle and thank the element of fire and the Mother for Her intercession.

Practice this technique for seven days, working with the same issue. Each day, before you begin, hold an unlit candle in your hand, put the picture of the goal into the candle, and then begin the same process that you did before (minus dressing the candle). Don't forget to add the feeling of success. Put a little of the oil or perfume on your hands so that you can use the scent as a mental trigger if necessary. At the end of each session, write down any experiences you may have had as well as any other pertinent information that comes to mind. On the seventh day write on the back of that slip of paper or card the words: "Fixation Spell Complete." Put the card and the candle away in a safe place until your desire has manifested.

With this exercise we didn't worry about the phases of the moon, the planetary hour, archetypes, totems, spirits, or particular day of performance. Right now you need to learn how to fixate your mind on a specific manifestation. Your desire centers on learning how to focus. The more you work with this type of induction, the faster you will be able to focus during a relaxed state of mind. This induction's main function concentrates on teaching you to draw your mind away from external sights and sounds that can cloud the mind and allow you to hold on to this type of focus for increasingly longer periods of time. When your desire has manifested, burn the card or paper and dispose of the candle.

On the eighth day, choose a new desire, and work on exercise two below.

The Relaxation Induction

The second type of induction in self-fascination techniques focuses on removing the stresses that cling to the body and mind. Here, we systematically relax all the muscles in the body. You can begin at the top of your head and work down, or start with your toes and work up. I prefer working from the top of the head down, and funneling any negative energy into the ground, where this energy will transform itself (through your visualization process). Notice that this technique has similarities to that of grounding one's energy so that we can work magick unfettered by self-imposed troubles.

Hocus Focus (Exercise Two):
The Relaxation Spell

Follow the instructions previously stated (don't forget the oil) except this time, close your eyes as soon as you set the lighted candle down. Yes, I know, you won't get to see the flame this time . . . bummer. Imagine the candle flame manifests inside of you as a white light that circulates from your crown to your toes (or toes to crown). Imagine this white light relaxing every portion of your body that it touches. You don't need to concentrate on every muscle, just feel the white light move up (or down) your body. Feel your mind and body relax and move deeper into a calm state of mind. It's okay to say to yourself:

My forehead is relaxing now. The muscles around my eyes are relaxing now. The muscles around my mouth relax. My neck muscles are relaxing. My shoulders are relaxing. My spine relaxes. My hips are relaxing now. My legs are relaxing. My feet are relaxing now. My toes are relaxing.

This method does not use more than one statement for each section of the body, and treats the body sections in large portions, for example *"my legs"* rather than *"my thighs, my kneecaps, my calves, my feet, my arches, my toes . . . ."* Don't worry if these muscles don't "feel" relaxed. As you move further into the method, your muscles will automatically let go and relax. Granted, the more you do this technique, the faster the technique will work for you. I've found that you'll come to a point where you can go through this technique quickly once you've practiced. This type of procedure, again, is called the relaxation induction. Once you have moved from your crown to your toes, you now can focus your mind on the mental picture of what you wish to manifest. If your mind strays, gently pull your thought process back. Do this procedure for seven days.

At the end of each session, write down any experiences you may have had as well as any other pertinent information that comes to mind. On the seventh day, write on the back of that slip of paper or card the words: "This is done." Put the card and the candle away in a safe place until your desire has manifested. Follow the same instructions for disposal once your desire has manifested.

The Progressive Relaxation Induction

Like the relaxation induction, this procedure systematically relieves stress in your body. Again, you may begin either at the top of your head or at your toes. Where the simple relaxation induction uses few statements, the progressive relaxation induction goes into detail. Pauses between each level of relaxation allow the information to sink in and give your body time to react to the statements. For example, I would say: *my thighs relax . . . loose and limp . . . my kneecaps relax . . . pause . . . my calves relax . . . pause . . . my feet,* et cetera. In a progressive relaxation induction you may wish to use the same induction more than once (head to toe, head to toe, head to toe). The more you practice this type of induction, the better for your overall health. During this type of induction you may be prone to images from the collective unconscious that relate specifically to your self-growth. Be sure to write these images down after your session.

Hocus Focus (Exercise Three):
The Progressive Relaxation Spell

Pick a new goal. Go through the previously stated steps except this time, after you close your eyes, you are going to tell each part of your body to relax, and between each statement you will either say "loose and limp," "safe and secure," or simply pause. Example: *My toes relax, my ankles relax, my calves feel loose and limp, my knees relax, I am safe and secure,* et cetera. Work through the entire body. Now concentrate on your desire. Keep careful notes of your experiences. On the seventh day write on the back of that slip of paper or card the words: "Fascination completed." Put the card and the candle away in a safe place until your desire has manifested. For you writer types, notice the removal of all passive voice in these relaxation statements. This type of procedure should employ active voice. When your desire has manifested, burn the paper and dispose of the candle.

The Indirect Induction

This technique uses analogies and metaphors rather than specific induction statements. Many of the vision quest meditation tapes available on the market today use this technique. You go into trance (alpha) by following an imaginary story line designed to take you into the alpha state. For example, you might hear instructions to walk down a path, and go *deeper* into the forest. One of the best indirect induction tapes I've ever heard is from Treena Sutphen of Sun Valley Publishing entitled *Angels of Light*. I use this tape for all of my students. Some tapes will employ the Relaxation Induction and the Indirect Induction in the same session, or combine the Progressive Induction and the Indirect Induction together. Again, for you writers, the statements will run smoother and carry more impact if you learn to eliminate passive voice and concentrate as much as possible on active voice. Further, try never to use the "it" qualifier. Always indicate the nature of "it" rather than using the word "it." If you talk about a waterfall, then use the word waterfall (or close facsimile) rather than including the word waterfall in one sentence, and in the following sentence calling the waterfall "it." This type of induction is wonderful for healing or raising your personal vibrational rate.

Hocus Focus (Exercise Four): Your Mental Sacred Space—The Indirect Spell

We're going to get a little more complicated with this one. Find a drum, rattle, or some other noisemaker. Take three deep breaths, then create sacred space in your mind. Build your sacred space in any way you feel comfortable. Once this sacred space sinks firmly into your mind, begin drumming in a soft, easy pattern. Focus on your desire. While learning this technique, keep drumming until you loose focus. Ground and center. As you get better, raise the level of sound until you reach a crescendo. Then ground and center. As with the other exercises, practice for seven days on the same goal. On the back of your three-by-five-inch card, write "Fascination completed" and put the card away.

The Rapid Induction

The rapid induction, which produces a trance state quickly, consists of short, rapid commands or specific body movements, such as discussed in my book *To Stir A Magick Cauldron*. This type of induction was practiced by Pow-Wow artists in Pennsylvania, Vaudeville, tent revivals, and illusions. You can still see rapid induction techniques in some magick shows and Las Vegas or New York City entertainment. Good speakers also use the rapid induction, though I don't think they plug into the idea of this procedure on a conscious level. The more experienced you become in your own work, the more you will notice rapid inductions within your personal progress.

The Confusion Induction

The last type of induction technique, the confusion induction, serves as a last-ditch effort for hypnotherapists who find themselves stuck with a client who has such an analytical mind that they insist on proving everything, and will dissect anything anyone has the presence of mind to say. While the client counts from fifty to one (or twenty-five to one), the hypnotherapist will count aloud in the opposite direction (one, two, three, four . . .).

Just so you know, con artists use the confusion induction and the fixation induction to put the proverbial bite on you. In Pennsylvania, there's a group known as the Gypsies whom every shop owner fears. Three of these people, often a combination of two men and one woman, will go to a cashier and insist on making change for a twenty while the cashier counts out change from the original order. These people speak rapidly, make lots of hand motions, and try to draw the cashier's eyes away from the till. They will often repeat what the cashier says in reverse, and they always exhibit extreme impatience, often to the point of rudeness laced with caustic remarks. Once these Gypsies have left the store, the poor cashier may find their till minus a stack of twenties.

The final exercise I have for you incorporates your free-form imagination. We all daydream about things we'd like to do, places we'd like to go, or what we want to become when we grow up, even if we're eighty years old. (Sometimes the structured inductions I've given you seem like so much work!) Turn your daydreams in to spell dreams with the following exercise.

Hocus Focus (Exercise 5): The Spell Dream

The spell dream consists of six frames in a mental movie. At first, we will work with stills—pictures that do not move, sort of like snapshots of the new you. Think of your ultimate goal and write this goal down. Underneath, number lines one through six. (For those of you who have experience with meditation, choose as many pictures as you can handle.) On each line, describe one picture of yourself either working toward your goal or the benefits that you want to reap when your goal has manifested. You can write as much detail as you like, for the moment.

Read the first description, then close your eyes and develop a still photograph in your mind. Open your eyes and write down a one-line summary of that picture. Close your eyes again and review the mental photo. Open your eyes. Do this visualization until that picture sets firmly in your mind.

Go to the next line and create your second picture. Follow the same procedure as in the above paragraph. Now, close your eyes and visualize the first picture, then the second. Practice until you can call up the two pictures, one after the other.

Go to the third line and create the next picture. Follow the same procedure. When you have set the third picture in your mind, close your eyes and flash the three pictures consecutively. Finish with the next three pictures in the same manner.

Every evening before you go to bed, or when you feel the mood to daydream sneak up on you, review your mental still pictures in a consecutive loop. Practice this spell dream until your desire has manifested. Remember to add positive emotions.

When you get very good at creating mental spell dreams, you can turn your still frames into a moving picture, where each frame blends into the next, with appropriate movement and sound.

Other ways to set your spell dream in your mind include taking actual pictures of yourself and pasting these pictures onto magazine pages or drawings you create. Or you can have a friend take pictures of you, including sets and props, with a 35-mm camera. You can also make a spell dream production with a video camera. View the pictures at least once a day in conjunction with your mental spell dream activity. The spell-dream technique also works in drum trancing.

Practical Living

Some students may ask, "Can I work on the same goal with all five techniques you've given in the hocus-pocus exercises instead of choosing one goal for each exercise?"

Of course you can, if you so desire. Check over your notes. Which type of fascination felt the most comfortable? Which seemed to work better for you? When you teach others the hocus-focus exercises, have them concentrate on the same goal, as you can teach these exercises in one evening.

One of the most important aspects of WitchCraft centers on knowing what you are doing and *why* you are doing it. The mysteries of the Craft were not designed to be a mystery to the practitioner, but to the *outsider*. That's why they we call our practices *mysteries*. And yes, we have two kinds of mystery teachings in the Craft—that of magickal application and that of soul evolution. At the moment we want to concentrate on working magickal applications that will blend into soul evolution if your workings rely on the principles of honor and integrity. Sure, we can get along blindly working magick for many years without honing our skills through the mental arts, but the enhancement of our magick evolves from our complete understanding of the mechanics of the techniques we use, hence the ability to traverse the untapped territory of the mind. Consider, then, how you can use these three types of inductions (fixation spells, relaxation spells, and progressive relaxation spells) in your current magickal work. Can you bolster your current magickal techniques? Might knowing the how's and why's now bring about faster results? Let's take this idea one step further. How can you use the art of magickal fascination in your everyday life?

The first technique we used—that of focusing on the candle flame—should have put you in a light alpha state. We call this procedure a **fixation fascination**. To make this understandable in magick-speak, we called this technique a fixation spell. Here your body relaxes, breathing and pulse are slow, and you should feel a withdrawal of self—your attention centers to a single activity, that of your desire.

The second technique should have been heralded by your closed eyes. Here you would lose the awareness of your surroundings while your awareness of breathing and senses intensify. Visualization comes easier to us. In magick-ese we called this procedure the **relaxation spell**.

The third technique should have further reduced breathing and relaxation of the body. We named this technique the **progressive relaxation spell**. You may experience a limpness of limbs, narrowing of your attention, increased suggestibility, loss of auditory receptivity, and environmental awareness as a higher degree of visualization ability. Here, the creative process heightens.

Finally, we experimented with the **indirect spell**, that of moving into a mental sacred space, then working magick from that point. Here, we narrowed our attention, increased suggestibility, and removed external awareness, yet we managed to work in a rhythmic sound.

The purpose of these four exercises (hopefully) showed you that your magick and your mind produce powerful results when intricately connected, and that this linkage makes it far easier for you to connect with divinity and walk in balance if you take the time to learn the art of mental fascination. You could use these techniques with any magickal practice—from cord and knot magick to the study and employment of herbs. Take some time and consider the different areas in which you would like to experiment with the four spellcasting techniques in this chapter, then make a simple list with two headings, Full Moon and New Moon, putting each need into the appropriate moon category. Work on these needs in the coming months.

The Six Major Types of Suggestions for a Trance State

Lest you think we've completed the process . . . fooled you. Once you have learned the art of using the various types of inductions, and have found the induction(s) that work well for you, it's time to look into what types of suggestions you should use to flesh out your spellcasting or goal-programming techniques. Overall, there are six types of suggestions you can use in a trance state.

Relaxation Suggestions

These work very well for individuals who have extremely stressful lives. You can use additional relaxation suggestions for goal programming and magickal work to instill harmonious living. Sometimes, we may experience an exceptional amount of tenseness during a goal programming or magickal working. Additional relaxation suggestions can lull you into a more focused state of mind.

Deepening Suggestions

These suggestions serve a variety of purposes, from moving you into a deeper level of trance, providing you with an activity that requires a single focus, to intensifying your trance state. In a normal fascination session for goal programming, you would first use your induction techniques, add additional relaxation suggestions if you feel it's necessary, then move into the deepening suggestions. You can word the deepening suggestions to match your intended goal:

> *Every time I hear the sound of the drum in this session,*
> *I will go deeper and deeper into a deeper trance state.*

Direct Suggestions

We have now traveled from the induction through the relaxation suggestions (if we needed them) and into the deepening suggestions (if we felt they were appropriate). From here, we move into the direct suggestions, the meat of our spell or goal programming session. Direct suggestions guide and instruct us as to what we want to manifest. In the earlier exercises, your direct suggestions encompassed your written goal. As the name indicates, the statements should be simple and to the point, and always said in the present tense, if you can manage it. For example, "I am a wise and powerful Witch." Although some hypnotherapists do not associate images with simple, direct suggestions, I do. I feel that your mind responds to the combination of direct suggestion and visualization (which uses the next type of suggestion, the imagery suggestion). I realize you may think I'm getting the stick end of the broom before the thatch end, but this is how I work with fascinations. You may feel differently.

With this example, we would say the words in our minds and then, if you lack an appropriate visualization, simply see yourself surrounded by white light, or you may see yourself looking like Samantha on *Bewitched*. Personally, I don't care what your visualization encompasses, as long as the visualization remains simple for you to conjure and positive in nature. As with one of our earlier examples, we linked a direct suggestion (your goal) to something tangible—the scent of the perfume, oil, or aftershave, so that you would have reinforcement once you returned to the waking state—and then we link the whole bundle to a positive emotion. Don't make your direct suggestions too long, as that will confuse the mind (though this borders on the posthypnotic suggestion, which we'll get to later). A direct suggestion relates to something you want to happen right away, this minute. Just so you know, other uses of direct suggestions include those vaudeville acts and stage performances we talked about earlier. One important reminder here—negative statements in direct suggestions are finger slappers—a big no-no. Words like "not," "can't," and "shouldn't" bring the brain to a screeching halt. Word your statements in a positive way: *"I am a wise person"* not *"I won't be stupid anymore"* (which also uses—you guessed right—passive voice).

Imagery Suggestions

Imagery suggestions augment direct suggestions (as in our wise and powerful Witch example); however, we can take imagery suggestions much, much further. We can create a full mental picture, complete with birdies chirping, clouds overhead, the sound of running water, fantastic foliage, and a gazebo right in the middle. This constitutes a mental picture of sacred space, as in our fourth hocus-focus exercise. Indeed, we can conduct an entire ritual in our minds without a single tangible tool or prop, and the goal will come out just the same as the goal would have manifested in the physical. Granted, this occurs after practice. Creating mental sacred space is exceptionally important for beginning meditation or for working on healing techniques for ourselves and others. Or we can see ourselves as we would like to be tomorrow, next month, next year, or in the next five years. I use this technique quite often, from planning a successive seminar for the following day to where I will be in my career in five years. Therefore we create mental pictures that have a specific purpose in themselves (to reduce pain, we might visualize a big monster that shrinks as we count down from ten to one) or that serve as a rehearsal for new behavior (seeing yourself as attentive to your spouse rather than biting his or her head off). You can use any type of positive image metaphor.

Have I confused you yet? Okay. Let's back up a bit and create a mythical situation. Here's Tina. Tina is a junior in high school and she wants to be involved with indoor guard (that's the boys and girls who twirl flags and dance to music with the goal of winning in competitions in big, smelly gyms across the district). Tina watched the kids last year and got a big thrill out of seeing them all move together (oh, a group mind thing), twirl the colorful flags, and basically look majorly hot. When the music starts and the crowd hollers, Tina feels the energy of the moment in her soul. Her blood sings. Her arms tingle. This is a major head rush. There's only one problem. Tina usually freezes when she has to do anything in front of others—a big stumbling block if she wants to be in guard.

Our Tina is a fledgling Witch, but she's learned enough in her self-study to know that the primary foundation of magick relies on the Witch's Pyramid—to know, to dare, to will, and to be silent—so when she considers how she will approach performing through magickal aid, she will try hard and keep her mouth shut about any magickal applications she chooses to do. There are lots of things Tina could do, as far as magick goes, but for the sake of our example here, we're going to use magickal fascinations.

Tina has three months to prepare before the coach posts the roster for indoor guard, but Tina won't wait until the night before sign-up, she's going to start now—first by practicing the routines diligently and by working magick. Yes, Tina, we should begin as soon as we can. Tina has already practiced the hocus-focus exercises I gave you, so she has a fairly good idea of how the procedure works. Now she's going to tailor those steps into a complete spellworking.

First, Tina sits down and writes out exactly what she wants to accomplish. She doesn't have to try out for guard in this case—but if she did, she would add that to her working. In Tina's school, anyone can participate as long as they are willing to attend the practices and work hard. Tina plans to do both. Now, Tina doesn't want to make this too complicated because she has to keep her grades up, work after school at the mall, and hang out with her boyfriend. She's also been cursed/blessed with a little brother, who exhibits an extraordinary sixth sense of curiosity. Her use of time and her tight frame for privacy are just as important to her as if she were an adult. (Do not glare at me Tina, I know you are *almost* an adult. Don't rush it.)Anyway, Tina will look over the list of inductions and types of suggestions and will choose which ones will work for her.

Tina writes down her primary goal: *To lose my fear of performing in front of others.* Tina likes to use candles, so she picks a white one to start. Later on, she may choose another color, but white is fine for the moment. Her parents tell her that taper candles constitute a fire hazard, so she uses the stinky-good-smelly air freshener candles you can buy at the supermarket in the cleaning aisle that come encased in little glass containers. Her parents label these candles "acceptable for strange teen use." In my day, we got a Boone's Farm Apple bottle from our older friends, stuck a multi-colored drip candle in the mouth of the bottle (because we thought those candles had magickal oomph), fired up the black light and away we went. Sigh. Back to Tina.

Tina checks her primary visualization: Herself confident and relaxed, twirling the flags with the other members of the guard. She adds sound (the beat of the music) and a big smile on her face. (The smile part is *very* important.) She thinks about how good she will feel if she wins. Her primary direct statement is: ***I am a capable and confident guard member.*** The progressive relaxation induction is too long for Tina, because she's pretty tired after an entire day of school and work, so she goes for the fixation method—that of her white candle, then she'll close her eyes, count down from ten to one, go to her sacred mental space, and launch into her direct statement with accompanying visualization. Sometimes she may use the progressive relaxation induction or a deepening suggestion, if she has the time or if she has trouble focusing. She plans to practice this mental programming every night she can. She knows it is best to do the technique for twenty-eight consecutive days but, after all, life must go on and some nights she may fall asleep and forget. That's okay. She'll remember to do the fixation spell the next night. She also knows, however, that if she lets too many days go by, all her work won't amount to much. Let's let Tina practice her fascination while we talk about more information you need to know.

Indirect Suggestions

We have two types of indirect suggestions: Those that bring a desired emotional state into focus and those that use metaphors and analogies to change a person's experience. In bringing about a desired emotional state, we could be talking about how Tina wants to feel when she performs, or we could be discussing a past memory that, for whatever reason, we need to relive in order to bring about some sort of healing. For example, if Tina had hurt her back when she was seven during a gymnastic performance, or if she simply fell at the wrong time and felt humiliation, these past experiences could be the direct cause of her fear of performing in public. We would need to go back and allow her to relive those experiences and give her positive reinforcement that she is well *now*, or that her humiliation was not the great threat to her psyche that she thinks it is. Indeed, Tina may have forgotten all about a slight injury or humiliation, but her subconscious stored that memory. Another desired emotional state for Tina to concentrate on would be through a keyword or other trigger. We employ these keywords and triggers during the normal suggestion period, or in the post-hypnotic suggestion arena (which I promise we'll get to soon). A keyword or sound does not have to link directly with the desired goal. For example, when I use hypnotherapy and healing techniques together, I tell clients that their keyword is "flower." Every time they see a flower, smell a flower, or say the word flower, their healing will be ten times (or one hundred times, depending on the client) faster than before. Keywords work amazingly well, but you must use them in moderation and be careful what you link and why. I've also used the word "snow" for the winter months, as one sees few flowers but lots of that dumb white stuff in Pennsylvania, especially during Farm Show week.

If we visit Tina again, we find that Tina chose the keyword "flag," as she'll be working with this tool. To help her reinforce this keyword, she hung a big flag on the wall over her bed. Whenever she spends time in her room, she will be reinforcing her goal. Every time she looks at the flag she will feel confident and strong. Therefore, Tina has added another direct statement to her fascination technique. *Every time I see a flag, touch a flag, or hear the word flag, I will feel confident and strong.* Thank you, Tina.

Post-Hypnotic Suggestions

These are designed to reinforce your behavior after a session or working ends. Therefore, Tina's keyword and additional direct statement would constitute a post-hypnotic suggestion. You can also add other statements, such as: *When I open my eyes, I will feel great,* or *When I open my eyes, I will feel rested and secure.* Post-hypnotic suggestions also function as bad-habit busters.

The Nuances of Fascinations and Other People

As with all procedures in magick and mental pursuits, little tricks of the trade will surface when working with fascinations. Although our primary use of fascinations in this book revolves around bettering the self, you need to know that fascinations work on others both directly and indirectly in a group setting, or when teaching on a one-to-one basis. I told you of a malefic use (the Gypsies—oh, and for those of you who wish to write me and tell me I'm being prejudiced because I'm calling them Gypsies, please don't bother; I didn't make up the name of this crime ring, they named themselves.) Ahem. On to business.

Direct Structure centers on what a teaching Witch should do for a student. The student seeks out the help of the teacher and goes through the training sessions, fully aware of what that session entails. These sessions focus on fascination techniques married to information on Craft Law, magickal practices, use of ritual, et cetera.

Indirect Structure, shorter in duration than a fascination session, is used to turn the tide of an emotional outburst or to convince one's opponent or friend to deal with a particular line of thought. A modern term coined for this procedure is called "pushing." Whether or not the pushee acts on the line of thought sent by the pusher remains entirely up to the pushee's subconscious mind. They still hold the reins of their free will. In Practical Craft Law there are only three times when the practitioner may use the art of Indirect Structure:

1. When the Witch (or those they feel responsible for) suffers from a physical or mental attack of some kind. Therefore, you act in defense.

2. When a Witch tries to buy property and no one will sell to them. (The rider to this law indicates the Witch *must* deal fairly with all parties concerned. Don't huff at me about this law—I didn't make it up.)

3. When a Witch wishes to promote harmony, whether in a circle of strangers or friends. I have a very special technique that I use that does not interfere with another's free will. I call it the *Angel Fascination*, and I'll explain this technique to you later in the chapter.

Using the direct structure, magickal teachers work with pre-written scripts, composed either by themselves or others in the field. In the past, most magickal teachers didn't write down these formats because one, fascinations were considered a mystery technique; and two, if these procedures were found in writing, the Witches surely would suffer the stake or find themselves dangling from the nearest tree. During medieval times, to practice the art of fascination fell into the category of utmost evil; however, we discover many other periods of history, especially in those revolving around the mystery traditions, that condoned the use of fascinations as a teaching tool. And three, not every Witch could write.

Teaching Wiccan theology through a scripted structure can result as a great asset to the student. Subjects that work well for this type of training include: the Oath, the Charge of the Goddess, the Charge of the God, the Ordains, the Tenets, the Principles . . . as you can see, this list could go on and on.

Before we go any further, I need to remind you that you cannot make anyone do anything against their moral fiber during either a direct or indirect format. I don't mean that you're not allowed (which you aren't) but that a person, any person, *will not accept a suggestion that goes against their personal virtues or moral code.* The fascination simply won't work; however, if someone does something they know to be inherently wrong, and you use an indirect format on them, they will stop—*as long as they subconsciously believe initially that they are acting in an improper manner.*

I've discovered that some North American Traditional elders use the art of direct structure when teaching students, and several have employed this technique for over twenty years. In the past two years I've included the direct fascination structure for my own students, and have found this technique exceptionally rewarding. Whether the format you use falls under the heading of direct or indirect structure, some standard procedures apply. They are:

Breathing: Deep breaths before you begin. Smooth, even breathing during a hypnotic session, whether you perform the session for someone else or for yourself.

Voice: Voice modulation should emanate as soothing, calm, and serene in most cases. Use rhythmic voice, where the level changes and penetrates the subconscious in a gentle, sing-song manner. Begin speaking normally, then drop to a monotone. Raise the pitch of the voice only with a command statement, and then keep those statements few and far apart. If you tape a session for someone, you can use the "loving voice," where the person can hear the smile in your voice on the tape. Normally, only one statement suffices. Command statements are okay for yourself, but will most likely not work on others as few people are willing to allow others to overpower them. Distort words by drawing syllables out slowly. String several sentences together with connective words, such as "and" or "when." This flow of words can mentally pull the individual into the fixation sequence. *Rhythmic voice in ritual or spellcasting tech-*

niques constitutes one of the most powerful aspects in a Witch's magick. We'll talk about this technique a little more when we cover chanting later on in the book.

Pauses: Learning to pause at various intervals in the fascination litany allows the subject to either follow instructions or gives them adequate time for a response. These pauses are important both in direct and indirect fascination, although you use fewer pauses when using indirect fascination techniques.

Use of Language: This also plays an important part in the art of fascination. When designing fascinations that involve meditation and vision questing, you should look for synonyms (words that contain the same meaning). Patterned phrases work very well in longer script fascinations. These phrases revolve around repeated suggestions that enhance understanding, comprehension, and ensure retention of the material. You begin with a full sentence, then repeat the last half of the sentence, adding a bit more. Use the last half of that sentence, then add again. This constitutes a building technique that reinforces the fascination. In the language of hypnotherapy, these sentences are called paraphrased suggestions. Timing cues are also important in direct and indirect fascination. For example: *"In a few moments you will relax completely,"* or *"At the end of one hour, you will stop studying."* Again, you'll find this technique in chanting magick.

Hypnotherapists and magickal teachers employ two kinds of fascination facilitation: **Authoritative** and **Permissive**. Authoritative, as you might have guessed, commands and directs the student. This technique alters behavior through repetitive commands given in a firm voice. Authoritative fascinations do not always work well, especially in group format, unless the individual giving the fascination appears to have some sort of power, either through known hierarchy or professional background, or being considered a trustworthy person. The authoritative technique does not work well with anyone who has difficulty relating to an authority figure, or who does not take direct suggestions well, or who feels that people in general spend hours plotting against them. Someone who has a suspicious nature will not process the techniques of an authoritative hypnotherapist. Females who rebel against male domination, and vice versa, will not stomach the authoritative technique from the opposite sex. Let me interject, though, that the authoritative words and tone of voice should be used in a past-life regression sequence to ensure the safety of the individual regressed. I've found that I need to function as the unquestioned "boss" in this type of regression sequence.

The permissive technique, which I normally use and am most comfortable with, generates a softer tone of voice to lull the subject into relaxation, whether that subject is myself or someone else. In essence, the permissive technique results in a seductive process—the hypnotist and the subject join as equal partners and, especially when strong, creative image inducers lace the session. The permissive technique works well in groups and brings about the best response from imaginative, creative people who have an authority complex. This technique works well for goal setting, positive behavioral enhancement, ritual, petitions, devotions, and spellcasting.

Walking the Line with Fascinations

Over the last few years I've learned to make my own self-hypnosis (or self-fascination) tapes. I've used them for increasing my magickal adeptness, goal programming, vision questing, meditation improvements, ridding myself of bad habits ("you will not judge others harshly," et cetera). If you plan to make your own self-hypnosis tapes, you will use many of the above-listed procedures. Witches were known to fascinate others with a look and the magick of voice. How did they do this? Well, not by staring down someone and saying, "You vill lee-sin to ev-ery ting I say!" That's only for the movies (and badly done, I might add). The premise fits, but not the circumstances or the bad acting. Getting others to do what you want *can* work, but to some Witches this technique walks the magickal line of ethics, and I agree that using the indirect structure in many cases could carry the label of negative magick (remember the Ordains).

You can't employ the indirect structure if you don't know how to go into the alpha state yourself. I have also found through experimentation and watching other hypnotherapists that they do go into alpha themselves when using the direct format for others, such as in a hypnotherapy session, especially if a session moves into an extended one. This type of indirect structure is okay, because you have already asked the participant for his or her permission to work the fascination. Before I use a script I've written for other people I always use the script on myself for several weeks to work out any bugs. I'll never forget the time when I was in the middle of a woman's session, said the keyword to take her into a very deep state of alpha, and woke up several minutes later to discover I'd put myself under! I was so used to listening to the permissive commands of my own voice when testing the tape that I obeyed them and bored myself right into deep alpha. To practice an indirect structure, you must be able to go into the alpha state and lead the other person into that state as well. When this happens, your minds will connect on a higher level faster and with better success.

Before I go any further, I want to caution you again about using the indirect format outside of training or healing sessions. This procedure isn't a toy to play with other people's minds. If you don't work in honor, you will get your carcass kicked at some point in time. Remember: what we put out, comes back. In the upcoming Angel Fascination, you will use the indirect structure to create harmonious, loving energy around you in a positive way, which will affect most people who come in contact with you, simply due to the nature of the vibrations you create. I don't want to confuse you, but I should add that the Angel Fascination employs the use of the direct format for yourself, but the indirect format *as perceived* by others, so what you are *really* doing rests on changing *your* energy pattern by an act of your will, not changing their energy patterns by *imposing* your will.

I think it is only fair to tell you that many non-magickal people practice the indirect structure without you ever knowing. Let's face it, people have been buying books on hypnotherapy for years, and most of these readers do not practice the Craft. Although many of the individuals who research and use hypnotherapy/fascination techniques are honorable, our society isn't a perfect one and there are people who will use the indirect format to get their way, either consciously or subconsciously. Some people naturally use indirect fascinations. Often they don't realize they are doing this technique, yet they work the technique all the time in day-to-day life.

How can you determine if someone tries to use the indirect format on you? Actually, it is pretty easy to tell. First, (in most cases, unless they exercise stupidity) they will not look at you directly in the eyes, but will look at the point where your nose meets your forehead when they speak to you. This feels like the person looks right into your eyes, but they really don't. Their eyes may take on a defocused glaze, and their breathing shallows. Finally, the voice pattern will exhibit a dead give away. If the tone sounds monotonous and soft, without the normal inflections you expect, they could be using fascination techniques.

Why would anyone want to use the indirect structure at all, considering you would be walking an ethical line? Well, sometimes rotten stuff happens. For example, a fellow student of my hypnotherapy teacher decided to go out to what he *thought* was a classy bar for some entertainment. While there, a fight broke out between two young bucks—naturally, over a woman. (The timeless, dependable structure of the human psyche.) The hypnotherapy student quickly determined which of the two young men would be more susceptible to the indirect format. The student stood in front of the young man, quietly spoke to him, looked at the point where the young man's nose met his forehead, and pictured the young man slowly backing away and walking out of the bar. The student's adrenaline was pumping, but he swallowed hard, pulled in his own fear, and kept talking, never allowing that mind-picture to waver. After two or three minutes, the young man backed off and left the bar, much to the amazement of the student.

How You Can Use the Indirect Format

A quick trick to going into the alpha state is to defocus your eyes. You know when you look at something long enough and you see two of the object instead of one? I don't mean crossing your eyes, as that will make you see two of things and would be bad for your eyes. You would also look silly to anyone passing by. When you defocus your eyes, a stationary object from six inches to several feet away appears to split in two. To help you learn to do this, several New Age stores sell what they call Theta Posters, which allow you to see a design within a design rather than processing the idea of two images of the same thing in your mind. These pictures appear to be massive dots but, as you focus, a three-dimensional image will appear. The theory is that the faster you can focus on the hidden object, the quicker your mind moves into the alpha state. This defocusing technique can be most helpful in spells, rites, rituals, petitions, and devotions.

An indirect format normally takes only fifteen seconds from the time you go into alpha to the time you complete the process. The next step, after going into alpha, is to look at the person where the bridge of the nose merges into the forehead, just like the student did. This process took him longer than the normal fifteen seconds because he was scared bodily-functionless and he was new to the procedure. At the same time, you must visualize what you want to accomplish.

How much practice does it take until you can achieve the art of indirect fascination? If you have faithfully meditated or have practiced some sort of self-hypnosis or magickal acts that depend on the foundation of the alpha state for several months, you should be able to do a wobbly indirect fascination immediately. You will get better with practice. That's why I gave you the four hocus-focus exercises. If you can't use your mind in the alpha state on command, it may take several months until you can practice the indirect format with success. So how do you practice without getting into ethical trouble? That's a tough one. I use the indirect format only for protection or when someone doesn't understand what I'm saying because they aren't *really* listening to the words coming out of my mouth.

For example, if you wanted to get Jesse-Lou to have sex with you and you've prepared yourself to do everything to get her there, including lying, cheating, and spewing promises that you never plan to fulfill, an indirect format would be cheating, and the old karma boot will wail you in the you-know-what when you least expect it. Just ask Jesse-Lou, for goodness sakes! If you needed to stop a fight, like the story of the hypnotherapy student, *that* would be acceptable. Never use the indirect format as a joke, because boredom entices you, or because you want something someone else has. Use your common sense and moral ethics. The rule of three definitely applies here, as well as our Witch motto: *Do as you will, but harm none.*

I could go into Western Occultism here, discuss magnetism, purple eye-light, and the evil eye, but now that we know the scientific basis for the art of fascination, why depend on folk tales to get the point across? Within every folk tale lies a grain of truth. Keep that thought.

The Angel Fascination

I use the Angel Fascination often. I've found that the energies of angels provide a safe, secure environment, make me feel better, and can assist others in their time of need without breaking any Wiccan Laws you may have internalized.

Angelic energy has been around since humans decided life included stuff they couldn't see with the normal eyeball. So, we're talking about beliefs and practices used before the inception of Judaism or Christianity. Angels don't belong to any one religious philosophy; their energies manifest as all-encompassing. I see them as bridges to all faiths. With this in mind, you may wish to practice any of the three variations of the following Angel Fascination. These procedure will only take a few minutes of your time.

1. Find a place where you will not be disturbed for approximately ten minutes. You may wish to turn down the lights, put on soft music, or light a candle. You can work this exercise with your eyes open or closed, but eventually you will need to be able to perform this glamoury with your eyes open.

2. Take a deep breath and relax. Ground yourself by imagining your legs have become the roots of a tree. Take another deep breath, then one more.

3. Imagine that you are an angel of perfect love and perfect peace. See yourself dressed in white. Feel the white wings on your back. Envision a white flame crowning your head. Hold the visualization as long as possible. Try to "become" the angel. You can use drum trancing or hum if you like.

4. Take a deep breath and ground. Imagine now that you are the angel of Celestial Power. See yourself dressed in gold. Feel the gold wings on your back. Move the air around you with the wings. Envision a golden flame crowning your head. Hold the visualization as long as possible. Try to "become" the angel of Celestial Power.

5. Take a deep breath and ground. Imagine that you are the Angel of Protection. See yourself dressed in purple. Feel the black wings moving on your back. Envision a blood-red flame burning at the crown of your head. Hold the visualization as long as possible.

6. Ground and center. Then cleanse your aura by imagining yourself surrounded by white light.

7. Repeat the visualization of the angel of peace, give yourself a suggestion as you learned in this chapter, then count from five to one, and open your eyes. Breathe deeply. Ground and center.

Glamouries

The Angel Fascination procedure falls under the category of a "glamoury" or "glamory" or "glamorie." Pick one, they all mean the same thing. When you work a glamoury the following may happen:

1. Your aura changes in color, density, and radius.

2. You temporarily change your personality.

3. You change the electrical flow in your body.

Let's go over the three manifestations in the exercise. The first, that of the angel of light, focused on perfect love and perfect peace, manifests in a non-threatening posture. People who live life in a harmonious way will perceive you as kind, strong, and generous. People who manifest violence may perceive this glamoury as weakness, so be careful when you use the Angel of Light. The second, that of the angel of inspiration and creativity, expounds a vivacious, exciting appearance. Those around you may feel exhilarated, confident, and eager to begin new projects in their own lives. The third, that of the Angel of Protection, explodes in "don't touch me" energy. Those who live harmonious lives will try to avoid you. Those who manifest violence exhibit confusion. This confused state may last only momentarily, but gives you enough time to cut and run. (And you'll live to fly your broom another day.)

I developed these glamouries after working for a year in a customer service position. I saw hundreds of people every day and found that dealing with difficult individuals required more than the average position description requirements. After several nightmares and generally stressed-out behavior (exhibited on my part), I realized that the techniques I normally used in my Craft goodie bag weren't working. I also realized that the more stressful the day, the less I remembered to ground and center.

After working with these glamouries for a few months, I asked various members of the Black Forest Clan to spare a few moments of their time. Each individual processes the "sight" of energy differently. Some feel energy fluctuations, some see changes in color in the aura, some see a haziness around the subject, and so on. First, without using eye contact (I covered my eyes), I went through the three angelic glamouries and asked them for their impressions. I didn't ask all of them at the same time either, because often people pick up on each other's thoughts and intuitions. Overall, two out of fifteen picked up on the manifestation of the wing movement. One picked up the flame above the crown. Fourteen out of fifteen felt or saw the energy changes and aura density fluctuations throughout the three types of glamouries. Fourteen out of fifteen experienced emotional impressions from the glamouries. With the Angel of Peace and Love manifestation, they felt loved, meekness, or safety. From the second glamoury they felt movement, excitement, or intense activity. From the third glamoury they experienced strength, power, and a few . . . fear.

In the next experiment I ran, I left my eyes uncovered, and moved the energy I created with the visualization through my third eye first, and then through my natural eyes. Their impressions were much the same, though intensified considerably.

When dealing with difficult customers, I used either the first or third glamoury. I saved the third for those customers who decided to spill their abusive behavior on me or on the people on the line who I was responsible for. This, thank goodness, did not happen often, but when the abusive behavior occurred, I no longer felt as stressed as I had before. In one case I actually burst out laughing in the woman's face. She walked out in a huff. I never saw her again. The glamoury does not eliminate stress from your life, but the practice does assist you in limiting the stress you manifest in your body.

Can you choose other images to practice glamouries? Yes, but I suggest you enter the manifestation process with care, because what you present, you may *become*. In ritual with a group of people, your High Priestess and High Priest may function on one of two levels. He or she may actually allow the spirit of the Lord or Lady to enter his or her body (called divine possession) or they may use a glamoury to manifest the desired energy. If he or she has good control with the latter, you won't notice the difference between divine possession and glamoury. Remember, though, a glamoury can turn into divine possession; or, if you are not careful, simple possession. This is why I chose angelic energies above other manifestations, such as animals or elements.

Glamouries come in handy when you need to present yourself in a particular manner. For example, when you prepare yourself for a job interview. How do you want the interviewer to perceive you? To achieve a specific effect you can choose your clothing (for women, makeup too) wisely, enchanting everything you wear. Then, right before you enter the office, you would "work a glamoury." Is this dishonest? Yes, if you do not plan to live up to the image you purport. No, this isn't dishonest if you choose to manifest on the job (and in your life) the glamoury you exhibit. If you cheat, you'll pay . . . perhaps dearly.

When should you *not* use a glamoury? Do not use glamouries if you take any type of mind-altering drug. Likewise, the influence of alcohol can screw up the energy manifestation from harmless to dangerous. Have you ever seen a mean drunk? Alcohol disturbs the energy patterns of the mind and spirit (not to mention the mess it makes of your body). Alcohol can also amplify a glamoury in a negative manner. A mean drunk *becomes* the energy of violence; because alcohol lowers inhibitions, the energy body of the drunk draws (like a magnet) negative junk around him or her. Think about it. Try not to use glamouries when you feel anger bubbling inside your personal cauldron. I know it's hard. Attempt to get your emotions under control first, or at least channel those emotions in a positive manner. If someone uses a glamoury that affects others in a negative manner, you have every right to shut down that glamoury. Call for white light in the form of ice water—that'll cool 'em off right quick. You can also imagine honey dripping all over their body. That works too.

How long does it take to learn how to manifest a glamoury? That depends on your persistence and personal training. It may take a week or two, or it may take a year or two for you to get the glamoury "just right." The practice involves experimentation, keeping good notes, and dedication. Learning to perform glamouries requires work. Who has the easiest time learning glamouries? Artists, musicians, and writers, because these people constantly work with bringing mental images to form.

Groups of people naturally manifest glamouries onto other people. For example, certain film stars, public speakers, and politicians have glamouries attached to their auras by fans (you know, the adoring public). These public glamouries manifest in individuals who have a high level of self-esteem that accepts the "bigger than life" persona the fans offer. Clothing, makeup, personality, and body language can enhance or detract from the fan-created glamoury. How the star internalizes that glamoury can make or break a popular individual's chemistry with the public. Many times a universally known person will self-destruct due to "public glamoury." The rush of performing and accepting the glamoury energy from fans will burn out the spiritual self of the popular person if he or she does not exercise great care. Heavy stuff, huh? The same thing can happen in smaller arenas as well, whether you discuss corporate functions or charity bazaars. Glamoury, to pound home the point, represents powerful magick that needs special handling by responsible people. Does that include you?

How long can an individual hold a glamoury? If you work on a particular glamoury for any length of time, your ability to sustain that glamoury will expand. Be careful. You can hone the Angel of Protection glamoury, but don't use this energy excessively unless you wish to have your entire world self-destruct. The same thing happens in the process of working with Dark Goddesses. Too much of any one thing in magickal applications will eventually turn on you. If you work with Dark Goddesses often, learn to work in equal balance with Light Goddesses. Excessive dark energy will manifest as poverty, continued ill-health, and so on. Always learn to work in balance.

In this chapter you learned the art of fascination and how this type of focus can enhance your spellwork. Granted, if you wish to become an adept in this area of study, you will need to research the topic further. You may wish to purchase books on hypnosis, take a correspondence course, or seek out a hypnotherapist who would be willing to teach you.[1]

You also learned about simple fascinations (those that take only a few moments to do) and complex fascinations (those that require a session of thirty minutes or more). Finally, you learned the old art of glamoury—use this art wisely.

I included fascination information in this book as I believe levels of the mind meld intricately to our magick and our religion. By understanding these levels we can practice our work with efficiency. Reread this chapter and keep practicing the exercises given. In time you will be amazed at your progress.

---

1. William Hewitt has several books available through Llewellyn on the subject of hypnotherapy. One good book in particular is *Psychic Development for Beginners* (Llewellyn, 1996).

4

Turning Your Environment Into Harmony

Your home should be a place of enlightenment, harmony, and protection. If your home doesn't measure up to your spiritual expectations, then the time has come for you to do something to transmute the negative energies that have collected there. Houses, like people, can and do harbor negative energy. To live a harmonious, magickal life, many individuals have found it necessary to cleanse the home mundanely and spiritually at least every four months. If you have someone living with you who has sucked in anger, sorrow, hatred, or other negative energies, you may need to spiritually cleanse your house often until that person either leaves or works themselves out of the negative state. No such thing exists in magickal housecleaning as "once and done"—just like mundane housecleaning, you have to keep at it.

The Craft teaches you to enhance your spiritual home (your body and mind) with every exercise, spell, and ritual you work. The Craft also instructs you how to create sacred space to do the work of the soul. I've designed this chapter to show you how to turn your home, whether you live in a Hollywood palace or a one-room apartment, into a place of sacred and secure living. You can be the most spiritual person in the world but if you live in a place that bombards you with negative energy, whether the energy has collected there or emanates from another person, just how spiritual will you turn out to be?

Mundane House Clearing

Let's start with a pitching spree, shall we? Put on some great music, grab some trash cans, and start cleaning house. If you think the task will reach monumental proportions, then work room by room. Get rid of all the broken stuff. Throw out those dead plants. Clean out the junk drawers and toss all that little clutter that manages to grow into mountains when you're not looking. Throw away all things given to you by negative people. I'm not kidding. If your sister-in-law gave you a great crystal bowl, but you dislike her intensely and never use the thing, why are you keeping the bowl around? What? Because it is worth money? Oh, please! If you can't bear to throw these things away, then give them away, or take them to the Salvation Army or another charity organization. Discard torn or stained clothing, anything that you'll never fit into again, or things that you know look terrible on you so you don't wear them. Take down pictures that don't appeal to you anymore. Jettison old projects you just never managed to finish, like that half-knitted sweater for cousin Alfie's baby who just turned twenty-six yesterday. If you can afford it, repaint. If not, wash the walls with holy water and fresh lemon mixed into your wash pail. Remove negative memorabilia. That boyfriend who betrayed you on the evening of August 10, 1972? Why do you still have the vacation pictures you took of the two of you in Disneyland the year before? Throw that crap away!

Now look again. Remove all visual clutter. Take a plastic garbage bag and start at one end of your house or apartment. Walk slowly through every room and dump what you can, put away what you can't. Everyday clutter breaks up the flow of energy in your home.

Even if you live with people who would not approve of a magickal cleansing ritual, there is no fool on earth who will turn down your cleaning services. Cleanse, consecrate, and empower all cleaning supplies. Hold that bottle of Windex in your hands and fill the bottle with white light. Ask the Mother to help you clean away all negative residue in your home. Do the same with your dust rag and the vacuum cleaner. While you work, light a white votive candle, asking the Lord and Lady to give you strength while you clean. In fact, it's been a while since I've done this myself. See ya later!

Whew! What a mess! You just don't realize how much junk you collect. I've got fifteen huge garbage bags full of junk here, and that's just from my bedroom! After I finish my cleaning spree (thought I'd take a break and get back to you), I'll go and take a ritual bath, asking the Lord and Lady to cleanse my body and my mind, before I continue spiritually cleaning my house. At this rate, it might take me more than a day to get the job done. That's okay. I'll take a ritual bath tonight when I finish the initial stab into the pit, then take another tomorrow, after I've completed the whole process.

Empowering Your Cleaning Supplies for Success

Moon Phase: New or waxing

Day of the Week: Sunday

Planetary Ruler/Hour: Sun or Jupiter

Angel of the Day: Michael

Candle Color: Orange

Quarter to Open: South

Element: Fire

Planetary Spirit: Astaroth

Archetype: Lugh

Totem Animal: Buffalo (abundance and good fortune)

1. You will need: Gold ribbon; basil, parsley, and willow leaves; lilac oil; mortar and pestle; a gold candle.

2. Gather all your cleaning supplies together. Put them on your altar or shrine. If you don't have one of these, use a table top.

3. Tie a piece of gold ribbon on each container. Crush the basil (for sympathy in objects and people), parsley (for prosperity) and the willow (universal love and abundance) together with mortar and pestle. Hold the mortar in your hands and ask Lugh to empower the herbs to bring success and universal love into your home. Add one drop of lilac oil for exorcism and protection. Sprinkle a bit of the herb into each cleaning supply container. Put some of the herbs in the bottom of a new vacuum cleaner bag.

4. Dress and empower the gold candle with lilac oil in the name of Lugh and Success. Light the candle and hold the candle out above your head. Ask Lugh to bless your home and cleaning supplies with success and universal love.

5. Cut an extra eleven-inch length of ribbon with your right hand. Hold the ribbon out before you and ask Lugh to bless your home and to bring success into your life. See the ribbon surrounded by the golden light of success. Tie the ribbon around your wrist. Say:

Every time I touch this ribbon, I bring success and
universal love into my life.

6. With both hands out before you, project success and universal love into your cleaning supplies (don't forget your vacuum cleaner).

7. Let the gold candle burn until nothing remains. If you have a candle stub, bury the stub in your back yard, or in a flower pot in your apartment.

As you clean your house, touch the gold ribbon and repeat the affirmation:

In the name of Lugh, I bring success and universal love into my home.

Spiritual Housecleaning

Your home should function as your sanctuary. Now that you've cleaned the place up, let's talk about the energies that curl patiently in the corners, hiding under the sofa or simply floating in the air. Your home should be the vortex of your energy, simply because you live there, think there, weep there, have sex there, love there . . . well, I could go on and on, but you understand what I'm saying. Your home should assist you in manifesting your desires, not defeat your purpose. By the time you finish working through the material in this chapter, your home will pulse with positive energy.

Your home isn't just "there." The place where you reside has a consciousness of its own. No one should determine what that consciousness should resonate except you. Endless forms of energy undulate in your home. From the ground on which your home or apartment sets to the highest peak on the roof, your house connects with a multitude of energy fields. Whether you believe it or not, your consciousness connects deeply with the place where you live.

Your house or apartment has an aura just like you do. What you do inside your house (or what someone else does) affects this aura either in a positive or negative way. If you clean away the clutter in your home (as we did earlier) then you acknowledge to the universe that you will not allow useless things to clutter your life. You have prepared yourself to move on to bigger and better things. If you throw out worn and broken things, and other trash, your comment to the universe indicates that you are willing to throw out the garbage in your life. When you mentally and spiritually clear your home, you are also mentally and spiritually cleaning your life.

My reasoning for physically and psychically cleaning my house may be different from yours. For example, when I do a housecleaning and clearing, I'm focusing on making my place a safe haven for others and myself. My intention also revolves around building power to protect and enhance my spiritual success. Finally, I usually get the cleaning bug when I feel my life is in chaos, and at least if I clean my house and put that mess in order, I'll be able to think better. There have been times when I've cleared houses or apartments after the occupants have experienced divorce, a run of bad luck, or nagging sickness. You can tailor your housecleaning ritual to the needs of yourself and others. When you clean your home mundanely and spiritually you will be causing an energy shift in the house or apartment. The more debris you cart away, the better, as this debris carries negative energy.

Don't Forget the Magickal Part of Your Life

Let's say you have practiced the Craft for about two years. You've progressed through many stages, collected lots of fun magickal gadgets, clothing, tools, and so on. Lately, though, a lot of your stuff has been sitting in a closet, gathering dust. You just don't use some of it anymore. What does this mean? Are you any less of a Witch? Not at all! You are simply growing and changing, which is exactly what you set out to do in the first place. So-o-o-o, what do you do with all that "stuff"? Time to recycle. Look through your things and determine what you want to keep (one or two things for sentimental reasons), what you can turn into something else (goodie! new projects!), what you want to give away, and what you want to discard. If you plan to trash the item, be sure to de-magick the piece in a small ceremony, then throw the item away.

I have a Craft friend who gets together with her coven members about every six months for a magickal rummage sale. Everyone brings the magickal items they don't want anymore, and then they barter them to each other. For example, one Witch may have collected oodles of candle holders but never bothered to buy an incense burner. This Witch could trade a set of her candle holders for another Witch's incense burner (who, by the way, has at least twelve of them!). If the rummage sale idea doesn't appeal to you, or you don't have that many Craft friends, you may wish to give your items away to one or two magickal friends, or perhaps a magickal pen-pal. Before either option, you should ritually cleanse each item so as not to give away any negative energies or energies that may not be appropriate for the other person. I've had lots of fun determining what I want to give to whom, and why.

Putting Housecleaning in a New Perspective

When you work a spell or perform a ritual, the first thing on the agenda involves the specifications of the project. This is true for a spiritual housecleaning as well. To continue this project, you will need some three-by-five-inch cards—one for the overall intention of your work, and one for each room in your house, including the attic, basement, and any large, walk-in closets (because closets can be little rooms within themselves). On the top of the first card, write the word "overall." Underneath that title, write down precisely what overall energies you wish to manifest in your home. You can have more than one, but don't have tons. Peace and prosperity go well together, so I'll use those two ideas throughout our example. Under that, write the following:

1. How that energy would feel to you if you could touch it. You might say "soft," "warm," "loving," and so on.

2. What color that energy brings to your mind.

3. What deity or deities correspond to that type of energy (in your mind, not someone else's).

4. What magickal symbol you would associate with that energy.

5. Write the totem animal that corresponds to that energy.

6. Write the element you feel corresponds to that energy.

Your cards would look something like this:

HOUSE CLEANSING—OVERALL

1. Energies—Peace and prosperity
2. Colors—White, green
3. Deity—Rosemerta, Celtic Goddess of Abundance
4. Magickal Symbol—The Goddess Symbol
5. Totem Animal—Dove
6. Element—Spirit

LIVING ROOM—HOUSECLEANING

1. Energies—Creativity and harmony
2. Colors—Orange, white
3. Deity—Brigid
4. Magickal Symbol—The Sacred Spiral
5. Totem Animal—Tarvos the Bull
6. Elements—All

Now, do the same thing for each room of the house. Here is an example:

BATHROOM—HOUSECLEANING

1. Energies—Spiritual and physical cleansing
2. Colors—White, blue
3. Deity—Epona
4. Magickal Symbol—Lagu (rune for flow)
5. Totem Animal—Horse
6. Element—Water

Okay, how did I make my correspondences? Well, I thought about it. I write my books on the computer in the living room; therefore, to me, my living room functions as the center of my creative energies. I also want to work in harmony, and since the whole family watches television in that room, I want them to be in harmony too. Orange, for me, corresponds to creativity. White stands for harmony. Your colors may not be like mine. You may see creativity as red, green, pink, or another color. I chose Brigid because I see her as the Goddess of creativity and healing. Finally, we use Tarvos the bull in our Black Forest rituals as the representation of the South, where creativity and passion reside. To me, he would be a logical choice; however, this choice may not suit your tastes. I had quite a time determining which elements to pick and finally decided on all of them—air for intellect and good ideas; water for the continual flow of ideas; earth for prosperity and stability in my work; and fire for continued passion and creativity. Let's do one more room to make sure you have the hang of this exercise.

Do you see how I got my correspondences? To me, the bathroom represents the area of the house where we do our bodily cleansing, and where I often do spiritual cleansings through sacred baths and, of course, my ultimate favorite, the holy shower. I associate the colors of white and blue with cleansing. I chose Lagu, the runic symbol for water and flow. For the deity, I picked Epona. For the Black Forest she represents the sweetwater of the West. Historical records associate the horse with Epona, so the choice for totem animal was easy here. Finally, the element of water definitely goes with the qualities of any bathroom (hopefully).

Organizing Your Spiritual Housecleaning

There are five main parts to spiritual housecleaning: one, removing all negative energy fields; two, filling the house or apartment with your positive energy; three, invoking divine energies to meet a specific need; four, aligning elemental energies to fit your specific needs; and five, securing the positive energies within the home. Keep these five parts in your mind as we go further into the art of magickal housecleaning.

Astrological Correspondences for Spiritual Housecleaning

To get the most out of your spiritual housecleaning, you may wish to plan your activities around auspicious astrological correspondences, especially if you have an essential intent for a particular room. I've listed some suggested correspondences to help you in your planning; however, learn to look at what fits your schedule as well as your purpose. Perhaps you have the intuitive feeling to do that housecleaning this week, then concentrate more on the days of the week and the planetary hours later, rather than worry about the moon phase or other correspondences. If you have time to leisurely plan, then by all means wait for as many compatible correspondences as possible. You may wish to jot down some of the following information on your three-by-five-inch cards.

General Whole House

Good Days: Sunday, Monday, Friday, or Wednesday

Good Planetary Hours: Sun, Moon, Mercury, Venus

Moon Phases: Full or new

The Moon in the Signs: Moon in Aries (new beginnings), Moon in Leo (strength), Moon in Virgo (practicality)

Asteroids: When Ceres or Pallas are in Taurus, Virgo, or Capricorn

Wiccan Holidays: Beltaine or Samhain, Summer Solstice or Yule

Standard Holidays: The day before Thanksgiving or Christmas

Candle Color: White

Angelic Influences: Four Archangels—Michael, Raphael, Gabriel, Uriel

Spirit: Marchosais (strength); Alloces (wisdom)

Deity: Hertha, Vesta, Danu, Dagda

Herbal or Floorwash: Wisteria and honeysuckle[1]

Totem: Frog (protection); goose (love of home)

Elements: All

Quarters: All

Rune: Odal (my house is my castle) or Dagaz (transformation), depending upon your intent

General Earth Mother Magickal Powder: Nutmeg, orris, rosemary, myrrh, benzoin, patchouli, allspice, chamomile, bay, cinnamon, cloves, orange peel, vervain (empower to Ana or Gaia)

Affirmation: *I bring the sacredness of the divine into my home.*

To Banish the House of a Particular Nasty

Good Days: Saturday (best), Sunday

Good Planetary Hours: Saturn (best), Sun

Moon Phases: Dark, full, or waning

The Moon in the Signs: Moon in Scorpio, Moon in Libra

Asteroids: When Vesta is in Aries, Leo, or Sagittarius

Wiccan Holidays: Samhain or Fall Equinox

Standard Holidays: Halloween or New Year's Eve

Other: Lunar eclipse

Candle Color: Black or purple-black

Angelic Influence: Michael or Uriel; Saturn Angels; Dark Moon Angels

Spirit: Vassago (protection)

Herbal or Floorwash: Angelica and clove

Deity: Cerridwyn or Hecate

---

1. Folk customs throughout America include several recipes for holy water that can be used as floor washes. These blends of water, a pinch of alcohol, and pulverized herbs were strained through cheesecloth and used as a general cleanser of negativity, or sprinkled about in an effort to rid negativity and/or heal people, places, and things. The basic formula is: 8 ounces water, ¼ ounce isopropyl alcohol, and herbs selected for their magickal properties.

Totem: Quail; panther; sow (totem of Cerridwyn); hounds (Hecate); alligator (survival)

Element: Water

Quarter: West

Rune: Algiz

Energy Movement: Widdershins

General Protection Magickal Powder: Cloves, rosemary, angelica, rue, basil, holly, ivy, marigold, mistletoe, sage, solomon's seal, vervain, and yarrow. All, or any combination of 3, 7, or 9 (empower to Hecate, Cerridwyn, or the Morrigan)

Affirmation: *I banish all negativity, now!*

The Intent of Creativity

Good Days: Sunday, Monday, Wednesday, or Friday

Good Planetary Hours: Sun, Moon, Mercury, Venus

Moon Phases: New or waxing

The Moon in the Signs: Moon in Aries, Moon in Gemini, Moon in Sagittarius

Asteroids: Pallas or Vesta in any sign

Wiccan Holidays: Candlemas, Beltaine, Spring Equinox

Candle Color: Orange, gold, or orange-red

Floor Wash: Frankincense, myrrh, cinnamon

Angelic Influences: Akriel; Angels of Vesta; Full Moon Angels

Spirit: Astaroth (success)

Deity: Brigid

Element: Fire

Quarter: South

Totem Animal: Whale (creativity)

Rune: Cen

Energy Movement: Deosil

Magickal Powder: Lavender, hyssop, patchouli (bless in the name of Brigid)

Affirmation: *I am a worthy and creative individual.*

The Intent of Prosperity

Good Days: Sunday or Thursday

Good Planetary Hours: Sun or Jupiter

Moon Phases: New, waxing, or full

The Moon in the Signs: Moon in Taurus; Moon in Cancer; Moon in Capricorn

Asteroids: Vesta

The Wiccan Holidays: Candlemas, Beltaine, Spring Equinox, Summer Solstice

Standard Holidays: New Year's Eve or New Year's Day

Candle Color: Green or orange

Element: Earth

Quarter: North

Floor Wash: Cinnamon and parsley

Angelic Influences: Barbelo (female—goodness, faith, integrity, success)

Spirit: Bune

Deity: Dagda (If you wish to work in balance, Dagda and Danu)

Totem Animal: Buffalo (abundance)

Rune: Feoh

Energy Movement: Deosil

Magickal Powder: Allspice, patchouli, myrrh, cinnamon, sandalwood, orris, orange peel (can also be used as an incense, oil, bath, or floorwash)

Affirmation: *My life fills with abundance and all my needs are met.*

Healing

Good Days: Sunday or Friday (Saturday for banishing illness)

Good Hours: Sun or Venus (Saturn for banishing illness)

Moon Phases: Dark Moon for banishing illness; New Moon for good health

Moon in the Signs: Moon in Scorpio for banishing; Moon in Leo for strength

Asteroids: Ceres in Leo (for good health)

Wiccan Holidays: Samhain for banishing; Beltaine for good health

Standard Holidays: Halloween for banishing; Christmas or New Year's for good health

Candle Color: Green (for healing power); black (for banishing illness)

Quarters: West and North

Elements: Water and earth

Angelic Influences: Gabriel, Anael; Virtues (for miracles)

Floor Wash: Eucalyptus, pine, and orange peel

Spirit: Buer

Deity: Ana, Sulis, Argante

Rune: Uruz, Birca

Totem Animal: Eagle, ox

Energy Movement: Deosil to promote healing; widdershins to banish illness

Healing Powder: Carnation, rose, gardenia; or angelica, boneset, chamomile, cinquefoil, horehound, bay, mistletoe, mugwort, and vervain (empower in the name of the Holy Mother)

Affirmation: *My immune system works in perfect order for my body every second of every day.* For banishing illness: *I banish illness from my body, now!*

Love

Good Days: Sunday, Friday

Good Planetary Hours: Sun, Venus

Moon Phases: Full

Moon in the Signs: Pisces

Asteroids: Juno (relationships)

Wiccan Holidays: Beltaine, Summer Solstice

Standard Holidays: Valentine's Day, Christmas

Candle Color: Red (for passion); rose (for true love); pink (companionship)

Quarter: West (to begin); South (to grow); North (to maintain)

Element: Water (to begin); fire (to grow); earth (to maintain)

Angelic Influence: Gabriel; Angels of Venus; Angels of the Full Moon

Spirit: Sallos (Love); Beleth (Passion)

Floor Wash: Jasmine, rose, and lavender

Deity: Venus, Pan, Branwyn

Totem Animal: Turtle (healing)

Rune: Birca (to grow); Gyfu (to form a partnership)

Energy Movement: Deosil

Magickal Powder: Patchouli, lavender, orris, lemon peel, bay, musk (empower to Venus)

Affirmation: *I bring the correct person to me who will fulfill my needs in a positive manner.*

Obviously you won't use all the correspondences listed. The magickal information under each topic gives you a selection of common energies to manipulate. What you choose and how you decide to manipulate that energy rests in your magickal lap. How did I get this information? By pawing through stacks of books and interviewing various magickal people, asking them what energies they felt were common to the desired goal.

Apartment Living

Not all of us live in a single home. Many urban Witches populate our major cities and small towns in apartment buildings, duplexes, condominiums, and single houses now functioning as several family dwellings. Even if you cleanse and consecrate your living space often, you still have to deal with the rest of the building, other people, and energies that you neither created nor invited. What do you do?

First, I suggest completing this chapter and learning how to cleanse your living area, then try some or all of the ideas given below:

1. On the outside of your front door, draw a pentacle or the Helm of Awe in clove oil or holy water. Do this every week on Sunday (best if done during the hour of the sun).[2] If you live in a high crime area, or for some reason you are having trouble with your neighbors, draw your selected symbol on the door every day.

2. Sprinkle holy water, basil, or salt (or all three) in the vestibule of the apartment building, outside the elevator doors on your floor, or at the top step that leads onto your floor.

---

2. Please see the Planetary Hour information in Appendix V.

3. Consider creating an elemental to guard the entrance to your apartment or living quarters (see pages 161–166).

4. Walk the perimeter of your building once a month sprinkling holy water, salt, or angelica as you go (if you put a bag in your pocket, no one will take notice).

5. Drop garlic cloves underneath your window (on the outside) and around all the doors that lead into the complex.

6. Hang a small mirror on your front and back doors to ward off negativity.

Magickal individuals who live in multi-family dwellings may find it necessary to do a thorough cleansing of their living area once a month, rather than every four or six months, simply because of the greater activity around them. If you share a wall with an abusive neighbor, try sprinkling basil mixed with angelica ground into a fine powder along your baseboard to keep the negative energies from coming through the wall (angelica) and promoting harmony (basil). Evict difficult neighbors with loving kindness rather than hatred. To do this, mix cayenne pepper, black pepper, yarrow, nettle, and angelica into a fine powder. Ask the universe to find the trouble-makers a home where they will find love and support and where they can evolve to a higher spiritual existence as you empower the powder. Place the powder on their doorstep during the dark of the moon, or on a Saturday in the hour of Venus. At the same time you should ask the universe to bring neighbors who are loving, open-minded, ecumenical, and courteous. Do not be surprised, however, if the universe chooses to allow them to remain, and sends you packing to a better home.

Noting Negative Energy Fields

Before you bounce around the house with bell, book, and proverbial candle, I want you to walk around your house with your three-by-five-inch cards and a pencil or pen. With your left or right hand extended, feel the energy patterns of your home. See where it feels sticky, light, or heavy; soft or hard; hot or cold. Briefly make note of these areas on the back of the corresponding card. Don't worry if you think you aren't good enough at sensing energy to do this, because your higher self can sense energies, you only need to shut out that argumentative, negative chatter of the logical mind. The more you practice, the better you will get.

Cold areas indicate emotional voids. Hot areas represent highly charged energy fields, usually due either to a preponderance of good or bad emotional residue. A heavy or sticky feeling may be a clue of build-up of energy-muck. Soft or light energy often appears in refined areas, such as your personal sacred space and around your altar or shrine. When you have finished the spiritual housecleaning steps in this book, your whole house should contain soft or light refined energy.

Magickal Minutes

How to Make Your Signature Magickal Powder

The use of magickal herbs varies widely within the Witch's cornucopia of spellcasting. Properly prepared powders made from herbs and other chemicals or ingredients may be blown into the air, sprinkled on the body, cast about an object, or placed directly in someone's pathway. **Note:** Never ingest magickal powders, and dry all herbs thoroughly before use. Although several tried and true formulas exist, the magickal person may use his or her intuition to create signature powders, meaning those powders that distinctively belong to that individual. Signature powders require a working knowledge of magickal herbalism, magickal correspondences, and the desire to experiment.

To prepare your own signature powder, you will need: Ingredients of your choice in the number of 3, 7, 9, or 11. A mortar and pestle. A signature chemical or ingredient (such as glitter, silver powder, gold powder, et cetera). A binding powder such as benzoin, mastic, or orris root. A firm belief in your choice of deity. A small glass container to hold the powder until the opportunity presents itself for use. A candle color of your choice. One bell. (**Note:** Magickal powders made during storms seem to carry a bigger "zapping" quality.) I have provided a general herbal listing in Appendix II to assist you in your choices.

1. Collect the appropriate ingredients. Cast a magick circle. Call the Quarters if you wish, or leave them closed as your general practice dictates.

2. Bless and empower all herbs and supplies. You may like to try the following exorcisms:

Hold your hands over the herbs and say:

> *I exorcise thee, O creature of Earth Mother, in the Names of*
> *Cerridwyn and Cernunnos, that you may receive strength, power,*
> *and virtue, attracting good energies and the correct spirits to banish*

all negativity within you, and may these energies and spirits
cause all hostile entities to retire.

Ring the bell three times.

3. Make your powder by adding the ingredients into the mortar slowly. Use the pestle to crush the ingredients into a fine powder. As you add each ingredient, state what the specifics of the ingredient are (for example, I add cloves for protection). Crush in a deosil movement for building, growing, loving energies. Crush in a widdershins pattern for banishing activities.

4. When finished, light the candle (if you choose to use one) and invoke your deity, archetype, angel, or general positive universal energy. Hold your hands over the mortar filled with the powder, and say:

In the name of ———— (your chosen deity) *and with the assistance*
of my ancestors I call the ancient power of the universe, which was
from the beginning and is forever through eternity both male and
female, one in Spirit, the original beginning of all things: all knowing,
all loving, all encompassing, all powerful, changeless, formless, light,
eternal, perfect. In the names of the Lady of the Moon and the Lord of
Death and Resurrection, in the names of _____ (your
archetype or other name here), *rulers of the elements, purveyors of*
wisdom, as above so below I empower thee now, in this time and place
to _____ (state your desired goal here). *With*
harm to none, corresponding to my free will. May the energies of this
powder not reverse, or place upon me any curse. So mote it be!

5. Thank the energies you have called. Take down the circle. Store the powder until use.

When you use the powder you should again invoke your deity choice, draw the rune Rad over the powder (so the powder will travel safely to your intended destination), then dispense the powder, saying something like:

Angels of air, dispense this powder and magnify its power a
hundredfold so that my desire may manifest as I will for the intent
of _____ (state your goal). *With harm to none.*
Away with thee to do my bidding!

Throw or dispense the powder.

Removing Negative Energy Fields

Your next step in a thorough spiritual cleaning begins in the basement or first floor (if you have no basement). Items such as a drum, a rattle, a singing bowl, bells, cymbals, or windchimes work very well for clearing a room of negative energies. If you don't have a rattle, an empty soup can with a handful of dried beans or unpopped popcorn will work just as well (remember to cleanse and consecrate these items before you use them). Other supplies needed to cleanse a home (especially for the first time) are: a white candle, holy water, a mister or completely clean empty spray bottle, salt, incense (with feather to help dispense, if you like), an item representing the element you've chosen for the room, and clove oil.

I put everything on a tray so that I can carry my supplies from room to room. I also choose one item that I will place in the center of the house to secure the overall energies I'm about to call. This item can be a sacred statue, a picture, a cleansed crystal, a simple creek stone, a plant, a small fountain, et cetera. The items don't have to look holy to be holy.

For this house cleansing procedure, I'm going to use the rattle and the drum, but this doesn't mean you can't use any of the other items listed above, such as bells, singing bowls, panpipes, a flute, and so on. If you don't want to use instruments at all, then try clapping or chanting. I use the drum because the sound breaks up oppressive and highly charged emotional energies. I live with six other people in my house; four of them are teenagers, which means my house gets highly charged with emotional energy. Both drums and rattles affect brain waves, moving you from beta to alpha. Chimes, bells, gongs, and windchimes work well for areas that don't experience onslaughts of emotions. For example, if you live alone, and life has moved along fairly well with no emotional upsets, then you shouldn't have many pockets of oppressive emotional energy unless your maniac sister just spent the night or the neighbor's kid had a nightmare in your guest room. Minus the visit from the ditzy sister or child, chimes, bells, singing bowls and such would work well to refine the energies of your home.

To begin, open all doors and windows in the room. Lay the drum and rattle in the center of the floor and bless them. Then begin at the center of the room and walk in a widdershins (counterclockwise) direction, playing your drum, moving outward in a spiral pattern until you reach the perimeter of the room. Your intent should be to break up negative and stagnant energy with the sound of the drum. Don't worry about the beat. Let the room tell you what pattern it needs, and let that pattern move through your hands into your drum. In shamanic Craft, we call this procedure drum trancing. Just let yourself go. You're not playing for an audience. You may wish to begin with a two-beat sound (like a heartbeat) and then let the drum and room work together. Some rooms may like fast drumming, where other rooms require a slower pace. Remember those "odd" spots you wrote down on the back of your three-by-five-inch card? Pay special attention to those areas, visualizing the negative or stagnant energy breaking apart. If it helps, you can visualize the negative energy as a dark fog;, just be sure you let go of the visualization as you drum or rattle.

Don't forget the closets. There will be times that you will move back to the center of the room and continue drumming for awhile, and other times, when you have finished the perimeter of the room, you might stop drumming with a verbal cry. Here at Black Forest, we finish drumming in our ceremonies with a howl, demonstrating that the drum, the human, and the sound are one. The howl also allows you to ground and center any excess energy we have raised, and is a thank-you to our coven mascot/familiar/totem, the wolf.

Magickal Minutes

Simple Drum Patterns

During our trips to various festivals, Mick and I have picked up a few beginner drum patterns for you to try. The word "Ka" means the center of the drum. The word "Tak" means the outer edge of the drum. Under each sound I've put the hands you can use.

(A) Ka-Tak (Pause) Ka-Tak

Right-Left (Pause) Right-Left

Sounds like a heartbeat.

(B) Ka-Ka (Pause) Tak-Tak-Tak

Right-Right (Pause) Right-Left-Right

Start slow. Raise energy by picking up the beat. This is a sexy beat, allowing people to sway and dance if you keep the same beat.

(C) Ka-Ka   Ka-Ka   Tak-Tak Tak-Tak

Right-Left Right-Left Right-Left Right-Left

We call this one "The Call." If you play it long enough, people will naturally gather around you. One fellow called it the Mamma and Baby Elephant beat or Marching beat. It's an excellent beat for calling Quarters, background for drawing down the moon or sun, or during initiations when the candidate moves around the circle.

(D) Ka-tak-tak-Ka-tak-tak-Ka-tak-tak-Ka

Right-left-right-Left-right-left-Right-left-right-Left

This one may take you awhile to master, but it appears to be a common ritual beat in the East, where continuous drumming makes up most of the event. You can raise or quiet energy with the tempo.

There are all sorts of drums on the market, but what if you can't afford that $450 djembe? Simple: turn a plastic or metal bucket over and use that. The bucket works just as well as a drum.

Back to our house cleansing/blessing procedures! Go to the center of the room again. Take the rattle and follow the same procedure. Sharp, quick raps, established in a pattern that you choose, work well in room cleansing. As with the drum, you'll find that each room may require a different rattling pattern, or a whole house may choose one pattern to begin, then move into another pattern as you finish; or you may wish to try the drumming patterns above, using your rattle. Let the house help you.

Now, go back to the center of the room and pick up the salt. Salt represents earth energies. Hold the salt in your hand, close your eyes, and become the salt—become the Earth Mother. Breathe deeply and take the Earth Mother into yourself. Whenever you work with any element, you should "become" that element, whether you work through house cleansing or you call a Quarter in a magick circle.

Here you have a choice. Some Witches like to move widdershins with the salt, where others will choose to move in a deosil direction. Do what feels right to you. Walk your spiral from the center to the perimeter again, sprinkling the salt lightly, keeping your intention pure. Do not mound the salt on the floor or you'll be crunching around from now until next Tuesday. A little bit will do. Visualize the negative energy dissolving and leaving the room. Work out to the perimeter of the room. Now, if you would be more comfortable walking in a widdershins pattern to banish with the salt, that's okay too. Use your instincts. Don't forget—do what feels right to you.

Go back to the center of the room. Light the incense and follow the same pattern as before. Incense, in Craft theology, represents the element of air. Breathe deeply of the fragrance and become the air. Close your eyes and become one with the element. You are the wind, the gentle breeze, the rise and fall of the lungs of Earth.

Repeat this process with the lighted candle. Become one with the fire. See yourself as the phoenix rising out of the ashes, the creativity and lust of the flames. You are the abundance and strength of the fire. Be the fire as you walk the room.

Put the holy water in the spray bottle. The finer the spray, the better. Become one with the element of water. Be the transformation, the cauldron of change, the chalice of no thirst. Be the delicate sound of the fountain, the cleansing surge of the waterfall. Be the water as you walk the room. Mist the room in the same manner in which you used the salt, incense, and fire. Don't get everything sopping wet. A fine mist here and there will do. You don't want your mother, spouse, or roommate coming home and asking if the house got hit by a flash flood.

To fine-tune the room, you may wish to make one more pass with a bell, singing bowl, windchimes, or wind instrument.

Making the Room Your Own

Close all the doors and windows. Move back to the center of the room and expand your energy field slowly. Feel your energy field move outward from your body with each successive breath (remember, we practiced this exercise in *To Ride A Silver Broomstick*). Continue this procedure until your energy reaches the perimeter of the room. Feel the room within you, and yourself within the room. Connect your essence with the room, then open your eyes. Concentrate on what happens in this room. Will this room function as a room of cleansing, a room of your creativity, a room of your love? Think about what type of energies you will manifest in this room. Take a deep breath, ground and center, then close your eyes and envision the room filled with a brilliant white light. Take your time. Don't rush. Some individuals like to use their drum to do this, others prefer to concentrate in silence.

Go back over the room with your hands, checking the energy of the area. If you feel satisfied that the negative energy has cleared, go on to the next step. If you aren't happy with what you feel, then use the rattle or drum again. If you have never cleared your house, or you haven't cleared your house in a long time, you may have to work a little harder to refine the energies. Again, to finish off the process, you might wish to use a bell with a light sound, windchimes, or a singing bowl.

Invoking Divinity into the Room

Now you will call divinity into the room, and your original intent comes into play. Would you like to call the Lord and Lady for peace, harmony, and protection? Would you like to call a specific Goddess, such as Rosemerta, the Goddess of abundance? For a child's room you may wish to invoke Diana, protector of children, or the angels of light. For your husband's hobby room, den, or office, you may choose the Green Man, Cernunnos, Herne, and so on. The basic question remains: Who ya gonna call? And *why*?

If you work with a traditional pantheon, be careful here. Eclectic experimentation might not be the best choice. Kuan Yin in one room may not get along with Hecate in the room next door. Rather than promoting harmony, you may whip up a magickal mess. If you work with a specific pantheon already, then stick with that pantheon unless that pantheon deals only with Dark Goddesses. I'm not saying black magick or evil stuff, I'm talking about crone energy, warrior energy, and the like. A house filled with Dark Goddess energy will not normally promote much prosperity and laughter. As in all things of the Craft, keep the essence of balance in mind as you work. So, be very, very careful when choosing archetypes. Even though much of your work might entail the energies of the Dark Goddesses, you may wish to fill your house with bright Goddess energy for a housecleaning procedure. If you like more eclectic practices, please research the deities you call into the various rooms. If you want to play it safe, just call the Lord and Lady. If you *really* want to be on the safe side, then call the angels.

Before we go further, some mystery traditions teach students that deity energy should not be invoked unless the practitioner works within the boundaries of a magick circle. Other traditions teach that you can invoke divine energy outside the circle but never inside the circle (this is not a popular belief among Crafters; however, this line of thought does exist). Finally, there are mystery traditions that teach the student that you can invoke divinity any time, any place, with or without the aid of the magick circle. Since there is no one right way to work with divinity, you will have to choose which mode of thought suits your practices and move on from there. I am in the habit of working with Spirit all the time so, for me, the magick circle rule does not apply; however, I respect those individuals who have learned differently.

Now, why would I suggest angels over the Lord and Lady? If you live in a home where you adhere to one faith, and your parents, in-laws, siblings, or spouse practice another faith and adamantly oppose your belief system, then they will unconsciously generate negative energy whenever they sense the psychic trappings of another faith. If this situation describes yours, then angel energy will do nicely. The angels act maturely and provide safety for all religious beliefs, without one stepping on the toes of another.

Back to invoking deity. How do we invoke deity? If you work with a specific female goddess, use the Goddess Position. For the God, use the God Position. However, always begin in the Goddess Position, not because females are better, but because you have an energy line in your body. Raising your arms with palms outward and feet spread apart assists you in the flow of your own energy without any breaks or gaps.

You can invoke deity with prayer, chant, or visualization. The choice lies in your magickal brain. In my home, I begin by ringing a bell seven times, as the number seven represents the calling of wisdom. Here's an example of a simple invocation:

Rosemerta, queen of abundance and joy, too gentle to be human,
too powerful to be elemental, holding in your arms the cornucopia
of life. Instill this room with your light, your love, and your laughter.
Descend upon this house, bringing prosperity and abundance.
So mote it be.

Or, you might wish to try this popular Pagan chant, "The Mill of Magick" (author unknown):

Fire flame and fire burn
Make the mill of magick turn;
work the will for which I pray,
Io Dia Ha He He Yea!

Air breath and air blow,
Make the mill of magick go;
Work the will for which we pray
Io Dia Ha He He Yea!

Water heat and water boil
Make the mill of magick toil;
Work the will for which we pray
Io Dia Ha He He Yea!

Earth without and earth within,
Makes the mill of magick spin,
Work the will for which we pray
Io Dia Ha He He Yea!

Seal all the doors and windows with holy water or clove oil, either mixture will work well. You can dab the window or door at all four corners and in the center, or you can draw pentacles with the liquid. Some magickal people seal the doors and windows at the top with a pentacle, then dab oil on the door handle, then above and below it, to symbolize "As above, so below. This place is sealed." Other individuals seal doors and windows with soft sounds from their rattle, drum, or tambourine.

Check your three-by-five-inch card now to review the color, magickal symbol, totem animal, and element you chose for the room. While standing or sitting in the middle of the room, envision the following:

1. The room filling with the color energy you chose.

2. Visualize the magickal symbol on the ceiling, the walls, or the floor (or all).

3. Invite the totem animal into the room.

4. Fill the room with the elemental energy you chose. In this case, do not envision the element as a "being" but as a pure, refined energy that represents universal concepts such as love, creativity, healing, trust, peace, and so on.

Complete the House

Follow the aforementioned procedures for each room in the house. When you finish, go to the room that most resembles the core of your home. In the Goddess Position, expand your energy field from the core (where you are standing) to the outer reaches of the house. Imagine that the entire house fills with pure, white light. Hold this visualization as long as you can.

Then say something like:

From foundation to roof; from concrete to timber;
I declare this house cleansed, consecrated and blessed.
In the name of _____. May all who live and visit here
find this house a sacred sanctuary, of love, of harmony, of peace,
of patience, prosperity, and protection. So mote it be!

Check the information on your card marked "Universal" and pull in the corresponding energies, watching them mix in your mind throughout the entire house.

How do you know your spiritual housecleaning has worked? You should feel better. Colors in your home may appear brighter, sounds may be more pleasing to the ear, or you may breathe easier. The emotional stability of others in the home should also improve.

Pointers for Cleansing the Homes of Others

You cannot compare another person's home to your own. Each place of residence, like each individual, will be different. If you plan to do a spiritual housecleaning for a friend, please take into consideration the needs of that person. Discuss with your friend the intent he or she would like manifested in his or her home. Follow that intent. You may suggest ideas, but when the time comes to perform the ceremony, please follow the wishes of your friend. Let's say that Susie doesn't like angels. It would therefore be inappropriate for you to use angels in your spiritual housecleaning of Susie's home. Perhaps your Catholic friend has difficulty with your alternative religion. He thinks the "other" religion is okay for you, but he would never consider practicing that theology. You would then ask him if he would prefer angels, Mary, Jesus, et cetera, as his deity choices. It would be terribly bad form for you to stick the Morrigan in the closet, just in case; likewise, choosing totem animals, magickal symbols, and the like, would be inappropriate for a friend who does not believe in these energies. As magickal people we need to keep the needs and desires of our friends at the forefront of our work.

If your friend's home has a high volume of traffic in the form of wild parties, you certainly have your work cut out for you. You could cleanse the place this morning, and tonight the house will teem with all sorts of astral nasties. In this case, you can create psychic energy nets to capture this unwanted energy, instructing your friend how to clean those nets. You can weave a net around a chosen object, or simply choose a corner of the room, to suspend the psychic net. Have your friend smudge the area (or the item) after everyone has wobbled home. I also seal all the doors inside of a home on both sides, even closet doors. This way if "something" does get in, whatever it is will get stuck, allowing you to cleanse the area quickly.

Don't ever be afraid when doing a psychic house cleaning. I did Casey's new home the other day. I started at the base of her house, in the ritual area. That part went fine. When I had just about finished, the door to a cement alcove, across the family rumpus room, squeaked open. And shut. And open. Hmmm. Something that had taken up residence in her home was not exceedingly happy that I was going about my business, and wanted me to know it. I double-warded the door of the room I was in, and remembered that to fear defeats your purpose. I took a deep breath, walked to the doorway, and said, "Shoo!" I could feel whatever "it" was move back in shock. Sort of a "Well! I never!" reaction. I kept going, paying special attention to that alcove on the other side of the room where the negativity seemed to collect. When I finished with the room, Casey came down the stairs. "How does it feel?" I asked her. She walked around for awhile, then said, "Calm. Much better."

"There was something hanging against that wall," I told her, pointing in the direction of the alcove. "Yes," she said. "I had a psychic in a few months ago tell me that when they erected this house, one of the workers carried a great deal of anger and negativity in his heart. She told me this anger lodged in one of the walls. Guess that was the wall."

"It's gone now."

"Good. My cat wouldn't go in there for love nor money. Maybe he'll go in now."

At that moment her cat meandered past, sniffed at the doorway, then sauntered into the alcove.

If you are cleansing a friend's or family member's home, do not do your cleansing with an audience. Not only do other people distract you, their non-belief inhibits your progress. For example, when I cleansed Casey's house, her son came to visit, carrying a great deal of anger with him. As I was attempting to clear the kitchen, he moved in and out of my path, stopped at the fridge to get a peanut butter cup, get a drink, meander around the room, and so on. It got to the point where I was tagging after him with the holy water like a frenzied mother. Embarrassing, to say the least. Then her daughter came to visit with her baby. To the kitchen they congregated. When I had finished the entire house, I told Casey to do the kitchen again, as I wasn't happy with the results in that room.

When cleansing people's houses, do the cleansing alone. Ask them to come in at the point in the ritual where they need to make the room their own. Then you should leave that room while they perform this function. Your energies should not be present when they make the room their own.

Finally, show your friends and family members how to do a full house cleansing for themselves, as well as how to perform quickie cleansings.

Spiritual Seconds

Get a big sheet of paper and draw your favorite magickal slogan on the paper. For example: This Home Is Inhabited by Beings of Light. Put a new slogan up every thirty days. To share your slogan with others, put your slogan on your answering machine.

Quickie Cleansers

Now that you've completely purified your home and instilled the energies you want, how can you continue to keep it that way, considering the ups and downs of a busy life? I know of several fast methods for cleansing an area, but remember the quickies function only as quickies. Never replace the full cleansing of your house with these fast methods. Quickies enhance and increase the longevity of your spiritual house-cleaning, but they do not replace the actual cleaning. Don't forget to reaffirm your intentions when using the quick methods listed below.

- Smudging with sage.
- Misting holy water from a spray bottle.
- Boiling herbs in water on your stove.
- Lighting a stationary thurible in the center of the room.
- Passing incense over the affected area.
- Lighting an empowered white candle at the core of the house or in the affected room, and encircling that candle with sea salt.
- Sprinkling a mixture of ground salt, basil, and rosemary, or one of the magickal powders you've made, lightly throughout the area.
- Using sound, such as drums, bells, rattles, chimes, musical bowls, tuning forks, singing bowls, and so on.
- Chanting.

Other ideas for keeping the home free of negativity include:

- Taking a ritual bath (or ritual shower) and smudging your clothes if you have had a particularly trying day.
- Keeping a vial of holy water or oil by the door that you can use when you come home from work, or when you have been out in public places (especially around the holiday shopping season!). I have a friend who

smudges herself in her garage every evening after work so that she won't carry the negative vibrations into the house with her. (She's a stockbroker in New York—say no more.)

- Putting salt on your tongue to keep from spewing negative thoughts into the world when you are angry. The salt dissolves the negativity.

- Fry sea salt in a frying pan on the stove or hearth until the salt stops jumping. Supposedly, you've just burned the tails off of unwanted astral nasties. Use the large, crystallized sea salt for this procedure, not the finely ground crystals.

- Formulate a magickal powder for emergency occasions.

- Empower everything you drink to keep your body in harmony with spirit.

- Bless your food at every meal.

Magickal Minutes

Energy Flow Differences

Practice feeling the differences in energy flow wherever you go. For example, what are the energies like in the different areas of your workplace, the mall, or your favorite restaurant? Take a pocket notebook along and write down your impressions. Soon, you will begin to see a pattern of how you perceive different forms of energy.

Blessing the Utilities in Your Home

Now that we've done the complete mundane and spiritual housecleaning procedure, we should look at specific items in your home that affect your well-being. They are your furnace, the water heater, the plumbing, and the electricity. Those of you who live in the southern areas of the country should include your trusty air-conditioning unit as well. I also include the phone in this category and, if you own a computer with a modem, throw that in for good measure.

Your furnace constitutes the sacred fire of your home. Each fall, you probably have a repairman come in and clean your furnace. (If you don't, you should.) To clean your furnace, if you use gas or oil, the repair person turns the pilot light off. Ask your repair person, when they are ready to relight the furnace, that you be allowed to do this function (with their guidance, of course). Ideally, you should carry the flame from your altar (or house shrine) to the furnace. However, if this isn't possible, ground and center and, as you light the flame, connect with the sacredness of fire.

You can say an invocation aloud, or you say the invocation in your mind (if you would feel embarrassed to speak in front of the repair person). Say something like:

> *Spirits of fire. I dedicate this sacred flame to Vesta. May she bring peace and prosperity into my home. As this sacred flame burns in her honor, may my house be warm and safe in the coming months.*

If you live in an apartment building, or for some other reason cannot light the pilot light yourself, or you have electric baseboard heat, then you will need to use a different method. For example, the first day in fall that the heat kicks on in your apartment, you can bless the heat registers in the same manner. If you have electric baseboard heat, you can clean the units, then bless them.

In spring, when you've shut off the heat for the warm season ahead, you can thank the spirits of fire for heating and protecting your home during the cold months, and bid them rest and renewed strength through the upcoming season.

Most hot water heaters these days, my husband tells me, are electric. With the hot water heater, you work with two elements—that of fire and water. Therefore, you would bless both as well as banish all negativity from the heater unit. An invocation for water would be:

> *Spirits of water. I call forth the essence of blessing and transformational change, and dedicate your flow and contents to Epona. May you bring forth harmony and peace in my home.*

Learn where the water main connects to your house, and bless that area as well. You can use the same invocation as above, or write a new one. Remember to break up any negative energy in that area with your rattle, drum, chimes, or smudging with sage. You choose. Don't forget the faucets in the bathroom and kitchen. You should be an expert at cleansing stuff by now.

Because your phone connects you to the outside world and connects your home to the universe, you need to take extra care when cleansing not only the phone but the telephone line. Your goal is to banish negative energy and deflect unwanted calls. Of course, the good old answering machine helps here; however, you should work on the energy coming through the line too. Wouldn't it be great if your phone was an instrument of wisdom? Well, you can empower the telephone in that manner:

Spirits of air, I dedicate this phone and the line to the energies of wisdom and harmony. May this phone exist as a vehicle of love and light, and may every word I speak through the receiver be filled with clarity and wisdom. Deplete and banish all negative energy that tries to come to me from the outside world. So mote it be!

Your computer can also function as a communicator to the outside world and, if you have one, it acts as some sort of vehicle through the written word, software packages, games, and so on. As smudging or misting your computer (and the supplies that go with it) would be, shall we say, unwise, then sound wins the bonus round for the best option in breaking up negativity around your workspace and computer. I opt for the Angels of Mercury (or Spirits of Mercury, if you so desire) for the dedication and empowerment of your phone or computer. Each time you buy something new for your computer, such as disks, paper, or toner for the printer, be sure to cleanse the items of any negativity that the supplies have managed to pick up from the manufacturing plant, to the store, to you. Write a computer blessing and save it in your word processor area. If you are really a computer wizard, you may wish to incorporate some sort of cleansing graphic that appears when you turn on your computer. Don't forget to dedicate and bless the surge protector too!

The electricity in your home relates to the element of fire. Bless and dedicate the fuse box and all lamps. Remember to cleanse, consecrate, and empower your light bulbs when you change them. Remember, become the electricity!

Buying Large Ticket Items for the Home

Before you romp out there with cash, plastic, or checkbook in hand, go to your guardian shrine (or altar if you don't have a shrine) and ask the spirits of your house to help you pick the right items for your home that will benefit you and the occupants as well as promote harmony and peace within your domicile. Ask for the best price available and the best quality for your budget. When you bring the item home, cleanse, consecrate, and bless what you purchased. Be sure to move into the item, making it your own.

When large ticket items break, go to your altar or house shrine and ask the spirits of the house to help you find the proper repair person who will fix the problem (the first time) at a fair price. If the item has to go to the junk pile, then thank the item for the service it has given you (remember, everything has a consciousness) and de-magick the item. Be sure to move your essence out of the item before you trash it.

Blessing Your Fireplace or Wood Stove

Light fires to warm the home at dawn on the first cool morning of the year. The hearth of your fireplace needs to be thoroughly cleaned, and all mechanics of the wood stove in working order. You should also have someone check to make sure the chimney is in good repair. A mason will examine the brick and mortar for you, as well as the chimney cap, and there are individuals who clean chimneys, usually listed in the yellow pages. The old adage "nine woods in the cauldron go" applies to making your first magickal fire. If you can get your mitts on these nine woods in your area, that would be terrific. If you can't find all the woods, then choose nine woods indigenous to your area. The only wood you should not use is the Elder, considered sacred to the Lady.

The nine woods are:

Apple	Love
Hazel	Wisdom, Divination
Ash	Healing
Birch	Purification
Elder	Evoking and Exorcising Entities
Oak	Solar Workings and Strength
Yew	Transformation
Willow	Magick
Thorn (Hawthorn)	Fertility and Happiness

Before you lay your fire, pass each piece of wood (tinder, paper, or firestarter) through salt and incense. Use your rattle or drum to break up any negativity attached to the wood. You can say something like:

*O thou being of wood, be welcome in my home. In the name of the
Immortal Lady and Horned Lord, I bless and free you from negativity.
Join with me to work my will on Earth. Assist me to build love, peace,
and harmony in my home that will extend outward into the universe.*

As you lay the wood, build a vortex of energy in the center of the grate. This fire will function as the need-fire of your home. Take great care in instilling the correct energies into your task. If you are upset with someone, stop, ritually cleanse yourself, then continue. Don't construct the fire while you feel emotionally distraught, as that energy will go into the wood. A nice chant for this task is:

By wisdom, by love, by power.

Before you light the fire, sprinkle the logs with frankincense and myrrh to conjure pure, spiritual energies; dried mint (or five finger grass) for prosperity; rosemary for conjuring protection; vervain to make the herbs "go"; dragon's blood for putting "vroom" in the room; and basil for the occupants to live in sympathy with each other. Throw in a capful of rum as your offering. Naturally, you could use the herbs of your choice—those I've listed here serve merely as suggestions. As you sprinkle the herbs over the logs, remember to reaffirm your intention.

Rather than lighting this particular fire with a long match or butane fireplace lighter, consider starting the fire from the flame of a sacred candle on your altar or shrine. Carry the candle slowly through the house to the wood stove or fireplace. As you light the fire, invoke the spirits of fire. You might wish to throw in a magickal powder made specifically for the purpose of blessing your home. An excellent Goddess of choice for your fireplace or wood stove dedication would be Vesta, the Roman Goddess of hearth fires (her equivalent is Hestia). This Goddess is worshiped, not in statue form, but in devotion to the sacred fire.

On the first day of March, the faithful renewed the fires of Vesta. Vesta was the Goddess of every sacrificial fire, whether in the home or the temple. She was worshiped along with Janus. His praise opened the service, and Vesta's closed it. Vesta's festival, the Vestalia, was held on 9 June.[3]

Hestia, of Greek extraction, was one of the twelve Olympians, known specifically as the Goddess of the hearth and home, and the sister of Demeter. Here is an invocation for Vesta/Hestia:

> *With the rising of the sun, with the coming of dawn, with the*
> *advancement of spring, I invoke thee, O spirits of fire, to cleanse,*
> *consecrate and bless my home. Vesta, guardian of the hearth flame,*
> *expand with the glowing orb in the sky, the lengthening light of the*
> *season. With this need-fire, my home will be filled with the positive*
> *magickal energies of the universe. Bless my home in the coming year.*
> *Fill our hearts and minds with abundance, protection, and prosperity.*

Chant:

> *The love, the joy, the peace, the beauty; return, return, return.*

(The heartbeat for drumming works well here. Tap-boom. Tap-boom. Tap-boom.)

---

3. *World Mythology and Legend* by Anthony S. Mercatante, Facts on File Publishing, 1988.

If you don't have a fireplace (and many of us, I realize, don't have such a luxury) you can use your cauldron instead, placing the nine woods in your cauldron (use a bit of alcohol mixed with your favorite herbs) and performing the ceremony. Do not use a charcoal grill indoors as this is unsafe, but you can set up a grill for this type of ceremony on your outdoor patio.

Blessing and Using Your Major Appliances in Magickal Applications

Not only can you bless your major appliances to keep them in harmony with the home and your chosen environment, you can use these appliances to work magick. Yes, your washing machine can be a magickal tool! The major appliances in your home include your stove, refrigerator, microwave, dishwasher, washing machine, dryer, freezer, television, stereo, et cetera. Not only does this make that $800 piece of equipment more valuable, using appliances for magick can be downright fun.

You can bless your appliances when you do your full house cleansing or you can save the blessings for a later time, depending on your schedule. I usually bless the appliances right along with my house cleansing procedures but you may wish to handle your appliances differently.

Every day you could use your appliances to enhance your prosperity, better your relations with others, raise your self-esteem, or assist you in recovering from an illness. All you have to have is a little imagination. For example, is there something bothering you that you want to get rid of? Write the problem on a piece of toilet paper and flush the nuisance away. Utter appropriate words as you watch your problem swirl away. Empower the water that runs through your coffee maker each morning to bring you spiritual enlightenment, courage, or a productive day. Magick your vacuum cleaner to suck up negativity. Empower your lawn mower to cut negativity from your property. Use the mulcher to put a protective blanket around the house. Bless your sprinkler system outside to feed positive energy into your lawn. Magick your pens and pencils to bring you wisdom, creativity, or clarity of thought. Enchant that summer fan to blow negativity out of your house. Imagine that every time you turn on a light in your home, you are turning on the light of spirituality in your soul. I could go on, and on, and on . . . however, you get the idea.

An Exercise in Creativity

Walk around your house and write down at least twenty objects you use at least once a day. Now contemplate how you can turn those ordinary objects into magickal practices. Work with each object and its associated magick for one week. Record your results. Place little sticky-papers with magickal symbols or your goals factored down to one or two words on the objects.

Major Renovations

There comes a time when renovations of one's property can't be sidestepped for the sake of a cheerleading uniform, a band trip, a school excursion to France, or sports gear; and so it was here, during the writing of this book, that my house finally declared war.

"The main beam is cracking," said my husband.

In a very small voice, I said, "Does this mean the house will fall down?" I was thinking of the tons of people here on circle night. I could visualize the disaster perfectly—I am a Witch, you know. There we would be, all thirty of us (give or take a bout of the flu, a broken car, or a fussy spouse) stomping around, banging drums and rattles, and the floor giving way. Down, down we would go like a bunch Pagan potatoheads, plummeting into the dank oblivion of the root cellar, where no human has gone before.

"We have to fix the main beam," repeated my husband.

"How much will that cost?"

"If your Dad and I do it, it won't be too bad."

So, I did what any intelligent Witch would do. I prayed like I'd never prayed before. "Please don't let the house collapse on us while they are tinkering down there," I asked the Goddess. I visualized bunches of big, strong, tough (okay, and cute) angels holding up the main beams of the house every night until they finished the job. I talked to the house constantly in my mommy voice. "This might hurt just a little bit, but then when we've concluded our little task, we can get rid of some of these yuckie, itchy uncomfortable walls and give you some nice new ones. You'd like that, wouldn't you? Hummm?" The house did not seem particularly amused, and sloughed off parts of the living room wall just to let me know we'd better make our promise good about that new stuff I'd guaranteed.

Every once in a while I would go down to the basement with my bell and incense to clear out all the negativity. I'd heard enough grunts, unusual expletives, and whining saw blades to know that constant cleansing was necessary. Even the dog cowered under my bedcovers as, each night, they threaded the jacks another turn. Surprisingly enough, the first time my home-brew crew put those jacks into place and began the operation, the house "felt" better. Sort of like an old lady who's suffered a twisted back for over thirty years and suddenly, through a miracle of conviction, could now stand with shoulders thrown back and spine straighter than her wooden walking stick. We could all breathe easier. The children even slept better. I got a monstrous cleaning bug up my broomstick, and the place began to look better than before.

During the renovation process, I snuck around and cleansed all the new materials and consecrated them to the God and Goddess. I even drew protective pentacles on the jacks and other equipment, just to make sure they didn't decide to have a mind of their own and try some crazy rumba while my construction team slaved away.

The point of this little exposé is to remind you that your intuition and creativity go a long way in the practical application of magick and spirituality in your life. Where, in any Craft book, have you ever seen step-by-step instructions on how to magickally renovate your house? We all think of renovation as a mundane thing and leave it at that—just like so many other situations in our lives. Every event in your life can have magickal or spiritual overtones, if you want it to. The decision belongs to you.

Other renovations you can turn magickal include:

- Room painting. Cleanse and consecrate all tools and the paint before you begin. Add a bit of holy water to the paint (just a drop will do). Chant as you paint.
- New flooring. Follow the same procedure.
- Removing layers of paint from woodwork and other areas.
- Installing new electrical lines.
- Installing new plumbing.
- Reroofing your house.
- Building a new addition. (Begin with a ritual for the blessing of the plans, and continue working magick as you complete each step of the building process.)
- Tuckpointing brick or stone work.
- Building a retaining wall.

- Installing new screen or storm doors or windows.
- Creating or replacing sidewalks.
- Installing new siding.
- Erecting a new chimney.
- Re-stoning or putting macadam on your driveway.
- Installing an electric garage door opener.
- Erecting a fence around your property or garden.
- Installing new closets.
- Turning your basement or attic into a family room or bedrooms.
- Adding a patio.

Creating Harmony in Your Office or Place of Business

What we do for a living directly affects how we deal with the world. How we deal with the world directly affects what we do for a living. How we perceive ourselves also affects our work and our environment, at home and at our place of employment. If you suffer from low self-esteem, your home life and career will suffer. Sometimes we blame our low self-esteem on our home environment or on our chosen employment. Just as you learned to cleanse and consecrate your home, you need to bring this same type of cleansing process to your job. This isn't always so easy. If you have an office of your own, lucky you. Half the battle is over. However, many of us don't have the luxury of an office alone. They've either crammed us into cubicles or rows of desks with fifty other co-workers, or we have a job in a factory, at a gas station, in a store, in construction, a hospital, and so on. You may be a mobile worker, where you travel from area to area in one building, or drive from place to place. Since there are so many different types of employment, let's work on some general cleansing procedures.

The first item on our agenda entails using the skills you learned in house cleansing. Remember how you walked around the house and made notes of negative energy pockets? Now you are going to follow this same procedure on the job; however, you will probably have to be discreet about the process, which could take you more than a day or two. Write yourself a list, then sort that list from the most troublesome spot down to those areas in which you feel comfortable. Since you most likely cannot mill around your place of employment with a tray cluttered by magickal tools, you will have to be a bit more imaginative. Here is a list of tips to break up negative energy and bring magick into your place of employment:

- Use a box of those candy Tic-Tacs as a rattle. You can empower anything that rattles. I've found that co-workers think it is funny when I shake my little box of Tic-Tacs. Guess that's because I've blessed the container in the name of Rosemerta.

- Draw protective rune symbols under your chair, under your desk, under your name badge, and so on. If you can't draw on the item, slip a piece of paper under the item (See Appendix IV).

- Keep your area clean. When you wash off your desk or wipe the seat of your forklift, no one has to know you are using empowered cleaner. When the next co-worker uses the same bottle, guess what? They'll be cleaning more than they thought!

- Cast a magick circle of protection around your desk or other equipment.

- Put a guardian on your desk. This could be anything from the statue of an angel to a simple creek stone with your name on it. I've seen great stones with little totem animals painted on one side.

- Make good use of holiday decorations by empowering them with intent, such as magicking for peace, harmony, team spirit, and the like.

- Keep an empowered hourglass (a 3-minute egg timer will do) in your desk drawer. When tensions get high, or the stress level is getting to you, turn the hour glass. As the sand slips down, imagine the tensions and stress dissipating.

- Sprinkle holy water around the area. Again, be discreet. Ooops, lookie there . . . I dropped a bit of water . . . I'll just clean that right up.

- Mentally cleanse all paperwork before you touch it. Imagine the paper glowing neon blue or brilliant white.

- Put a magick mirror on your desk, in your van, on the work table, et cetera, to ward off negativity and allow you a complete view of things going on around you.

- Use magickal powders to aid you in the various ups and downs of work life. Keep your signature powder handy to make the situation or place your own.

- Feed co-workers goodies that you have cleansed, consecrated, and empowered with intent, such as love, team spirit, harmony, creativity, and so on. If you worry about ethics, add the rider "that the universe deems necessary for each person." A candy jar on your desk can work wonders if you are truly imaginative, too.

- Empower every piece of paper that leaves your desk to go to someone else with love and harmony.

- Banish negative energies every time you throw a piece of paper away.

- Ask your guardian spirit to be with you before every meeting.

- Fill every room you walk into with white light, even if it is the stockroom or utility closet.

- Every time you punch the time clock, think of a positive affirmation to say in your mind.

- Use either a letter on the keyboard, wing-ding, or symbol to end each e-mail. Empower this symbol for protection and harmony.

- Create a mini shrine or altar in your desk drawer. A packet of salt, a vial of water, a small feather, and a lighter . . . who would know?

- Empower all pens and pencils and any other tools you may use in your job, such as an air hammer, the keys to the service van, drill, et cetera.

- Cleanse and consecrate all manuals.

- Write a negative situation on toilet paper and flush it down the commode. You know, the new kind of Bathroom Banish!

- Place a bowl of potpourri on your desk.

- Keep as many plants in the area as permitted. Of course, this means you have accepted the responsibility of taking care of them.

- Hang windchimes to break up negative energy and increase the flow of positive energy in the area. Some Feng Shui experts believe that windchimes in a house are unlucky, others don't seem to think it matters. Since they can't agree, my advice is to experiment for yourself. Both schools of thought believe that windchimes hung outside bring good luck.

- Dress an important document with magickal waters (healing waters, prosperity waters, success waters, et cetera).

- Hang an empowered air freshener in your work vehicle.

- Place empowered gem stones (rose quartz, turquoise, smoky quartz) under rugs, seat cushions, in glove compartments, desk drawers, file cabinets, and so on.

- Put empowered ribbons in books, desk drawers, In/Out bins, around plants, et cetera.

- Hang empowered photos on walls or place on your desk in a small frame, or clip to the visor of a vehicle.

As you can see by the above list, there is no limit to being a magickal person at work without letting the world know just how magickal you are. You can also use any of these ideas in the home environment.

Magickal Minutes

Think of fifteen things you routinely do at work that you could change into a magickal application to improve both yourself and the environment. Begin practicing the new magicks you've invented!

Magickal Secrets

Although it bothers me to say so, some of us, for whatever reason, must keep our magickal practices quiet. We may not have the luxury of setting our favorite things out in the open, or working our magick when others hang around. I've jotted down a few ideas to help you stay magickal and still remain in the closet until such time as you can freely practice your religion. Even if secrecy isn't on your agenda, you may find some of these little tips helpful.

- Incorporate angels as much as possible in your decorating scheme. Most people do not question the positive energy of angels.

- Display a large statue of Mary. The Catholic shop will love you, and who's to know it's your rendition of the Goddess?

- Use a window seat to store magickal supplies.

- Sew herbs and magickal powders into the lining of your drapes. Place packets of herbs or powders under rugs.

- Glue an appealing poster to the top of a card table, add a protective coat of varnish, then store in plain sight. Use this table as your altar.

- Draw protective sigils on the back of floor mats.

- Turn a ladder into steps for success by painting the ladder in bright colors and adding plants as decorative objects. Paint magickal sigils under the rungs to help your prosperity (and plants) grow. As the plants grow, so does your prosperity.

- Hang environmental posters that match the Quarter energies in the room you do ritual.

- Paint the inside of glass jars with pretty colors. Allow to dry. Set them on a high shelf for storage of small candles, packets of herbs, crystals, talismans, and so on. Tie a ribbon around the mouth of the jar. Visitors will think this is a cute, decorative idea, and the shelf will be too high for them to peek inside without dragging out your dining room chair and overtly teetering on the brink of destruction.

- Cover your walls with environmental throws that feature wolves, bears, dolphins, or other totem animals.

- Keep magickal supplies in empty animal food boxes.

- Keep larger magickal supplies in large, opaque plastic boxes. Store under the basement steps. Although I have a magickal cabinet, I have two green boxes that sit under my altar (which is a huge coffee table with a big stone on top). I have easy access to my supplies when I need them, and they fit well under the table when not in use. Out of sight, out of mind.

- Decorate your home with hex signs. Your mother will think you went American traditional. In a way, she'll be right.

- Cut a hole in the wall the size of a heat vent. Place your magickal goodies in there and cover with a metal register covering.

- Cut out several vertical feet of space in a wall between two studs. Slip in shelves. Hinge a magickal painting or wall hanging over the opening.

- Slip stick incense into drinking straws. Keep the straws in their original box.

- Have a piece of opaque glass cut to fit over the top of your kitchen table, coffee table or bureau. Keep magickal notes and other important documents under the glass.

- Use an empty suitcase to store magickal tools.

- Convert a bread box to store magickal tools or notes.

- Hang a towel rack six inches from the wall at the back of a closet. Hang your book of shadows there.

- Install a wall dispenser that normally holds liquid soaps. Fill with holy water or your favorite anointing oil. Or buy the countertop dispenser, use the soap, clean the dispenser and fill it with holy water or oil.

- Paste a heavy Velcro strip to your wand and paste the other half of the strip under your altar, or make a cloth sheath for wand storage and put the Velcro on the sheath, then hang under the altar or your bed. Do the same for your athame, but only if you don't have children in the house. (Never put your athame where a child could find it.)

- Paint protective symbols under your basement steps.

- Buy trial-size products, use the contents, then convert them for storage of oils, powdered incense, magickal powders, or holy water. Color code the bottom of the container with a bit of nail polish or a marker so you don't forget that the holy water is in the shampoo container and the magickal powder for success in the mouthwash bottle. An old shoe polish bottle—the kind that has the little dauber brush in the cap—is great for storing your anointing oil.

- Store magickal supplies in an old backpack or beach bag.

- Use buttons, change, safety pins, or toothpicks in a jar to work on abundance and prosperity spells. Add an item each day to increase your prosperity.

- Turn a large coffee can into a cauldron. Line with disposable tin foil. Store under the sink in the kitchen.

- Draw magickal sigils in holy water or oil underneath your dining room chairs. (Especially the one that your mother-in-law or that nosy neighbor always plops in.)

- Draw a magickal symbol for abundance beside each deposit entry in your checkbook.

- Soak your broom in holy water. Not only will the salt water mixture keep your broom lasting longer, this will also help you spread cleansing energies when you banish those unwanted dust bunnies.

- Mist ironable clothing with empowered water. Iron. Chant as the steam rises.

Ghostbusting

Clearing houses of ghostly friends or enemies can get fairly complicated, and perhaps dangerous if you don't know what you are doing. Recorded cases exist where a house or dwelling remains haunted no matter what one magickally or mundanely does to the house; however, these incidents remain few and far between.

I'm not an expert at ghost busting, but I have managed to clear several houses containing some unusual energies. In a few cases, the owners viewed these psychic irritations as ghosts. Since I've never met a ghost face to ectoplasm, I can't tell you for sure (though in one of my books I did relate the story of my children and their ghostly encounter, which I have no doubt existed, and in which I immediately ousted the bothersome wraith). For whatever reason, Spirit does not let me visually see ghosts. I can't decide if this rests on the fact that I'm a Virgo, thoroughly grounded, or simply too stubborn to allow anything to manifest in front of my eyeballs. I have been physically touched by a ghost, smelled perfume, felt hot, cold, or emotionally uncomfortable—but never has any floatie-thing made an impression on my retina. This is not to say, of course, that I don't believe in ghosts.

Humans have experienced several types of ghostly encounters. We have the kindly, almost nanny-type (either male or female), the just-leave-me-alone-and-I'll-go-about-my-ghostly-business type, the prankster, and (at worst) the nasty ghost. Most people don't want to get rid of categories one and two. Homeowners feel, well, more at home if they can share their space with a friendly ghost. Some people like category three (the prankster) and others can't be bothered. No one, at least that I've ever met, likes the nasty ghost.

Before you decide to take on any sort of ghostbusting activities, you should make note of the following:

1. What kind of ghost do you think you've encountered? This will determine what, if anything, you plan to do in the house as far as cleansing and consecration. As I said, some people like to keep their ghosts, others do not.

2. Do teenagers, mentally challenged, or mentally unbalanced individuals live in the house? If any of these categories apply, then your ghost may not be a ghost at all, but a manifestation of a human. I watched a television special about a particularly nasty ghost in a house where the family went through a terrible ordeal. Some of the people in the house experienced physical attacks. This family did everything from calling in a psychic, a priest, and finally the paranormal people. In the end, nothing worked and they were still stuck with their ghost. As I watched the show with my daughter, I turned to her and said, "Check out that kid. Look at her eyes. There's your ghost, which isn't really a ghost at all." The family unit contained a mentally challenged girl in puberty. It was obvious to me that this girl manifested all the problems. You could see the unbalanced energy in her eyes. I can't believe that at least the psychic didn't pick it up.

3. Has the house experienced some sort of extreme upset in the past or present? Many nasty ghostly occurrences may result from the production of negative thoughtforms due to a violent crises, such as spouse or child abuse. Every time someone in the home gets angry, this anger feeds the thoughtform. A negative thoughtform has no mind of its own, and only feeds on negative energy. The more negative the emotions from the occupants of the home, the more movement they will experience from the thoughtform.

4. Do you feel that you meet the qualifications of a ghostbuster? Arthur Ford and Sybil Leek had a particular technique for their ghost-busting practices. Arthur would hypnotize Sybil, then she acted as a medium. In some cases they led the spirit to the light, in other cases they were unsuccessful. How confident are you of your own abilities?

5. If you tremble at things that go bumpity-bump or if you break into a cold sweat at the thought of a ghostly encounter, don't offer to rid your friend's house of a troublesome banshee.

In the 1990s, séances and mediumistic help doesn't appear to be the norm for ghostbusting, rather, the focus now lies on cleansing and consecrating the house, allowing the universe to take the ghost wherever he, she, or it needs to go. Granted, the individuals doing the cleansing and consecration appear to have some minimal talent for sensing the presence of otherworldly beings, but the days of Hollywood hype have frittered back onto the silver screen where they belong.

6. If the owners of the home have convinced you that the house has an unwanted presence, or if you sense this presence yourself, you should cleanse and consecrate the home by working within a magick circle, and you may need a stronger itinerary than the one I've given. If possible, work with an experienced magickal partner. My daughter, Angelique, and I have worked as a team when we think a home contains more than a nanny-type entity. If you decide to work alone, at the very least you should be confident of your magickal skills, including protection magick, circle casting, and warding. If your magickal training is lacking knowledge in any of these areas, I highly recommend you leave your magickal paws off the situation and find someone who does have these skills. I once knew a young man who prided himself as a Witch so much so that he offered to accept a hefty payment to bust a well-known haunted house. To make a long story short, he found himself ousted by the ghost, vaulted by the seat of his pants through a front

window and smashed into the shrubbery by the front door. Not a good thing. To be fair, he appeared to have things under control until the young woman from the paranormal foundation who came with him scoffed at his magick circle, stepped over it, and they both found themselves whirling around the room before their behinds hit the foliage outside. Our friend decided the fee wasn't worth it and refused to reenter the house. I don't blame him. He certainly hadn't made buds with that determined ghost.

7. Please be aware that some people create astral nasties either subconsciously or consciously, and then run after you to fix them. These psychic pains-in-the-you-know-what are the result of an overactive imagination. I've found this to be especially true with magickal teens and magickal young adults. For some reason these young people associate WitchCraft with grumpy spirits. Thank you ever so much, Hollywood. They expect to have testy spirits and so they manifest these stupid things. The problem here lies not in your banishing techniques, but in the difficulty of wresting the belief of the thing from the teen or young adult. Belief, as we know, can be a powerful force, and has manifested because the kid is bored, has low self-esteem, or worse. The person in question may come from a dysfunctional family and this may be a psychic way out—a way to occupy the mind with something that isn't real, keeping the teen from concentrating on what is real. These cases require a massive amount of your time, not in ghostbusting, but in counseling and pulling the person into a serious reality check. If you aren't willing to expend the time, then don't get involved.

8. If you have determined that the house is really haunted, be sure to check out the history of the house and the property as much as possible before you go about your spiritual busting business. This information could come in handy as you clear the house.

9. Finally, there are such things as transient activity, meaning that magickal people, because of their work with energy, will manage to draw curious and downright nosy energies. Don't get excited about this. If you keep your home cleansed and consecrated, you should have no trouble whatsoever.

Should you charge for the cleansing and consecration of another's home? If you want to. You do expend a lot of time, especially if the house or apartment covers a lot of territory. Right before I do a house, I go to the store and purchase spring water, sea salt, cloves, garlic, candles, and other supplies. When I get to the home, I usually hand the owner the receipt for reimbursement. Everything I purchase stays with the homeowner so that they can use the supplies themselves when they want to try cleansing the house, or wish to use some of the quickies I've mentioned. I don't charge a fee for house cleansings, but if the owner offers a donation I don't refuse, as I fully understand the process of the exchange of energy through my Pow-Wow training. To refuse a donation constitutes a snub and leaves the homeowner in your karmic debt.

In this chapter you learned that your home and work environment reflects your energies and the energies of others. When we want to change ourselves, we need to change our environment to match our ambitions. You also learned that you can take routine functions and turn them into magickal applications.

I realize that several methods exist for spiritual housecleaning. The applications given in this chapter represent only a few types. In various Wiccan traditions you'll find several types of housecleaning rituals, which usually follow the energies intrinsic to the tradition (shamanic or ceremonial) and the specific deity and Quarter definitions of that tradition. If you practice traditional studies, you may wish to incorporate ideas from the information provided in this chapter and write your own cleansing ritual to fit your current mode of study. The following format shows an example of a house blessing ritual written by Jane Shipley and Cynthia Lollo, members of the Black Forest Clan, on December 21, 1997.

House Banishing and Blessing

First choose the best time. We decided on the Winter Solstice—the New Year and new beginnings; also, the Yule in 1997 was full. We thought about what we wanted to include and what our goals were. We decided on peace, love, harmony, protection, success, enlightenment, and hope. It took us some time to determine how we wanted to energize these goals. We chose runes, herbs, oils, a jar of new pennies, and the pentagram.

Runes: Feoh, Odal, Sol, Wyn, Algiz, and Dag (Feoh: To make it go and monetary wealth; Odal: Shift from egocentric to clan-centric, home and hearth, and security; Sol: Success, enlightenment, and guidance; Wyn: Joy, pleasure, and hope; Algiz: Protection, connection between Gods and Man, Goddess and Women; Dag: Ritual fire of the hearth, powers of day and night, and polarity)

Oils: Clove, rose, cinnamon, sandalwood, lavender

Herbs: Mistletoe, valerian, rosemary, dill, and a special tobacco mixture

Tobacco: Ceremonial Mix—bear berry, red willow, osha root, mullein, yerba santa

Incense: Pine

We wanted to include the guests, so we gave each guest a job to do (herb person, penny person, oil person, and so on). We also chose a chant:

> *Peace, love and harmony,*
> *bless all who dwell inside of thee.*

Before the guests arrived, we did the banishing so as not to make the ritual too long. Then we cast a circle to encompass the entire house. We called the Quarters, took a smudge stick of sage, and went widdershins three times in each room, chanting:

> *Out with the negative, never to return,*
> *in with the positive with no concerns!*

We began in the basement and worked our way to the top floor. We blessed and consecrated the herbs, pennies, and oil before our guests arrived.

When our company came, we anointed them with the oil mixture. At the chosen time we began the blessing. Again we started in the basement. At each portal/door/window, Cynthia drew a pentagram within a circle with scented oils. (We used the stopper of an oil container instead of a finger, so as not to smudge the sigil later.) At each point of the sigil, we drew a rune and explained the rune's significance. The rest of the group drew each rune with their fingers in the air as we called out the name. We entitled this procedure the "Rune Chi," and Jane acted as the Rune Chi Master (or leader).

Next, the person previously chosen to hold the herbs sprinkled the herbs over each window sill, portal, or door. Then, the individual chosen to hold the pennies placed one penny in each corner of each room we entered and on each corner of each portal, door, or window. As we completed each room, we finished with our chant:

> *Peace, love, and harmony,*
> *bless all who dwell inside of thee.*

We returned to the first floor at the completion of our work and stood before the altar. We thanked the God, Goddess, and Quarters for their assistance in our house banishing and blessing. Then we dismissed the Quarters and released the circle.

After grounding and centering, we broke out the food and drink!

Blessing Sigil

Done on the window, door, portal, lightly in oil with the glass stopper (wand). Later, when cleaning the home, especially the windows, use five squirts of window cleaner for each pane of glass, saying the following:

With earth, air, fire, and water, I cleanse this window,
but I do not remove the essence that was placed here during
the house blessing, for I know the Goddess would not want me
to have dirty windows!

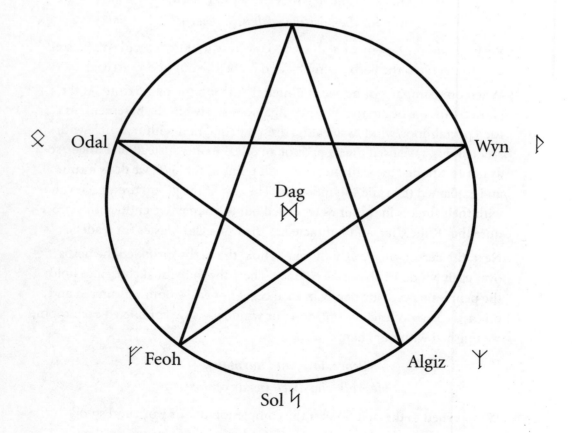

For further information on magickal households, you might like to read:

Feng Shui for Beginners—Successful Living by Design by Richard Webster. Llewellyn, 1997.

The Magical Household by Scott Cunningham and David Harrington. Llewellyn,1983.

Sacred Space by Denise Linn. Ballantine Books, 1995.

Feng Shui—A Layman's Guide by Evelyn Lip. Heian International, Inc, 1979.

Feng Shui for the Home by Evelyn Lip. Heian International, Inc, 1986.

Feng Shui for Business by Evelyn Lip. Heian International, Inc, 1989.

5

Linking Spells and Fascinations

When you ask experienced Witches how they cast a spell, most of them will say, "Well, you just do it." Gee, that's a big help, isn't it? Although on the surface you think this question would be simple to answer, it isn't. When asking most Witches how to cast a spell, or what spell to use when, or how they determine which magickal application they will incorporate in their spellcasting, most of them will give you a blank look. You see, this simple, basic question has many possible answers. That's why I get tongue-tied on every radio show I do when someone asks, "Yes, Silver RavenWolf, Witch and author of umpty-dumpty books, how *do* you cast a spell?"

"Ummmm . . . focus?"

When considering how to cast a spell or what spell to use, most Witches rely on gut feelings before logical thought, though logic does come into play during the working at some point. Most Witches do what feels right, trusting our intuition or higher selves to guide us. Good spellcasting rises out of our mental oven, sort of like Grandma's famous sticky-buns. Put a pinch here, throw in a finger measurement there, stir until it feels right, let rise by eye-measurement, add that special, secret ingredient . . . scary, huh? Remember, though, that Grandma's cooking usually pops from the oven as a culinary masterpiece. After you practice, so too should your spellcasting techniques improve to the point where you don't need to follow a spell book religiously and you will learn to substitute similar ingredients rather than spend eighty dollars for a special herb just because "the book says so."

When someone writes me a letter and asks me for a spell or ritual, let's say for self-improvement or for more money (I have e-mails on my desk for these two), then I know the following about the individual:

- They have not reached a personal level of self-confidence in their training.
- They haven't figured out that the best rituals and spells to use manifest from their own creation.

I consider spellcasting both an art and a science that depends on one thread of belief: That you understand the world is an abundant place, and you *deserve* to partake of that abundance. If you do not believe in the power of spellcasting, then you won't succeed. Where, then, does this power come from? Ultimately, the power comes from Spirit; however, I've found that other energies involved in spellcasting, depending on what I wish to call or utilize, can be helpful. For example, you may choose the element of fire for creativity, the properties of a special herb such as dragon's blood to give magickal powders more oomph, an astrological application, or the thoughtforms that surround an ancient talisman. In essence, most spellcasting techniques combine various energies that are mixed, measured, or formulated into a single practice. And that's the key word: Technique. Count how many Witches live on this planet and you'll find an equal number of spellcasting techniques. It is up to you to determine what techniques work well for your energy pattern and your particular belief system.

Some magickal practitioners incorporate music with most of their workings, others like to use herbs eighty percent of the time, still others desire to use crystals or gems. Certain Witches may not feel comfortable with lots of baubles and Witch's tools, and work more with natural magicks such as ice or fire, wind or earth. Still others rely on the mind as the most important magickal tool in their compendium of occult goodies. True elders of the Craft usually fall in the last category. (Remember the story of Lord Serphant's wiggling fingers and "Look, Silver, no tools!") I don't mean that elders never use tools; however, if they found themselves caught in a windstorm without any underwear, they'd be fine.

When considering what type of spell to use, Witches turn to applications they have studied. For example, if a Witch decides to concentrate on herbs this month, then most likely they will use herbs as much as possible in their spellcasting techniques so that they can understand how herbal applications work for them. The same goes for gems, magickal alphabets, candles, mental magicks, astrological correspondences, the tarot cards, runes, the Seals of Solomon, incense, magickal powders, and so on. So stop worrying that you might do something wrong. A spell does not need complicated steps or require ninety dollars worth of herbals to work. Goddess knows we've whomped up enough Pow-Wow magick with bits of string and a rattle or two without any complications at all around here. Yes, I realize the sense of exaltation when you learn the more complicated techniques (or priceyness) of spellcasting, but you are not any less of a Witch if you don't know them right this minute.

When someone asks me how to cast a spell, hundreds of replies race through my mind. Should I tell them about moon phases, herbs, candles . . . oh draught, how about focus, divinity, archetypes . . . blast! Try explaining the concept of "Spirit" to them and see where you get—nowhere in a hurry. Basically, I throw up my mental hands and draw a blank. How do you begin, anyway?

With a desire.

Here's another question for you to ponder. Must you have a spell book to cast spells? My answer falls in the no category. A very wise Witch I know, who was one of Sybil Leek's students, Lady Phoebe of Coven of the Catta, says: "The best spells you can make are the ones you create." She's right; however, you first need to know the mechanics of spellcasting before you begin to brew your own, and you need to have the courage to experiment. Remember, Grandma learned her style of cooking from her mother, or perhaps her Grandmother, and she more than likely had many failures until she got those sumptuous dishes just right.

For example, I've learned all the basic spellcasting techniques[1] such as the appropriate timing, wording, care of tools, and so on, and I've also studied the properties of herbs, gems, alphabets, the runes, blah, blah, blah. *Now*, I can experiment. I'm into making magickal powders (see For Your Book of Shadows, Part II), so I may sit down and throw a bunch of herbs together and grind them up. I list each herb before I throw that herb in the pot and what I know about each plant (magickally speaking). Then I mix my ingredients together and wait until a situation arises where I think this powder may work. Then I experiment with the powder. Sometimes I fail. Sometimes I succeed. I keep notes for future reference.

Almost every magickal practitioner I know has gone through such stages of learning. For a year or more the magickal person may study and work with herbs, then move on to something else. They may stop using herbs altogether, or use herbs on a minimal basis for the next two years, then, in year number four, back to herbs they go with added zeal. I've seen the same thing done with runes, drumming, chanting, the tarot and other mystery teachings. *The important lesson here lies in the spiritual*

---

1. See my books *To Ride A Silver Broomstick* (Llewellyn, 1993) and *To Stir A Magick Cauldron* (Llewellyn, 1995).

growth of the magickal person. Sometimes magickal people need to work with one type of magick and then, when they have learned enough to reach a new stage of spirituality, their interest will wane and they'll move on to something else. In time, the magickal person realizes that his or her expertise has grown largely based on previous studies. We can say the same for ritual. A magickal person may begin with short, limited rituals, move onto a more ceremonial, rigid practice, then drift back to lighter, shorter ritual work. None of these ritual techniques are wrong as long as these practices do not intend to harm. Variety fills the need of the practitioner at that particular stage in his or her spiritual growth. As Ray Buckland says, there are Cadillac spells and there are Toyota spells—you need to get used to working both.

Remember: There is *no* wrong way to cast a spell or do ritual as long as you do not intend to harm anyone; however, you will find that throughout our community, certain *preferred* ways manifest in some groups. In the magickal world, who you may associate with governs acceptable forms of training in the magickal arts. For example, in Wicca, we often teach students to cast a magick circle before any spellworking or ritual application; but in American WitchCraft (which the Pow-Wow Doctors/Artists employed) the conscious raising of a magick circle doesn't exist, nor did Pow-Wow's consider the magick circle a necessity in spellworking. They did not employ formal ritual, as we understand it, in their practices. If anything, the early American Witches practiced spontaneous ritual (which we will cover in Chapter 6).

To begin casting a spell means we must begin at the proverbial beginning—at the desire—the reason you want to cast the spell in the first place. Spellcasting, from the moment you determine to cast your first spell, grows into a process of skill building and spiritual maturation. Truly, spellcasting involves designing a spiritual plan that you will follow, whether you wish to work for money, love, health, or the well-being of the planet.

Choosing a Goal

I'd like you to take a few moments and do some serious thinking—not that mind-chatter jumble that you normally do, but focused considerations. I'd like you to choose a specific goal, as you did in Chapter 1. By the way, did you finish that exercise? Well, keep at the goal if you haven't finished. You will benefit from the process . . . . Now then. Do you have a particular problem that nags at you constantly but you've tried to ignore? Or do you have a dream you've not implemented because your fear stops you? I'd like you to write down the problem or goal you would like to work on.

Can you use the same goal you may have worked on in previous chapters? Yes, if you have finished with your exercise in that chapter. No, if you haven't. And no, you may not choose more than one goal or difficulty for this exercise. You see, that's the biggest problem with humans. We have so many things we desire, or things we wish to fix, that we get muddled and end up not doing much of anything at all. Throwing magick at a bunch of things constitutes enchanted Russian roulette. You may get lucky, or unlucky, depending on which end of the revolver you're staring at. I've provided a space for you to write your goal, or you can put your goal on a piece of notebook paper. Leave your goal to sit for awhile. We'll get back to it further on in the chapter; however, I'd like you to choose a goal now so that you can refer back to it as we work through the next several sections. I suggest writing your goal in pencil because, as you study, you may make some changes. If your goal remains the same once you've worked through this section, that's okay too.

Write your goal here:

Correlations between Hypnotherapy and Magick

I once heard someone complaining because she went to a hypnotherapist to lose weight (with a weight-loss goal of fifty pounds) and to stop smoking. The hypnotherapist handled the weight loss and the smoking as two different issues in one session. The waitress lost five pounds and kept smoking. Why didn't the session work? Unless the hypnotherapist could figure a way to link the two issues together in the mind of the client, he had already stacked the deck against himself before he began. You see, both of these issues required major changes in the client's mental, physical, and spiritual self and perhaps her weight problem and her smoking habit stemmed from two different psychological issues. Therefore, one session would not make much of a dent in the client's difficulty. The rule of thumb for hypnotherapy sessions rests on six sessions per issue. If the hypnotherapist can't correct the difficulty or set the goal in the client's mind after six sessions, then usually the hypnotherapist refunds the client's money (at least in this neck of the woods). Granted, these six sessions may occur over a six-month period while the client carefully follows instructions, like listening to the tapes made for them every day throughout the treatment, allowing them to slowly manifest the desired change.

The same premise operates in magick. Unless your goals link together either by similar issue or by building some sort of bridge that makes the issues compatible, most magickal teachers will tell you not to mix issues in spellcasting. Like hypnotherapy sessions, one can't always expect to cast a spell once and have the problem go away or the goal manifest. Of course, with smaller subjects, you might blast the problem or find success immediately but, when dealing with the larger issues, the spellcasting technique builds on each session. You never really know how many sessions it will take to manifest a desire or correct a problem. Granted, if you work under a deadline, your instinctive need will help you to push harder at accomplishing your goal; but you must exercise caution. If you push too hard, you may emotionally strangle your magickal intentions by limiting your possibilities. Unlike the six-session theory for the professional hypnotherapist (and not all follow this practice), spellcasters may simply continue at regular intervals until the goal manifests or the problem turns into a solution.

To move things along faster, you can set a time limit without limiting your possibilities of manifestation. (As in the hypnotherapist's choice of a limit of six sessions—to give the client an outside-imposed deadline that they may not set for themself internally.) For example, if you want a car, but someone provides transportation for you right now and that person doesn't mind ferrying you from here to the netherworld, you may take your good old time to manifest the goal because you don't experience any outside pressure. Giving yourself a deadline, then, can help your spellcasting expertise grow.

Why am I talking about hypnotherapists and spellcasters as if they function in the same manner? Because they do. In reality, they use many of the same practices and techniques, albeit with a different focus (sometimes). Both the hypnotherapist and the spellcaster use the power of the mind to reach a desired goal, either for themselves or for someone else. Also, most hypnotherapists do go into alpha right along with their clients. When two people experience the alpha state together, more probability exists for thought transference, opening a vast avenue for the greater chance of client healing. When you work magick with a partner or in a group, the same line of reasoning applies. When you have taught yourself the art of fascination, then you too will act much like the hypnotherapist when doing magicks for yourself and, most importantly, for others.

Your Personal Magick Cycle

I've discovered after many years of my own training and then training others that each of us has a personal magickal cycle. During the year, we experience periods of heightened activity as well as times of quiet introspection and non-productive time. We need our busy days and our leisure days to remain healthy and in harmony with the universe. Our magickal work functions in the same manner. We naturally gravitate toward doing magickal work when our personal cycle moves from a time of rest into a time of activity. Haven't you ever watched television, read a book, or involved yourself in a mundane project and suddenly felt "in the mood" for magick? I know I have. Usually these moods hit me not when the moon is in the proper phase, not when the correct planetary hour is available, and not when a particular planet is in a certain, auspicious sign. I've learned that when the power flows through my body, tingles in my fingers, and increases my senses, that it's time to rock 'n roll. If I follow these moods, then I reap the rewards. If I don't, then I miss out.

Sometimes our magickal expertise may cycle with the seasons. You may feel very productive in the spring and winter months, but find yourself unproductive in the summer and fall months (that's me). Someone else may find himself or herself very productive on the cross-quarters but low in activity level over the Quarters. Each person is unique in his or her personal cycle. Certain times of the day may affect your productivity. I'm not worth anything, productivity-wise, during the daylight hours. My creativity blasts into orbit from midnight to dawn. From dawn until dusk, my engines just don't fire properly. I finally had to quit a part-time job because I realized that the morning hours and I dislike each other, and I had no hope of winning the overall battle. This holds true for my magickal work as well.

One can work magick, however, despite a fallow cycle. It is here where things like correspondences, correct planetary hours, moon phases, and so on, increase in importance in your work. I have days when I can simply hold out my hand, focus on my desire, and the thing is done. There are other days when I require such things as correspondences, tools for focus, incense for the mood—you get the picture.

Magickal Correspondences: What Do I Use Them For?

Almost every how-to magickal book on the market gives you various listings called *magickal correspondences*, and this book is no exception.In many magickal books these lovely tables and columns brim with neat and nifty information that may include the subjects of herbs, planetary influences, candle colors, angels, gods and goddesses, metals, moon phases, magickal alphabets, magickal symbols, et cetera. You'll find daily correspondences, weekly correspondences, and monthly correspondences. With all this information, every single spell or magickal application should work perfectly, right? Wrong.

The word "correspondence" (in magickal applications) means stuff that goes together, things that match, symbols whose energies blend well with each other, or ideas that carry historical representations. These symbols enhance the practitioner's planned application. For example, the color red vibrates close to the same energy frequency as the emotion of passion. Historically, the color red conjures an association with the element of fire and the root chakra. The heart shape travels through the collective unconscious as a symbol for love. Mythos, created by the human mind, tell us that Aphrodite stands for that elusive energy known as love. The soft scent and vibrational pattern of a rose blends easily with thoughts of love. Make that rose red, cut out a red, paper heart to depict the fires of passion, call on Aphrodite and you have the makings of a simple spell for conjuring love with the help of the correspondences you chose: red, fire, heart shape, Aphrodite, rose. If we look at a table of correspondences for the appropriate day to cast our spell, we find that Fridays constitute love days, and that Venus, the planet associated with love, gives us a good choice for a planetary hour. Through our choices we kept one keyword, "love." With these symbols the magickal practitioner uses sight, smell, touch, and emotion to focus on a chosen desire—that of love. If we throw in a full moon or a waxing moon, we've added a planetary body whose energies affect the chemistry in our human bodies; again, the full or waxing moon finds historical association in lovers trysting under a full moon, and the waxing moon's association with growth—in this case, the growth of love.

Correspondences don't make the magick, *you* do. Consider correspondences as fine-tuning devices, or that special ingredient in your favorite dish that gives the food an extra zing. Although correspondences carry energies of their own, their function relies on your focus. Throwing a bunch of stuff together (as in our previous example), like a red candle, a red paper heart, rose petals, and calling on Aphrodite on Friday in the hour of Venus during a waxing moon won't secure the love you need by itself. Correspondences initially help you to focus on your desire.

Correspondences have energies that you can manipulate. The more correspondences you use in your magick, the better chances for success *if* you remain focused on the application and *if* the universe has determined that your goal should manifest. Since not all goals and desires would be good for you, the universe may not dispense the energy in the way you wish or in the time-frame you desire, no matter how many correspondences you use.

Must you use correspondences in your magickal and ritual applications? No. Some factors do override the energies of a correspondence. Emotion, for example, plays a big part in magickal workings. If your need carries a high emotional level, such as how you feel during an emergency, and waiting for the right correspondence (the moon phase or the correct planetary hour) isn't possible, your energy level may override the need for the use of those types of magickal correspondences.

Magickal training will also enhance the use of correspondences. If you have learned to focus, practice routine meditational exercises, work with energy flow in the body and in other areas, have a good relationship with Spirit, and so on, then these aspects of your training will enhance the use of correspondences.

As mentioned earlier, magickal correspondences work well in our fallow times—when our energy level feels low. Every individual experiences slow periods, and sometimes these vacant stretches can last six months or more, depending on the various issues and entanglements in our lives. In these times, the more correspondences you use, the better your chances of success in a magickal or ritual application.

Must you use only the correspondences listed in magickal books? Nope, although I'd work with these correspondences first to get the hang of what I'm doing. After you find your comfort zone with published material (such as a spell book), learn to create your own correspondences, but do so carefully. Experiment on a small scale and work up to bigger projects. Any spell book you buy represents someone's (usually the author's) experimentation with various correspondences.

Some correspondences will work better for you than others. Magickal practitioners have found this particularly evident in color magick. Certain colors vibrate better or will flow easier for one person than for another person. Again, this circumstance depends on magickal training, experience, social background, personal history, and individual energy fluctuation—all the factors that make you an individual. Don't let those lists and columns of magickal correspondences confuse you anymore. Take your time, experiment, and build your skill level with the tried and true methods, as well as your own.

All Spellcasting Should be Thought of as Success-Making

No matter what type of spellcasting you perform, your primary goal concentrates on success. Rather than naming our work "spellcasting," perhaps we should rename the work as success-making. This leads us into an important set of thought processes that we need to examine. First, as I mentioned earlier, the world is an abundant place. There's plenty to go around, so we should not feel embarrassed to work toward our goals. Spirit has provided everything we need to exist on this planet.

Secondly, there is no such animal as asking for too much. Neither poverty nor avarice are a part of Wiccan training. Causing others to suffer poverty, or stealing from them, constitutes avarice. Witches don't do that; however, feeling that you don't deserve to have what you want is not a part of our religious or magickal training either. There are other religions that want you to believe that going without will strengthen your soul—not Wicca. Spirit does not want you to feel guilty about pursuing the best you can be, or wanting the best for yourself and your family. Spirit will help you work toward your goals as long as you are determined not to hurt yourself or others in the process of gaining your desires. In order for your spellcasting to work, and work consistently, you must believe with all your heart that it is okay to want and to have success.

Finally, we should normally not limit the possibilities in our success work. If we place finite thoughts on how, when, where, and why our spellcasting should manifest, we effectively put restrictions on our work that limits our possibilities. By limiting our possibilities, we emotionally strangle the outcome of our magickal workings. Envision your goal as a river. If you build dams at the tributaries, or in the main body of the river itself, you have effectively limited and controlled the course of the water flow, perhaps in a direction that could cause destruction. Rather than choosing to control the outcome of the work, allow Spirit to control the outcome for you. Learn to surrender your need, allowing Spirit to intricately design all aspects of the end result. This will permit the universe to manifest what you need, when you need it.

Allow yourself to play with creative possibilities in your spellwork. Don't assume that your life churns in a continuing cycle of roadblocks. Always work your magick in a manner that will open new pathways for you, rather than set you on an inter-state without exits.

If you think about it, every human-made object you touch was once a creative idea for someone that blossomed into a physical manifestation. Therefore, every object designed by humans carries the excitement of creation and completion. From this book in your hands to the chair you sit in—all were once thoughts that mani-fested into something physical. Spellcasting follows the same premise: from thought to form.

Spellcasting Should Never be Used for One-Upmanship

As spellworkings encompass focused prayer and the connection to divinity, one should never cast a spell to spite someone or to gain authority "just because." Bluntly, don't use spellwork to keep up with the proverbial magickal (or nonmag-ickal) Joneses. Abundance for you will not be the same as abundance for your next-door neighbor. Working magick to get a sport utility vehicle because your brother just got one is downright silly. Maybe you really need a refrigerator because yours experienced an invasion by a creative black fungus. Okay, so you can't drive all over the place showing off your new sport utility refrigerator—sometimes we just have to learn to make the right choices.

Mum's the Word

Although I've covered this topic in my other books, I'll discuss the necessity for silence briefly here to ensure a good, overall coverage of spellwork. Don't emotionally strangle your spellwork by telling everyone what you are doing. And I'm not just talk-ing about magick here, either. The negative thoughts and emotions of others who do not believe in your spellwork will limit your magickal expertise. To know, to dare, to will, and to be silent all have their meanings in Craft teaching. On a mundane level, the negative thoughts of others can defeat even your everyday purposes. I learned a long time ago that to feed those who are not close to me with private information fuels unnecessary gossip. I don't mean you can't talk about anything, but choose your words wisely when communicating with others. People often judge others not by what is said, but by the attentiveness of the listener. If you blab often about your personal travails, you lower your respectability, whether you mean to or not.

What Is Your Pattern?

Humans live as creatures of habits and patterns. The woman who continually chooses the abusive male and the man who is always broke right before payday both represent psychological patterning. Granted, there are mundane things we can do to change our habits and patterns. The woman could investigate her childhood and teen years to determine what triggers led her to a poor choice in a partner, and the man could learn to budget that paycheck with the help of a financial counselor. By incorporating magickal practices and mundane solutions, we can rise to be the best in body, mind, and Spirit. Many times our needs flag because we don't realize that our habits or patterns have lead us in that direction. When we propose to work magick toward a goal, we need to pinpoint any significant patterns in our lives that need revamping. Are you practicing a poverty pattern? Perhaps an ill health pattern? How about a poor choice in love pattern? Once you have learned to face the fact that you have created the habit, you can work on breaking that habit. Because habits and patterns are natural for us, we need to investigate and remove old patterns, then replace them with new ones.

You will also discover patterns and habits in your spellwork. These develop over time and act as triggers to your higher mind. Perhaps you will always begin a spell or ritual by lighting a particular color of candle, or burning incense as an offering to Spirit, or by dusting off the altar or shrine. You may adjust the statue, touch the picture of your mother, or blow your nose! These patterns are harmless, yet they become an integral part of you and your magick. Practicing a standard altar devotion before every act of magick or ritual gives us the positive patterning we need to focus on our intent.

Asking Spirit for Help

The very next step in spellwork or ritual consists of asking Spirit to help you. Yes, that's right. Before you gather any tools, choose your correspondences, formulate your petition, or cast that magick circle, you should hold a conversation with Spirit. Spirit may manifest as the Lord and Lady, the Goddess Diana or Aradia, or the God

Herne. It doesn't matter how you envision Spirit. I don't care how you incorporate Spirit into your psyche, just as long as you incorporate something! You don't have to do anything ornate; talking to Spirit in your head will do. If you want to mosey out to the front porch and watch the sun rise while you ask for help, that's cool. If you're stuck inside and making dinner, that's okay too. Spirit listens wherever you are, whenever you call!

Ray Malbrough, author of *Charms, Spells & Formulas* (Llewellyn, 1986), says:

> It can take an individual from one to four years to really learn how to practice natural magick. For the first year of training the student's primary concern should be their own spiritual development through meditation and daily devotion. The student must also learn how to pray. There is no such thing as opening a spell book to page 63 and your problems are instantly over. Anyone who believes this is suffering from delusions and lacking wisdom. For wisdom is the stripping away of all delusions, whether self-induced or through the influence of others. Books give knowledge and books give inspiration, but books alone do not give a person power. Power only comes through the persistent struggle in one's life for spiritual development.

Power rises through the release of negative habits and patterns, and the realization that nothing will manifest properly until we jettison our fears. Ray also adds:

> Remember, a spell that worked for one person may not work for another. All spells are individually tailored to suit the needs of yourself, or for whom you are working and his or her situation.

He has another tidbit of information for those of you who wish to work magick for others.

> If a person's problem is to teach them a lesson, then it may not be wise to interfere. Indeed, you run the risk of having a string of bad luck. If the universe wishes your friend to learn a valuable lesson and you interfere, you will pay the price to get them out of the situation. It may be wiser to give the proper guidance and help your friend diagnose a spiritual plan that will help them through this lesson. Don't merely throw magick at a piece of their problem.

Learn to work mundanely, spiritually, and magically for the whole situation. Then your spellwork will succeed!

Designing a Spiritual Plan

Designing a spiritual plan isn't as difficult as the task may sound. After you have outlined the situation or the goal, consider what types of activities you could incorporate to solve the problem or meet the desired end. Think carefully about the impact of your actions. What do you need to change mentally, physically, or spiritually? A mere removal of a mental block, or something more serious? A spiritual plan involves mundane decision-making, meditation, and the willingness to work toward your chosen desire. For example, let's talk about money magick, a subject near and dear to all of our hearts because in our society, we see money as power and survival. To work money magick we need to learn that money, in and of itself, is not power. Our entire society empowers this delusion. This is silly. Money is nothing but bits of paper and ink, or pieces of metal, even plastic! Money is a vehicle, a tool—nothing more, nothing less. When working financial magick, we need to consider what we need the money for, and if this need will ultimately create harmony or disharmony in our lifestyle.

For many people, money magick doesn't work because they haven't followed a spiritual plan to get what they need. In a veritable tizzy, some people throw magick at the immediate problem rather than consider the whole picture. Sometimes this hit or miss magick will work, and sometimes it won't. I'm not too proud to tell you that I've thrown magick for money when the bank account was empty. We all have. This is why some magickal teachers have said, "Use magick as a last resort." What they really mean is, consider the entire situation, design a spiritual plan that involves working with body, mind, and Spirit, and then plan your magick accordingly. They don't mean, "Wait until the world buries you."

You see, putting magickal training into words is not as easy as you might think. Some people will take your words literally, and others will process the information you give them figuratively. When training others, we have to mean what we say, and say what we mean. I was always the type of person who took the words literally—now, I know better.

As you become adept at spellcasting and ritual, you may design master spiritual plans that you can share with others. If a friend comes to you with a problem of low self-esteem, you may have followed a spiritual plan for yourself that you now wish to share with your friend. Developing master plans will help you think creatively and logically about a situation. Your accurate record-keeping techniques come into play here. You can refer back to your written plan and change whatever aspects necessary to relate the plan to your friend. At the same time, you can explain to your friend the theology of a master plan, allowing them to understand that magick doesn't consist of a snap of one's fingers. Depending on the problem, there may be several steps that you and your friend can discuss to ensure a positive outcome of the situation. Most people do very well if you give them an outline of what to do. This outline assists them in firming their desires in their mind, and allows them to put the necessary effort required into making the hoped-for change.

Most spell books I've seen do not contain a complete spiritual plan for any situation or issue. They contain a portion, or one aspect that you can incorporate into your spiritual plan. Think of a spell book as containing possibility cores—each spell providing a block of information that you can build your spiritual plan around.

Don't Let Your Magick Move into Obsession

If you smother your magick, then the magick will die. Sometimes we want something so badly that we create more blocks than pathways to a desired end. This is why many magickal teachers in the past said, "Do the magick, then forget about it." What they really meant was: "Don't obsess over the outcome, or influence the future with negative thoughts."

If every time you think of the future, you see problems, difficulties, and negatives—stop that thought. If, for some reason, you feel too emotionally charged, upset, or sick to formulate a good thought (which can be difficult at times), then simply envision the future as "bright." Just think of white light, or a golden horizon, or some sort of visualization that contains brilliance and light. I've noticed that during illness, we mentally fight the disease until the condition of the body plummets to where we can no longer think properly—this is the danger zone, the time when we relinquish and say, "you've got me." At this point, negative thoughts march forward, eager to create gleeful chaos and overtake the mind. When we are physically ill, we have the ability to make extremely detrimental futures for ourselves without realizing what we have done. One way to help ourselves when we tuck that sick body into our comfy bed is welcome our bed partner, the friendly continuous-playing tape recorder, in with us, and slap on a store-bought self-help tape or, even better, one we've made ourselves, just for those "sickie" moments in our lives.

Our magickal teachers have tried to tell us that it isn't necessary to regiment the future with our thoughts. We need to allow the universe to be creative as we are creative.

Good Spellcasting Techniques Rely on Your Personal Power

Do I mean you should be able to light up a Yule tree bulb by sticking it in your mouth? No. By your personal power I mean your confidence in yourself. An adept Witch does not concern himself or herself with what others think , because they know that all their actions have manifested in a positive, harmonious manner. Right? Getting tied up in personal politics or the negative experiences others manage to create need not affect the confident spellcaster. I'm not saying you should be a snot about it; I'm saying that if you move in harmony, you need not fear. Good spellcasting techniques transfer positive energy into the future. Poor spellcasting techniques transfer fear into the future. Which would you choose? We need to learn to move through our fears, use them when necessary, and set them aside when the situation dictates. The purpose of fear is to keep you from hurting yourself and others, thereby giving you the reigns of control in certain situations; however, as humans we often fear needlessly. We need to jettison those needless fears to become powerful.

I had a student, let's call him George, who really put himself through a massive head trip. George was a first-year Wiccan student who had just lost his girlfriend to another Wiccan student. We'll call the other man Larry. What began as a simple breakup between two incompatible people quickly mushroomed into a magickal nightmare. You see, George believed, for whatever reason, that Larry was out to get him. Not only did Larry want his girlfriend, said George, but he was adamant that Larry meant to curse George right out of existence. You know, this kind of nonsense is why standard religions turn up their noses at magickal people. Now we know that George was using Larry as a scapegoat. George didn't want to admit that he and the woman were incompatible, rather he wanted to remove the blame (or perception of failure) from himself and give that burden to Larry. How nice of George to do this.

Day by day, George empowered Larry with his (George's) negative thoughts. George, through his own fear, talked himself into a major mess. To make matters worse, George told everyone that Larry was out to get him. Now, other people got involved, spreading rumors and really complicating the issue. It got to the point where George suffered financially, mentally, and spiritually. Why? Because George couldn't admit his own shortcomings and let go of his own fear. George empowered Larry rather than empowering himself. And Larry? To be honest, he was laughing his ass off. He'd never done anything to George, except fall in love with his ex-girlfriend.

Here's another one. Amy and Lisa owned a business together. Over time, Amy wanted to take the business in one direction, and Lisa wanted to take the business in another. Each secretly feared separation, so they didn't say anything to each other right away. Each empowered the other with negative thoughts of what they could possibly do to each other when the time for the split actually came. After awhile, Amy and Lisa act out the negative scenarios they managed to create and the situation ends badly for both. Indeed, they eventually take each other to court, and both lose their proverbial shirts.

What should George, Amy, and Lisa have done when each realized that their ultimate goals had marched out of the picture? To begin, they should have talked to Spirit. From that point, they all needed to project peace, calm, and harmony into the future. It is easy for us to project fear, but it is not so easy to project positive circumstances, until we learn to practice that type of projection. What else could these individuals have done? Think about it.

Spiritual Seconds

Each evening for the next thirty days, sit calmly on the edge of your bed and think about tomorrow. No, don't *worry* about tomorrow. Project positive energies into the day ahead. You can visualize sending white light, or see yourself briefly through moments you expect to be important in a positive manner.

Magickal Minutes

Pick one thing you've been worrying about. Write the worry on a piece of toilet paper. Flush the worry down the toilet. That's right. Give up the worry. Push yourself into positive action rather than passive reaction. Visualize the best happening, rather than the worst, as the paper gets sucked down to the sewer. Do this faithfully every evening until the situation resolves itself.

Magick Makes a New You

Any type of magickal application or ritual changes your being on various levels, including mental, spiritual, and physical. Therefore, you need to think carefully about the magickal and ritual applications you plan and perform. We consist of many selves. I'm a wife, mother, writer, teacher, diviner, orator, et cetera. All these selves represent a part of me. During my life I have added new selves, allowed some of the old selves to mature, and tossed out other old selves who would be detrimental to my overall happiness. I've even created temporary selves to handle a situation or do a job. Sometimes people call these selves "the masks we wear," but I'm not so sure they represent masks at all, as these masks function as a part of us for good or ill. Just as we unconsciously create new aspects of these selves when we perform magick and ritual, we can consciously re-pattern our lives with magick and ritual, thereby ultimately changing ourselves. There isn't anything wrong with making a "new self," no matter how old you are. This new self integrates some of the old while cultivating the new. This is a part of maturation.

Most spellcasting has a lot to do with your attitude about yourself and others. I'll never forget the sugar bowl spell. Years ago, I threw a big party at my house for magickal and non-magickal people. We had at least forty-five adults and about twenty-three kids here. As I don't have a particularly large house, you can guess the overall atmosphere—chaos.

I have a habit of inviting people I don't know to these parties. Usually, the people have worked with magick in some way or another, and want to stop by because they've read my books or have attended a local seminar. Anyway, I invited one fellow and his friend over for the party, thinking they might enjoy talking with several magickal people who I know act in a trustworthy manner. Eager to attend my party, the young man didn't tell me his friend was scared bloodless of Witches. I mean, this guy must have seen and believed every horror movie in Hollywood, and then some. He also failed to mention that his friend was psychologically unstable.

So, there we sit around the dining room table—several Wiccan friends, the white-faced friend, my daughter, and some of my relatives. I have no clue that this man thinks we plan to sacrifice him. The party roars around us—the fellows are shooting the you-know-what on the patio, the kids are playing tag in the backyard, there's a clutch of people gabbing in the kitchen, music blaring, laughter roaring, somebody yelling "We're ready to fry the flesh!" (meaning that the grill is ready for the hot dogs and burgers), et cetera. I don't see the manic flicker in the eyes of the white-faced friend because I'm too busy having a good time with my friends. Down the stairs clomps my oldest daughter, then in the throes of beginning puberty. Yap-yap-yap at my face, turning on her heel, yap-yap-yap, growl over her shoulder and then she marches in a huff back up the stairs. Evidently someone had borrowed her nail polish and didn't put the bottle back. Just what I'm concerned about with over seventy people in my house—the search for a missing bottle of nail polish. Blue metallic, no less. I don't think so.

"Put her name in the sugar bowl," says one of my Craft friends.

I raise my eyebrows. "What will that do?"

"Sweeten her up," says my friend.

We all laugh. Okay, so we cackled.

Up from the table bolts the white-faced friend. Zoom! Out the door he flies screeching into the back yard. What the heck?

"Uh-oh," says my friend.

Another friend twitters politely from behind her palm, which now covers her mouth, her eyes larger than most pentacles I've seen. "I think we did a no-no," she says demurely.

"I think we should seriously do a sit-com," says my youngest daughter.

"Do you want me to go after him?" asks another friend.

I sigh. "No, my party, my head trip. I'll take care of it."

Needless to say, I spent most of my evening trying to explain to this man that we had no intentions of hurting him, nor did we plan to manipulate anyone else. "But you said you would put your daughter's name in the sugar bowl!" he said.

"When I put my daughter's name in the sugar bowl," I said patiently, "I was not planning to manipulate her. I was planning to manipulate my own reactions to her. If I change my attitude toward her, then I will be opening a line of communication between my daughter and myself. Therefore, I'll be able to understand her better."

I didn't convince the guy of anything, and personally, I could have cared less as he fulfilled his own desires that night—gaining the attention of just about everyone at the party. Anyone who carries that much fear in their hearts and needs that much negative attention from strangers that they would believe such superstitious nonsense needs counseling, big time. Nothing I could have said would have helped him, but the event did help me to formulate how a particular spell worked and helped me to understand my own thoughts on magick. In all fairness, I received a very nice letter of apology from both guests, and I hope that life has treated them well.

Say What You Mean, and Mean What You Say

Now let's look at that desire of yours again and see what we can do with what you've written. Does your desire in any way incorporate fear or worry? Have you considered a spiritual plan to build around your desire? Have you inadvertently given your power over to another person or to the situation? If so, you need to take your power back and reconsider what you truly want. Have you taken into consideration your personal, magickal cycle? Are you throwing too many desires into one cauldron? Consider rewriting your goal before we move on. Again, you may wish to use a pencil, because you may want to do another rewrite before you've finished.

As I mentioned earlier in this book (and in my other books as well), before you begin any spell or magickal working, you must learn to be specific. It won't hurt to practice saying what you mean and meaning what you say in every facet of your life, but being truthful and exact in magick about what you want will serve you better than making fuzzy statements and expecting the fuzz to wear off by the time the magick is through and the goal manifests. Check your goal for clarity. Rewrite the goal a couple of times if you have to. When satisfied, transform your goal to a piece of paper. Again, you may want to use a pencil. No, we haven't finished!

Don't be in a rush to cast this particular spell, because I want you to work on the internalization process. This internalization process is how you let your subconscious mind know that you are getting ready to magickally boogie. In other words, get your creative juices flowing before you march up to your shrine or altar and cast that spell. Any good writer can tell you that they may mull over a particular chapter, the plot, a character, the ending or beginning of a story for weeks, maybe even months, until they feel they are ready to sit down and write that particular portion of the story. The same idea applies when a Witch formulates a spell or ritual. Not only does the intent need to be there, but the Witch needs to believe what they are writing, and they must be able to connect with the words on a mental-visual scale. This is why some of the best spellcasting done by experienced Witches doesn't come from a book but from their own creative essence. Granted, you can find spells in books that "speak" to you. For me, the words of Doreen Valiente or Z. Budapest often mesh with how I feel and what I need to do, so I borrow heavily from them in my own workings when I design my spiritual plan. Their work becomes the core of my outline. I know I'm not a great poet, and that most of my poetry sounds like a country hoedown, so if I can find something that speaks to me, then I prefer to memorize the passage, or at least read that passage over and over again until I can get the feeling I want immediately, before I cast the spell. If I can't find what I'm looking for, then I wing it on my own.

Jack Veasey, whose work you've seen in this book and in *To Stir A Magick Cauldron*, actually brings me poetry instructions to his study night here at my house. He learns magick while I waddle around trying to improve my poetry so that I can write better spells. No kidding. When we exchange gifts, I'm always giving him books on how to practice magick and he is always giving me books on how to write poetry. My last wonderful gift from him was *The Complete Rhyming Dictionary*,[2] which says on the cover: "The essential handbook for songwriters, poets, students, teachers,

---

2. By Clement Wood, published by Laural/Dell, 1991.

speechmakers, and members of the performing arts." I think I'll write Dell and ask them to add "Also for Witches, Druids, Ceremonial Magicians, and all manner of magickal practitioners." Think they'd print it?

So, ruminate over that goal. Play with the words (but keep the clarity, mind you). Have a little fun with it. In fact, make it crazy and have a laugh, then take a more serious view. Try to make it rhyme, if you can. For some reason, the subconscious likes rhymes and holds onto them with stronger mental associations. At this point, you should have several aspects to your original goal. Let's go over them, just to be sure:

1. The original goal.

2. The re-written goal.

3. The workings of a spiritual plan to go along with that goal.

4. Your goal rewritten as a simple spell, considering rhyming techniques and specifications. You shouldn't have more than a line or two on your paper.

Once you feel satisfied with what you've written, take piece of paper number four (I'm sure you've written this spell over and over again, right?) and place this paper on your shrine or altar.

Checking the Outcome

Most adept magickal practitioners have learned the wisdom of checking their work before they actually perform the spell. To do this you will need to become well acquainted with some sort of divination tool. I suggest trying several until you hit on the one that works best for you. Examples would be: tarot, runes, I Ching, pendulum, crystal ball, playing cards, the cartouche, et cetera. You don't require a complicated layout, a one or three card reading (for runes or cards) will do.

I use my runes. First, I blow in the bag three times, shake the bag, then pull out one rune while saying:

> *Enchanted runes, whisper to me,*
> *what pattern will this magick be?*

Positive answers speak of success of your endeavor, negative answers would speak of dangers, difficulties, blocks you may encounter, et cetera. If you receive a negative answer, reword your spell, reevaluate your spiritual plan, or consider moving in a different direction. Check that solution with your divination tool as well. If your answer speaks of success or moves in the direction you wish, then go forward with your working. There will be some workings in which the tool will always indicate a negative response. This could mean that you are working against karma or moving against your mission in life. Heed the warnings well. If your divination tool says, "All systems go," leave your paper on the altar or shrine. If you need to make changes, then rewrite your goal and put it back on your shrine or altar.

What if you want to work a spell now, and you don't have any type of divination skills? Not to fear. Talk to Spirit or ask your guardian angel to clearly show the pathway that is appropriate for you to follow. Ask Spirit to guide you through your spellwork.

Putting It All Together

Are we done yet? No. We've written our goal, we've designed our spiritual plan, and we've checked the outcome with our divination tool. Now what? You see, a spell is sort of like a head of lettuce—there are lots of outer leaves around the heart, or core, of your desire. Some of those outer leaves in your spellworking could be:

- The choice of Divinity.
- The choice of magickal correspondences.
- The choice of sacred space versus circle casting.
- The choice of calling Quarters, one Quarter only, or no Quarters at all.

Take a few moments now and make these choices. Write them down on a piece of paper and set them aside for the moment, as we continue learning about good spell-casting techniques.

Incorporating Divinity into Your Spellworking

Once you have chosen the representation of divinity, you need to connect yourself with that power. Although Witches connect mentally and spiritually with the power of divinity in ritual and in spellworking, they often use verbal communication as well. Verbally calling on divinity tells your conscious mind that you're not trying to pull any tricks and that you are very serious about this working. The sing-song of a rhyme, when spoken aloud, also strengthens the spell, as the vocalization of rhyming words harmonizes the energies around you, making them more conducive to your working. When writing a rhyming communication for divinity, keep in mind this easy rule: Each line must have the same number of syllables, and each line, or every other line, should rhyme. For example:

> **Dark Goddess hover near** (7 syllables),
> **lend to me your blessed ear** (7 syllables).
> Or, **Dark Goddess hover near** (7 syllables),
> **grow with the night,**
> **lend me your power** (9 syllables),
> **bless my work with your ear** (7 syllables),
> **may your strength build stronger in this hour** (9 syllables).

Here we've used the magickal numbers seven and nine. Granted, the rhyme sounds lousy (which is my point), but I'm focusing on the rhythm of the words at the moment. If we incorporate action with our words, then we would have something like this:

> **Dark Goddess hover near, lend to me your blessed ear.**
> (Action: Light a candle to the Dark Mother.)
> **Guardian wolf, I call your power. Lend your strength,**
> **a protective bower.** (Action: Light a candle to your guardian.)

Your physical actions, spoken words, and mental connection to deity or other energies will assist in the success of your magickal application. The idea revolves around doing everything in harmony, from words to actions to thoughts. Take some time now and write an invocation to the deity you have chosen for the goal we are working on.

Achieving Your Basic Psychic Magickal Level

No, we are not ready yet. Put your invocation to deity with your goal on the altar or shrine. Right now, we are going to work on achieving your basic psychic magickal level. I've chosen to use the work of William W. Hewitt here. I like him almost as much as I like Doreen Valiente and Z. Budapest. As you can tell, I'm a big believer in not reinventing the magickal wheel. If someone else has an excellent key or practice, my raven eyeball is right there, trying to figure out how to incorporate the practice into exercises for my students. Hewitt is a master at teaching psychic development and positive mental programming. Granted, I took his exercise on page 53 of his book *Psychic Development for Beginners* and changed it a bit for you magickal people, but the main thrust of the exercise belongs to him.

Remember the candle exercise at the beginning of the book? Now, I want you to light another candle, darken the room, and relax in this quiet place, as you did before. You can put on soft music if you like.

- Close your eyes.
- Visualize a spiral staircase with ten steps curving down to the bottom floor.
- Visualize yourself standing at the top of the staircase.
- Take a step down to the ninth step and mentally say:

Deepest psychic and magickal level.

- Then step down to the eighth step and mentally say:

Deepest psychic and magickal level.

- Then step down to the seventh step and mentally say:

Deepest psychic and magickal level.

- Then step down to the sixth step and mentally say:

Deepest psychic and magickal level.

- Then step down to the fifth step and mentally say:

Deepest psychic and magickal level.

- Then step down to the fourth step and mentally say:

Deepest psychic and magickal level.

- Then step down to the third step and mentally say:

Deepest psychic and magickal level.

- Then step down to the second step and say:

Deepest psychic and magickal level.

- On the bottom step, mentally say:

I am now at a strong magickal and psychic level that I can use
for successful magickal and psychic performance. I can reach this level
whenever I wish, with my eyes either open or closed, simply
by desiring to be here and counting down from three to one.

- Open your eyes.
- Repeat the exercise with your eyes open.

The nice thing about this exercise is that not only will it improve your overall magickal performance, but your everyday psychic performance as well. And, if you are a tarot or rune reader, then I suggest practicing this exercise with every ounce of your being. You won't regret it. In essence, each time a client sits down, you can simply say to yourself, "Three, two, one," and then begin the reading (providing, of course, you have been a good student and have been practicing this exercise faithfully).

Practice using this exercise every day for at least two weeks before moving on to the next stage. At the end of two weeks repeat this exercise, except add this sentence:

To perform successful magick, all I have to do is say the words
'Three, two, one,' then focus on my desire, followed by
blowing softly into the air.

That's right, kid: put your lips together and blow. Practice using this extended exercise for one full month. During that month, when you work magick, be sure to practice what you are telling yourself that you will do. You will say the words "Three, two, one" after any spellcasting, focus on your desire, then blow softly. Be sure to keep a record of your successes or failures.

Testing Your Abilities

Okay, you've been doing Hewitt's exercise and added RavenWolf's one-two-three, focus, put-your-lips-together-and-blow. Now what do you do? Pull this technique into your everyday life. For example, I wanted to go home from work early, just because I wanted to. Without anyone noticing, I focused on the woman who was in charge smiling and telling me I could go home, then blew into the air slightly. I added the statement, "With harm to none." Ten minutes later she said, "I'm going to cut some hours today. How would you like to go home?" Some magickal people may stick their broomsticks or wands up in the air and say, "Well, gee, that's easy. I expected you to give us better stuff, RavenWolf." My response to this is: If you don't have the basics down, then you can't do the big tasks when you really need to. And, your spellcasting techniques should not be like Russian roulette, where you worry about the outcome. To be certain, to be confident, to be proud of your accomplishments, and to raise your self-esteem, you need to practice, practice, practice to the point where you will achieve a positive outcome ninety-five percent of the time. Besides, Hewitt's exercise is a wonderful way to truly live a magickal life and have fun with it!

That Spell

No, I have not forgotten the spell and your invocation that you put on your altar or statue. In fact, you are going to incorporate that spell and Hewitt's exercise.

The final nuances of spellcasting include magickal correspondences, to circle or not, and to call Quarters or not. Take some time now and determine what correspondences you will use (check the appendices, or come up with some of your own), and write down any supplies you will need, or notes you might want to refer to. Once you have gathered this information, check your spiritual plan, then wait for the timing you chose. If you are a beginner at spellcasting, don't get too wrapped up in correspondences just yet. Try working this spell without them, so you understand how it feels to cast a spell. If you consider yourself experienced in spellcasting techniques, by all means pull out all the bells and whistles you desire.

Now . . . it's time to do that spellworking.

1. Go to your shrine or altar and get your spell.

2. Create sacred space, cast the circle, and call the Quarters, if you so desire. Light an illuminator candle so you can see what you are doing.

3. Use your invocation you wrote to call on the assistance of deity.

4. Hold the piece of paper with the spell on it in your projecting hand.

5. Say your intended goal out loud.

6. Do Hewitt's exercise (pages 153–155).

7. Hold the paper to your breast and say in your mind: "Three, two, one!" Visualize the desired outcome of the spell, then blow softly.

8. Do this each evening until your desire has manifested. If you like, you can carry the spell with you and read it whenever you like. Yes, I know this is against the old rule of cast it and forget it. The idea there was to keep you from worrying that the desire would not manifest. However, you are a big boy or girl now, and you know not to feed negativity into your spells. If, however, you have a tendency to worry, then you will indeed negate all the positive effort you are putting forth with this exercise. If that is the case, then leave the paper on the shrine or altar and only touch it when you work the spell. If you have learned to control your thoughts and turn negative thoughts into positive ones, then please carry the paper with you and review it at your leisure.

9. When your desire manifests, thank deity, then burn the spell paper and scatter the ashes to the wind.

Gee, that was awful short for all that work, huh? Once you get the techniques of spellcasting down, it won't seem so involved. Indeed, you may learn to skip or combine steps, especially for more simple desires. We can lengthen the same spell in the following manner.

1. Go to your shrine or altar and get your spell. Mine's going to be for protection.

2. Create sacred space, cast the circle, and call the Quarters, if you so desire. Light an illuminator candle so you can see what you are doing.

3. Use the invocation you wrote to call on the assistance of deity.

> *Dark Goddess hover near, lend to me your blessed ear.*
> (Action: Light a candle to the Dark Mother.) *Guardian wolf,*
> *I call your power. Lend your strength, a protective bower.*
> (Action: Light a candle to your guardian.)

4. Hold the piece of paper with the spell on it in your projecting hand.

5. Say your intended goal out loud.

6. Do Hewitt's exercise (pages 153-155).

7. Hold the paper to your breast and say in your mind: "Three, two, one!" Visualize the desired outcome of the spell, then blow softly.

8. Now begin chanting the following while lighting your thurible. (Oh, what goes in the thurible? Let's see; if you chose to do protection magick, you'd throw in some rosemary, a little angelica, some lavender to scare away bad astral dreamy stuff, some vervain to make it go, some dragon's blood for more power, and anything else you feel appropriate. Add a dash of Epsom salts, a bit of alcohol, a piece of paper with the rune Algiz on it for protection and fire that baby up.) Keep chanting the following until the fire goes out:

> *Earth and water, wind and fire;*
> *raise the energy, higher and higher.*

Ta-da! Instant spell. As the smoke from the thurible floats about the room, release the protective energy you raised. And, if you really want to get hot, you could bang on that drum or rattle your heart out. Then ground and center. In this little spell we started with the beat of seven, funneled that energy into the first candle, went on to the beat of nine, placed that energy within the second candle, finished with a repetitive beat of five (the power chant), and scared the crap out of anyone or anything that had his or her evil little gaze plastered in your direction. Ah, they won't be back. We've also followed the rule of three times. In early American magick, you always followed the rule of three, and I'm not talking about the following poem: Three times three, whatever you send out comes back to thee. That's a good rule to follow, but that's not the rule I mean here. When you worked chants, breathing, or spells, you always did them three times, or performed actions within sets of three. Here, the first candle was one, the second candle was two, and the thurible was three. We followed the rule of three for standard magickal applications. Now you try. Don't forget—when your desire manifests, thank deity, then burn the spell paper and scatter the ashes to the wind.

So what's the big deal about spellcasting anyway? Casting spells are a Witch's way of achieving focused prayer. Spells can be a vehicle or tool used to raise your self-esteem, give you control of your life and environment, and keep you in constant touch with divinity. As I've said before, there are those Witches who prefer ritual over spellwork, and those who prefer magick over ritual. There are Witches who choose meditation over both ritual and spellcasting. Are any of these Witches wrong? No. How you seek relationship with divinity is your business and not subject to approval or condemnation from any other magickal or mundane individual, and how you seek to spiritually mature, whether through spellwork, meditation, or ritual, is your choice.

As with all of my books, I try to show you how I have achieved success. I try to incorporate as many standard magickal (community-wide) practices as I can; however, many adept magickal practitioners will see personal nuances within my work. My main goal revolves around getting you thinking and doing in a safe and meaningful way.

Magickal Minutes

The Tornado Charm

Many Pow-Wow practitioners used the Tornado Charm to conjure healing or prosperity magicks. Think of a single goal, then factor that goal down to one to three words. Write these words on a piece of plain white paper. If you have used more than one word, do not put spaces between the words. For example: Healing for Annette, would be HEALINGANNETTE.

On letter is then dropped for each successive line, until you have:

HEALINGANNETTE
EALINGANNETTE
ALINGANNETTE
LINGANNETTE
INGANNETTE
NGANNETTE
GANNETTE
ANNETTE
NNETTE
NETTE
ETTE
TTE
TE
E

Now your charm looks like a little tornado, and that's exactly how the charm will act in the astral realms. You lift the paper up, allow the request to form a tornado, then let this imaginary tornado spin a moment in your hand. If you can visualize well, then add color to the tornado. Release the tornado. Put the paper under a wish candle, in your pocket, or under your pillow until the wish becomes form. At this time, bring the tornado back into your hand and watch the tornado diminish until it has disappeared. Then burn the paper, releasing the magicks, and toss the ashes outside.

The Ritual Spell

Jack Veasey writes: "The following poem is designed to be a complete spell in and of itself. To use it, first familiarize yourself with its rhythm, then write an additional stanza with that same rhythm, expressing a wish that you would like to see manifested (most lines in the poem are eight syllables long, and simply writing lines that length should be close enough). Then face North, relax, and say the poem with total concentration, inserting your own new stanza into the space indicated." If you visualize the occurrences described in the poem taking place as you say the words aloud, so much the better.

If writing verse is not your forte, there are other ways of using the poem as a spell. For instance, when you come to the space for a new stanza, you could simply meditate for a moment, visualizing your wish coming to pass. Adding the stanza has the advantage of bringing the total number of stanzas up to the magickal number of nine and of adding something to the poem that is in sync with its feelings and rhythm. It will feel right read aloud, which will enhance its impact.

Jack structured the poem in such a way as to systematically accomplish the following: The poem grounds and centers you, and triggers an alpha state; the poem banishes negativity; casts a circle; calls the Quarters; invokes the Goddess and the God; raises a cone of power, and instructs the power to manifest with your wish; thanks all the invoked spirits/energies and gives them the direction to return to their original state; opens the circle and releases the raised power onto the astral; and states two magickal fail-safes to ensure proper astrological correspondences and prevent reversals. Whew!

Jack adds:

> You need not stand at an altar or shrine to perform this poem/spell, as the words transform any area into sacred space. If you do perform the poem at your altar or shrine, it is advisable to devote the altar or shrine first. While the poem includes a proviso protecting against bad astrological correspondences, checking the correspondences and performing the poem at an auspicious time can only increase your chances of success.
>
> I would also like to here acknowledge my debt to the brilliant Doreen Valiente. Her *The Witches Rune* inspired this piece, which attempts to perform the same functions, but also cover some ground not overtly dealt with in that great poem, haunting and compelling though it certainly is.

A Rune for all Reasons

Up through my roots, down through my wings,
into my core, energy sings.
Through mind gone still, through words that dance,
descend upon me, sacred trance.
Let all impediments to grace
now be banished from this place.
Salted water, smoke of sage,
cast out all trace of doubt, fear, rage.

Rise up, flame, and circle 'round—
within, protection will be found.
The forces raised within your frame,
Circle of Power, you'll contain.

Linking Spells and Fascinations

Spirits of East, South, West, North,
I summon, stir, and call ye forth.
Graces of thought, change, feeling, fact —
these gifts now let your strength attract.

O Lady, Queen of Earth and Sea,
come to my aid, I cry to Thee.
O Lord of Air, O Lord of Fire,
come and bring form to my desire.

O light that rises, light that spins,
I raise you as the Work begins.
O swirling cone of power, I pray
that you now do as I now say.

(Here, insert the new stanza stating your wish.)

O Mighty Ones, you are released
with thanks and love by this your priest*
O Circle, open your embrace.
O Power, to your task make haste.

Sun, Moon, Stars, Planets, now hear ye—
align yourselves compatibly!
Let no reversal trouble me—
as is my will, So mote it be!

* The word "priestess" may be substituted for the word "priest" if that
feels more comfortable—but there is nothing wrong with a woman
simply using the word "priest" inclusively, as in more conventional current religions (female Episcopal priests, for instance, don't call themselves "priestesses"). Keeping the rhyme and rhythm, for magickal
impact, is worth considering.

In a group working you could employ the grapevine dance while reciting the
poem, building the power for a specific working. Others use the rune as it stands,
then move into other aspects of ritual to satisfy the needs of the working. I know
several solitary Witches who activate their shrines each day by chanting Jack's rune,

and I know one individual who uses this poem in replacement of the LBR (Lesser Banishing Ritual). What a wonderful gift Jack has given us. I applaud him.

Accessing Your Higher Mind

In my opinion, the main reason why we have appeared on the earth plane revolves around our efforts to raise the vibrational level of our higher selves, as well as assisting others to raise the level of their spirituality, too. Our job is to create. The constant stress we humans encounter doesn't help us to reach higher spiritual planes; however, this exercise done twice daily at your shrine or altar will assist you in reaching your ultimate level of spirituality.

1. Kneel at your shrine or altar and light one white candle.

2. Ask your guardian to assist you as you tap the higher levels of your spiritual self.

3. Turn on your stereo, tape deck, or CD player and listen to soft music.

4. Sit comfortably in a chair by your shrine.

5. Close your eyes and do Hewitt's exercise (pages 153-155). When you get to ten, imagine that you walk into a beautiful field that has a set of spiral marble steps rising from the ground. There are twenty steps. Say to yourself:

   I am going to climb the steps to
   my spiritual self, my higher mind.

   Slowly count up from one to twenty as you imagine yourself walking up those steps. Don't worry if you can't do it the first time. Your conscious mind may try to fight you and keep you from going up the steps. It likes its favorite vices and will not be excited that you wish to overcome them. If you can't make it all the way up, ask your guardian to appear and walk up with you. If you still can't make it up the stairs, don't despair, you can try again later in the day, and then again tomorrow. Keep trying until you get all the way up those stairs.

6. You are now at the top of the stairs. In front of you sits the Goddess and the God (or just the Goddess, or just the God—this is your mind, you know). Ask divinity to help you in certain areas of your life, or ask for wisdom, or whatever. Keep up a rolling conversation until you either lose your train of thought or feel you have garnered a satisfactory dialogue.

7. When finished, imagine yourself walking down the stairs. Count from one to five and tell yourself you are wide awake. Write down anything you heard or saw in your meditation. Allow the white candle to burn as long as possible. You can use this candle over and over again, as long as you use the candle for this work only. Many Witches I know inscribe runes, symbols, or words in a magickal alphabet on the candle. When the candle finishes, bury what is left in your "Witch burial place" on your property. Rule of Witch-thumb: bury the good stuff on your property, but bury the bad stuff off your property, or put the bad stuff in natural, running water, or throw the bad stuff at the crossroads at midnight and ask Hecate to take the evil away.

This simple meditation of accessing your higher mind can prove invaluable if you work with the sequence on a regular basis. You can also use the sequence to talk to friends and family who are deceased, discover the truth about nagging questions, work on self-esteem, goal programming, getting rid of bad habits, et cetera.

For example, let's say you want to banish yourself of a bad habit. You perform a ritual on the dark of the moon, leaving a petition at your altar or shrine. At the end of your ritual, before you close your circle, sit down and use this meditation sequence to access your higher mind and obtain the help you think you need to banish the bad habit. To raise energy, you might want to try this chant:

Crone and sage, crone and sage, wisdom is the gift of age.
Sage and crone, sage and crone, wisdom's truth shall be my own.

You might trying playing with your drum or rattle by repeating the word "Wisdom" many times to incorporate Spirit's knowledge into your life. After the sequence is over, write down your impressions, then close the Quarters and deactivate the circle.

Creating an Elemental

Many teachers feel that a knowledge of the reality of non-physical entities is essential to your progress on becoming an effective Witch. There are two broad classes of these entities or spirit beings—those that you create and those which already have a life of their own (nature spirits, devas, daemons, et cetera). These elementals can come in handy when employed in your spellcasting techniques.

Self-Created Elementals

There are two basic types of elementals you can create:

1. Timed Elemental: Created to perform a specific task, as an extension of your will, within a specified time limit.

2. Untimed Elemental: Created to be your eyes and ears—an extension of your will that maintains its existence for an unspecified period of time. Some magickal people call this type of elemental a "watcher." Odin's ravens, Thought and Memory, fall into this category.

How to Create a Timed Elemental

The most important factor in creating an elemental rests on your ability to plan properly. Before you begin, you should set down on paper the specific task you will impart to the elemental you create, as well as the time limit in which the elemental should operate. You can't have the elemental bumbling around out there, unsure of its mission, mucking things up for other people or for yourself. This type of elemental represents your pure thought and, therefore, you are responsible for anything it does.

You do not need to create this type of elemental in a cast circle, though for some practitioners this is a necessity; however, I do suggest building your thought creation in sacred space. To refresh your memory: sacred space is any area that you have cleansed and consecrated. You can also open the Quarters in sacred space, if you so desire. For example, if you need information from somewhere, you may wish to open the East Quarter and ask the element of air for assistance so that the elemental procures the correct information. The East can also act as a traveling portal for your elemental, where the elemental would leave by the East and return through the East gate.

You don't need any physical tools to create the elemental; however, many Witches and magickal individuals do use props, such as incense and candle color selected to match the intent of the working. For your training exercise, we will use a white candle and any incense that appeals to you. While following this procedure, please, please find a place where you can work undisturbed. People entering the room, turning on lights, or talking loudly will disrupt your concentration. Elementals such as these can manifest with other people in the room, but guests need to practice silence and respect through the operation. For example, for a training exercise, one of my students created an elemental to assist him in his music career while our coven encircled him. Coven members remained silent. Their task centered on watching the energy flow and giving their impressions of the process afterwards.

Linking Spells and Fascinations

1. To begin, seat yourself in a comfortable place where you feel protected and loved. In sacred space, light a candle and incense and, in peace and quiet, meditate until you are mentally and physically at ease. Use your 3-2-1 deepest psychic magickal level exercise to assist you (pages 153-155).

2. When you are ready to start, begin a chant in your mind of exactly what you wish to accomplish, and what the task will be that you wish the elemental to undertake (this is a process that is similar in the creation of a cone of power). Examples here would be:

   a. Money—*Bring to me abundance in a positive way, so that all my needs will be fulfilled. Return at the success of this task.*

   b. Information—*Bring to me information on Harold's project so that I make a wise decision on my involvement within twenty-four hours.*

   c. Health—*Help me find the right healer for my condition within seventy-eight hours.*

   d. Love—*Go to my sister Mia in Seattle, Washington, at 413 Harvard Place, and take with you my loving energy. Protect her while she goes through her divorce. Return when the divorce is completed.*

   Notice that we have given the elemental a specific time limit on two of the requests, and an open time limit on the other two; however, the instructions clearly state that at the completion of the task, the elemental should return.

   Only give the elemental one task at a time. For example, don't send the elemental out for love and money; choose one theme or the other. When you feel satisfied that you know exactly what you want the elemental to do, go on to the next step.

3. Once the specific task form is fully placed in your mind, narrow your thinking down to one phrase and say this phrase in a chant form, like this:

   a. Money—*Abundance to meet my needs.*

   b. Information—*Project information within twenty-four hours.*

   c. Health—*Find a healer within seventy-eight hours.*

   d. Love—*Love and protection for Mia.*

   Once you have worked your words into a smooth, moving cadence, then you are ready for the next step. You can use your drum or rattle here, but you will have to put the instrument down for the next step. If you are working with someone else, that person could continue the rhythmic pattern for you while you follow the remaining steps.

4. Now hold your hands about six inches apart with your palms slightly cupped and facing each other. Imagine a triangle of energy radiating from your third-eye chakra (forehead) and heart chakra to a mid-point in your cupped hands. Energy color from the third-eye is purple; green from the heart chakra. If you find visualizing a color too difficult, think of pure, white light.

   Imagine a pyramid of power, the sides taking in all of your head and chest area. Pull this energy into your hands.

5. Call on the gracious Goddess and the great God to give life to the elemental that is being created in your hands. You can call on a specific set of deities, or you can use Lord and Lady references. Although you could call on one particular god or goddess for this task, we've found that using the balanced energies of Mom and Dad works better. Be sure to thank them for their help. You can now feel the elemental grow with the rhythm of your breath as you begin your chant again.

   Take your time with this step. Don't rush the creation of the elemental. If you do, the elemental may not mature and you'll find yourself right back where you started from.

6. As you breathe, let your palms move slightly back and forth, toward and away from each other in a pulsing motion in rhythm with your breathing. Take deeper, longer breaths, moving your hands further apart, until the elemental becomes a large, swirling ball of energy within your hands. Remember to keep up your mental chant of your one-line command and keep the vision of the triangle of power (energy) flowing from your forehead and heart to the form in your hands.

7. Breathe right into the elemental, visualizing your breath as the breath of life. From the Goddess and God within you comes the gift of life to your creation. If you are nervous about this, simply do your 3-2-1 deepest psychic and magickal level and merge with the elemental to give it your support. You are now in the alpha state (altered state of consciousness). Here, if you like to make things complicated, is where you can govern the appearance of the elemental, if you want to. For example, if your sister would feel good about having an astral cat hanging around, you can give the cat form to your creation.

8. When you feel confident, rise to your feet and command the Elemental to go forth and fulfill its mission. You may say something like this:

*Elemental from my hands of birth, go forth and fulfill your
mission of protection and love to my sister, Mia. When you have
completed your task, return yourself from the state in which you came!
With harm to none, as I will, it shall be done!*

Surround the elemental with a mental circle of protection and throw it into
the air. Spread your arms wide in the Goddess position, repeat your one-line
command and end with:

*So be it done; 3, 7, 9, 21;
end ye well, that's here begun!
So mote it be!*

If you have given your elemental a time limit, be sure you remember what
you told it and be available for information collection at the end of the set
period. Once the elemental has passed on the information, the being will
return to the pre-birth state, as were your instructions when you released it.
If you have given the elemental a task, wherein the elemental did not have
to relay any information to you, it will return to the pre-birth state
automatically, as were your original instructions. Never, ever, leave an
elemental you've created floating around out there without anything to do,
or fail to give specific instructions of where the elemental should return
at the completion of the task.

How to Create an Untimed Elemental

In creating an untimed elemental, such as Odin's ravens (Thought and Memory),
you will use the same instructions as in building a timed one, though your commands will be a bit different. For example, when considering your statement of purpose, it may sound something like this:

*Be my watcher; alert me of any information that is vital
to my well-being and spiritual path.*

A chant might be:

Watcher, protector (or, as in the raven totems)
Thought and Memory, information bring to me.

If you are really creative, you can put physical objects on your shrine or altar that
can house your untimed elemental when the elemental is not out and about, pranc-

167

ing through the universe on a specific command. You can merge your elemental with a wolf totem and place those combined energies within the statue. Simply touch the statue when you want a task completed (sort of like calling the mythical genie from the lamp). Before you send this combined energy away, give it specific instructions on what you want done, then remind this energy to return to the vessel immediately after the completion of the task.

For example, you would say something like:

Elemental from my hands of birth, go forth and fulfill your mission of protection and love to my sister, Mia. When you have completed your task, return to the wolf statue and remain there until I call you again. With harm to none, as I will, it shall be done!

Surround the elemental with a mental circle of protection and throw it into the air. Spread your arms wide in the Goddess position, repeat your one-line command and end with:

So be it done; 3, 7, 9, 21; end ye well, that's here begun! So mote it be!

Are there other ways to create elementals? Certainly! The instructions I've given you provide one methodology. You may discover a better way, or a different way, in your own research.

6
Detailing
the Ritual

Much of Craft activity, especially in a group environment, revolves around ritual. Why do we do this? Why have ritual at all? Why do we always use the same basic components in ritual? Why have rules for ritual? What is the point?

In a lecture on the subject of solitary Wicca in March of 1990, the late author and magickal practitioner Scott Cunningham stated that "There is no such thing as a solitary Wiccan. To me, the whole purpose of Wiccan ritual is to expand my awareness of the God and Goddess within. The more I expand this awareness, the more I realize I am never alone."

Reasons for Ritual

Whether our chat centers on solitary or group ritual, we will eventually meander into the reasons why humans feel the need for the practice of ritual.

Reinforcement of your faith through worship. By our very nature, humans gravitate toward ritualistic behavior. For example, most of us celebrate our birthdays every year, regardless of our faith, economic background, age (well . . . maybe after awhile we'd rather not celebrate our birthdays), et cetera. Many of us develop ritual behavior in situations other than those considered celebratory. A friend of mine goes to work a half-hour early every day so that she can have coffee and something to eat before her shift starts. Another friend of mine likes to read the paper or listen to music on headphones during the morning and evening subway ride as part of his morning ritual. Some of us bend the spines of books we read, others leave the bindings in pristine condition. Each of us incorporates rituals or patterns of behavior every day. Isn't it natural that we incorporate ritual or habitual patterns of behavior into our religious practices as well?

Ritual, in worship, gives us a comfortable structure in which to honor our chosen divinity. Repeated behavioral patterns, such as ringing a bell, smudging with sage, special words of opening or closing, or acting out a communion segment, bring about repeated positive results. In honor of divinity, ritual sets aside a chosen segment of our time wherein we focus only on our interaction with Spirit and the movement of divinity within our lives.

Ritual serves as a mental launching pad for physical, spiritual, or mental manifestation. I think one of the most exciting aspects of the Craft lies in the fluidity of the belief system, wherein no matter what our problem, need, or desire, we can interact with divinity at any time or any place without obtaining the approval of another human being or a structured organization. Ritual provides a format in which we can safely conduct such magickal workings either alone or in a group situation. The Craft does not require you to contact divinity in a specific manner, therefore rituals that you write yourself allow you to personalize your association with divinity and lets you bring your special needs into focus. Ultimately, you have full reign over how you choose to manifest change in your life. Of course, this also means that you must accept the responsibility for your actions.

The structure of Wiccan ritual as we know it today allows you to create a compendium of fascinations that will act as a catalyst to a better you. You can fill your ritual with many gestures, procedures, or words, or you can choose a selected few techniques to accomplish your chosen desire. Regardless of the ritual format you choose, you can fulfill your needs and desires through an outline of your creation.

Ritual provides socialization with others of like mind. An important part of Wiccan group work includes the enactment of ritual, whether the format encompasses the basic building block of honor or work. Humans are tribal in nature and enjoy group religious functions. The positive aspects of group socialization can be uplifting and nurturing to Spirit. When many people join in spirit to accomplish a specific goal, a vortex of positive energy emerges into the universe, helping to move our spirituality closer to the source by changing things for the better in our world. When you move about in any social environment, your energy field merges with those of like mind, allowing you to communicate not only on a verbal and physical level but on a psychic and spiritual level as well.

Over the years, rules for group interaction have entered Craft ceremonies just as rules enter all types of group function, whether we are talking about a softball team, a civic organization, or a yearly town celebration. Rules enhance and protect the activities of the group. Therefore, in the Craft, we have two types of rules: Those which help to facilitate and protect group functions, and those which assist in heightening our spirituality, not only as a group, but as an individual as well. When rules serve as a detriment to the group, we should either rewrite them or get rid of them.

Ritual allows you to gain control over your life no matter where you are or what you are doing. The best example of this statement came to me in e-mail form from a reader of one of my previous books.

Dear Silver,

Thank you so much for writing *To Stir A Magick Cauldron*. You can't know how much that book helped me in my time of need. I had just gotten the book in the mail when I received a phone call that my aunt, who lives over a hundred miles from me, tried to commit suicide. My father told me to stay put, and he would call me back as soon as he could. Silver, what could have been the worst two hours of my life turned out to be one of the best learning situations of my life. I took my new book and started to page through it. I found the parts about daily devotions, then flipped to some of the rituals. Right there and then I decided that I would do a ritual to help my Aunt, to let her know that we all really love her, and not to give up. I used your book as my altar, right in my lap! Since I'm not very experienced, I called the archangels at the Quarters. I asked them to watch over my Aunt and to deliver my message of love to her. I invoked the Lord and Lady and asked for their healing assistance, should the universe deem it so.

Silver, it worked! My father called me back and said that my aunt was out of the danger zone, and that she would recover. After she got out of the hospital she went into counseling and she is doing wonderfully. But, best of all, when I thought I could do nothing but sit there and chew on my fingers and cry, I found I could do something! I discovered that the Craft is an interactive faith, and that I don't have to sit around and wait for life to bop me on the nose. I can fight back!

The most exciting aspect of ritual lies in its ability to assist us in controlling our own lives. Even if we fail in our ritual focus, for whatever reason, the fact that we performed the ritual put us in the ball game of life, rather than cowering on the sidelines. You haven't done everything you could do until you have performed ritual.

Ritual serves as relaxation. One of the finer aspects of ritual involves its ability to put you into a non-stressful thought process. When you have completed any ritual, you should feel better than when you began. Ritual represents part of our spiritual journey and, in that format, should provide us with feelings of joy, euphoria, relaxation, and a sense of mystery. Solitary ritual wins in this particular category, as no one can judge you, either on purpose or by accident, on the rituals you perform in solitude. The one major downfall in group ritual centers on individual opinion, and you'll always find one person who feels he or she must fulfill a divine duty and tell you what you did wrong and how the ritual could have been done better (if they were doing it, of course). This is not the main focus of ritual, but it can slide that way much too easily, defeating the process.

Here is my rule of thumb. Take it or leave it, but this is what I teach my students. *Anyone who appears at a ritual was supposed to be there. Anyone who doesn't show up, wasn't. Anything that happens in ritual was supposed to happen, for whatever reason. Anything that doesn't happen, wasn't supposed to. Just because we are in ritual doesn't mean we aren't supposed to learn any lessons.* For example, several years ago a High Priestess in Philadelphia ran a large group ritual. After the ritual, one person made it a point to tell at least twenty-five others that the High Priestess "forgot" to make sure everyone had grounded and, therefore, she was incompetent. Okay, so maybe she didn't include grounding 101 in her final closure of the circle; however, I don't remember reading anywhere in any Wiccan law, including the Ordains, that a prerequisite of magickal applications includes perfectionism and subsequent sainthood. If something goes wrong in a ritual, whether that ritual be of a solitary nature or group participation, then view the error as a lesson, rather than a detriment of your (or someone else's) character. Ritual always makes the ordinary extraordinary; don't defeat the mystique.

"If at any point," writes a friend of mine, "we feel that the ritual has not achieved its purpose, or we feel that our abilities and performance are being judged, then it is time to stop and think. Have we allowed the ritual to become more important than the spiritual journey? Ritual is not the path . . . it is the reminder that there is a path."

Ritual creates positive pockets of energy all over the planet. Each time an individual or group performs Craft ritual (for honor or for practical reasons), that individual or group creates pockets of positive energy that lasts long after the ritual chants die away. This energy assists in uniting us with divinity, and allows divinity to move freely about the planet. Think of every ritual that you do as the creation of a power cell or energy line for positive manifestations for the good of all. If you are out in the woods and create sacred space by cleansing and consecrating an area, when you leave that area, you leave the vibrations of your ritual. The plants and animals in that area will benefit from the work you do there long after you've left.

Ritual manifests harmony. In the Ordains, one of the laws states that ritual seeks to manifest balance. You give your energy to the act of ritual and, in return, Spirit empowers all within the circle. I love to watch the faces of the Black Forest Clan when they complete ritual. When I see big grins and flashing eyes, I know that we have completed our task. It doesn't matter if someone forgot their lines, or if we all burst into laughter over a blooper. It's the smiles, the laughter, and the sense of harmony that's vitally important to good ritual.

Why Do Most Wiccans and Witches Use the Same Basic Components in Ritual?

In Craft ritual we often follow the same basic components. They are:

Creating sacred space. We cleanse the area to remove any negative vibrations that daily living may have infused in the area.

Casting the circle. We cast the circle to protect us from outside influences and provide us with a contained area that will hold the energy we raise until we choose to release that energy. In essence, the magick circle becomes our church or sanctuary for the divine.

Calling the Quarters. We call the Quarters either asking for their protective energy or to pull positive, natural energy into our working.

Invoking divinity. We draw divinity into the circle so that we may either honor that divinity or ask for that divinity's energy assistance in our working, or both.

Stating the purpose of the work or celebration. We state the purpose to help our minds focus on the primary working or ceremony.

Working magick (or recognizing the celebratory reason). We work magick to support the purpose of the focus, or to conduct an honorary celebration that corresponds to the focus of the ritual. Consider the magickal working as the engine of the ritual.

Raising energy. Raising energy provides the fuel for the engine in the ritual. We raise energy to accomplish our task, whether that task functions as celebratory or otherwise.

Observing communion. We observe communion to ground ourselves after working ritual, and to recognize within ourselves that we honor divinity.

Thanking divinity. We thank divinity because we are good Witches and are grateful that divinity has aided us in our working or celebratory function. Thanking divinity gives back energy to the universe and ensures a cyclical return should we do magick or the celebration again.

Releasing the Quarters. We release the Quarters so that we don't hold unnecessary energy in any one particular place. When we send this energy back, it can go somewhere else, again returning in a cyclical pattern, should we have need of it. If we forced the energy to stay, then we would short-circuit the energy pattern. If you give the energy the choice to stay, then that is another matter entirely.

Opening the circle. We open the circle so that we may once again move freely through the area. If you do not open the circle, then you will continually rip and tear it until the energy dissipates in a chaotic manner. We also open the circle to acknowledge the completion of the ritual. Finally, we open the circle in an orderly manner so that we can direct that energy in a specific way. For example, you may place the circle energy in your tools, in yourself, in a loved one, and so on.

Grounding and centering. We ground and center ourselves to help our bodies slough off any extra energy. Consider the excess energy like fat cells that your body doesn't need.

Of course, we can remove some of these procedures and still have a generic Craft ritual. For example, you may choose not to cast a magick circle. You may choose not to call the Quarters, or to call only one Quarter. You may choose to eliminate communion. So, what do you have left?

> Creating sacred space
>
> Invoking divinity
>
> Stating your purpose
>
> Working magick (or indicating celebratory honor)
>
> Thanking divinity
>
> Closing the ritual

We call the former ritual (the longer one) a **detailed ritual.** The latter (the smaller procedure) is known as a **simple ritual.** Some magickal practitioners feel you do not need a magick circle if the working consists only of calling divinity. Their reasoning: Why do you need a protective circle to protect you from deity? Conversely, some magickal practitioners feel that every performance should rely on the magick circle, regardless of what or who you call. Take your pick. Now here things get a bit more complicated. In all, there are five types of ritual format—formal, complex, informal, basic, and spontaneous.

Ritual Formats

Formal and Complex Ritual

The **formal ritual** consists of several scripted steps, includes a compendium of tools, and usually takes at least forty-five minutes to an hour to perform. The ceremony covers a complete cleansing and consecration of each person involved, as well as the act of communion. You'll find an incredible number of details in a formal ritual. A **complex ritual** might not carry an entire script (an outline does the trick), however all the steps mentioned previously apply, including circle casting, Quarter calls, invocation, the working, and communion.

You can take any of the rituals or spells provided in this book and turn them into formal or complex rituals if you so desire. Formal and complex rituals use many steps, each reaffirming the desired goal. The main difference between a formal ritual and a complex ritual resides in the **script**. The formal ritual relies completely on a script without deviation. A complex ritual holds the same steps as the formal ritual, but the complex ritual does not need a full script and changes to the existing script, as well as individual ad-libbing, are acceptable. Where a Gardnerian or Alexandrian group will normally use a formal ritual, a shamanic group, such as the Black Forest Clan, will use the complex ritual.

The formal tri-circle ritual should be looked at here so that we can review the differences between the various ritual formats. I decided to include a formal group ritual because I know that many solitaries get together to do ritual but have little material available to them to understand how a formal ritual progresses, from start to finish. So, even if you do not ever plan to work formal ritual or work a formal group ritual, please read this section to heighten your awareness of what a ritual like this would entail, should you find yourself part of one.

Our sample ritual has the following players:

The Elder

The High Priestess

The High Priest

The Maiden

The Temple Summoner

One person for each of the Quarters (with rattles)

The Drummer or Official Rattler

Coveners

Therefore, we have at least ten individuals with specific parts to play. If you don't have that many people, you can double up duties. For example, the High Priest and the High Priestess can call the Quarters, which cuts out four people right there.

As you read through this ritual, think of the ritual as a mind play. Look at the cast of characters again and attribute some individual characteristics to them. Then, as you read, you can "see" these people going through the motions of the ritual. Also notice as you read that the Drummer has a very important part to play—he or she acts as the affirmation of the intent of the entire ritual.

Master Shamanic Tri-Circle Formal Ritual: Erecting a Shrine

Supplies: Ice, salt, incense of your choice, white taper candles or oil lamps (for illumination), a white pillar candle, oil of your choice, sterno or tea candle in a small cauldron, your thurible cauldron, herb mixture, pumpkin spice, Epsom salts, matches, and gin. A red taper candle for the South, an incense holder for the East, a bowl of water for the West, and a large crystal for the North (keep the Quarter supplies at the foot of the altar). A libation bowl. A chalice, juice, cakes, and a tray (put these items at the foot of the shrine or altar, off to one side). Drums and rattles. Set up the shrine complete with statue, chosen first offering, and sacred objects. Before the ritual begins, the Temple Summoner or the Maiden makes sure that all these items are ready.

Astrological Timing: Full or new moon (as you feel appropriate)

Planetary Hour: Sun, Moon, Mercury, or Venus (your choice)

Good Moon Cycles:

Runic Correspondences: Birca (Birth)

Do not perform while the moon is void-of-course.

1. **Personal Preparation.** When working in a formal group environment, set aside a few moments before the ritual to walk the area, meditate and prepare yourself for the coming events.

2. **Creating Sacred Space and Taking Position.** The Elder walks the pre-ritual area, contacting the devas and asking for their acceptance, assistance, and protection.

   The Coveners wait off-site.

The Drummer takes up position near the altar or shrine, but back a little so that he or she doesn't impede the course of the ritual. The drummer says:

We gather together to perform the ritual of (state the purpose here).

The Drummer begins a soft, steady beat.

The Maiden of the coven creates sacred space by cleansing and consecrating the room or outdoor space with the four elements. The High Priest and High Priestess wait, one on each side of the altar, while the Maiden performs her duties. The Temple Summoner stands beside the High Priestess. The individuals who will call the Quarters take their positions at their respective Quarters. The Elder stands behind the High Priestess. Although many of these characters will move throughout the ceremony, each individual (the Quarters, the Elder, the Temple Summoner, and the Maiden) will keep these same positions as "home" positions. These individuals also remain silent throughout the ceremony unless directly spoken to by the High Priest or High Priestess.

The Quarters begin to rattle their instruments in accordance with the beat of the drum.

The Maiden anoints the four corners of the shrine table with oil. She may draw a banishing pentagram, a crescent moon, an equal-armed cross, or the rune algiz. Then she anoints the center of the shrine table with the same symbol. She rubs salt into the four corners, followed by the passage of fire and air over the surface.

The Drummer and Quarters stop. The Drummer says:

We have prepared the area for (state intent of ritual).
So mote it be!

All: *So mote it be!*

3. **The devotion of the altar.** Everyone turns to face the altar or shrine. The Drummer changes the beat, stopping whenever the High Priestess speaks, then continues as she works until near the end of the devotion, where he or she increases the pace of the beat. The Quarters can shake their rattles as long as they don't overcome the Drummer. Here, in a shamanic circle, the Drummer is as responsible for the energy flow as the High Priestess. Sometimes the Elder will act as the drummer, since they understand the complex nature of ritual energy.

The High Priestess performs the Altar Devotion, as set forth below.

The High Priestess lights the fire candle (located at the South on the altar or shrine stone), then holds the candle up at eye level, and says:

O creature of fire, work my will by my desire. Black Forest ancestor,
light my way; aid the magick cast this day.

She sets the candle down in the South, lights the incense, and says:

O creature of air, I cleanse and consecrate thee by the ancient energies
of the East. I remove all negativity in this world and in the world of
phantasm. Blessings of the ancient ones be on you now. So mote it be!

She sets the incense down, picks up the fire candle, and says:

O creature of fire, I cleanse and consecrate thee by the ancient energies
of the South. I remove all negativity in this world and in the world of
phantasm. Blessings of the ancient ones be on you now. So mote it be!

She passes her hand over the flame three times (or does the banishing pentagram) to banish, then holds her hand steady to bless, imagining a sparkling light surrounding the candle. She says:

At the West is ice (water). *Creature of water, I cleanse and consecrate*
thee in the names of the ancient energies of the West. I cast out all
negativity in this world and in the world of phantasm.
Blessings of the ancient ones on you now. So mote it be!

She passes her hand over the water three times (or does the banishing pentagram) to banish, then holds her hand steady to bless, imagining a sparkling light surrounding and infusing the water. She says:

At the North is salt. Creature of earth, I cleanse and consecrate thee
in the names of the ancient energies of the North. I cast out all
negativity in this world and in the world of phantasm. Blessings
of the ancient ones on you now. So mote it be!

She passes her hand over the salt three times (or does the banishing pentagram) to banish, then holds her hand steady to bless, imagining a sparkling light surrounding and infusing the salt.

Detailing the Ritual

The High Priestess holds the bowl of water in her hands and raises the bowl out before her, silently in communion with the Gods. She moves the water bowl to the center of the altar. She places three pinches of salt into the water (or balances a little salt on the athame blade and sprinkles the salt into the water) three times. She stirs thrice with her finger (or the blade).

The Drummer begins to pick up the beat. The Quarters shake their rattles attuned to the beat. The High Priestess picks up the athame, and says:

As the rod is to the God, so is the chalice to the Goddess.

The High Priestess begins to lower the knife into the water. As the knife is inserted into the water, she says:

And together, they are One.

At this point, the High Priestess envisions the water exploding with divine energy. The Drummer speeds up the beat; the Quarters follow. The High Priestess then removes the knife. With her hand or with the knife, she imagines that the altar (or shrine stone) represents a giant cauldron. Beginning at the North (as all things come from the North) in a clockwise, spiral motion, she stirs her hand over the altar five times, imagining the energies mixing together.

The High Priestess taps the hilt of the knife or her fingers soundly five times (one for each element plus Spirit) at the right lower corner (the corner closest to her right hand if she is right-handed, the corner closest to her left hand if she is left-handed) to seal the power of the altar.

The devotion is done. The High Priestess grounds and centers.

The Drummer and Quarters stop.

The High Priestess says:

So mote it be!

Everyone present says:

So mote it be!

The Drummer says:

We have devoted the altar for the purpose of
(state intent of ritual). ### So mote it be!

All: ### So mote it be!

179

4. **Calling the primal elements.** Fire and ice represent the primal elements of the Black Forest Clan's traditional ceremonies. By bringing the energies of fire and ice into the area, we create balance among ourselves and push those energies forward into the world of form for the benefit of others.

The Drummer begins a slow, steady, soft beat, and continues throughout this step of the ritual. The Quarters can use their rattles if they do not overpower the drum.

The Maiden lights the need-fire in the cauldron at the center of the circle, altar stone, or shrine stone.

The High Priest says:

Fire . . . First of the elements of creation given to our Clan by Brigid and Lugh. This fire embodies the force of the rapturous, infinite Spirit. With this symbolism, I will be free and pure in the names of the eternal ones. Burn brightly, waxing fire, in this hallowed place and fill me with your passion and your purity. Empower me on this eve (day) *of magick.*

The High Priest puts his hands over the ice, and says:

Ice . . . From the frigid realms of the North, given to our Clan by the Morrigan and Herne. The ice was formed, which cools and freezes. May this ice fill this place with balance and bless this circle with perfect peace and perfect love. May I draw forth the courage of the ancient ones, my ancestors, whom I honor. Everything comes from the North.

The Drummer and rattlers stop.

The Drummer says:

We have called the primal energies for the purpose of (state intent of ritual). *So mote it be!*

All: *So mote it be!*

5. **Self-Purification.** For anyone to function within the magick circle, the adage goes that all must be purified.

The Drummer begins (the Quarters do not participate) with a slow, steady beat.

The High Priest holds the ice water up to the Gods, and says:

O Hooded Lord and Veiled Lady, who have formed me from dust
and water in thine image, bless and sanctify this work for the
cleansing of the body, mind, and spirit. Let no deceit nor ignorance,
pain nor fear, dwell within my human form, O most powerful
God and Goddess. Give me thy grace, purified and cleansed
by water and salt. So mote it be!

All: *So mote it be!*

The High Priest dips his finger in the water (by now the ice has begun to melt) and draws a banishing pentagram on the forehead of the High Priestess. Then she does the same for him, who then does the same for the Maiden and those who have Quarter positions within the circle area. Other times the High Priest anoints the High Priestess with oil, then asperges her with salt water. She, in turn, does the same procedure for the High Priest. Naturally, these procedures differ from group to group. If a circle is to be cast around a lot of people, then each person is anointed at this time by the Maiden. If the circle is to be cast before the people enter, then the next step is performed.

When all have been anointed, the Drummer stops.

The Drummer says:

All have been purified for the purpose of
(state intent of ritual). *So mote it be!*

All: *So mote it be!*

6. **Casting the Three Circles.** The Drummer begins a slow, steady beat. The Quarters rattle in alliance with the drum beat.

    The Maiden asperges the four directions with salt water. Then she blows incense in the four directions. The Temple Summoner makes the first circle on the ground with the staff or sword (or his finger), beginning at the North, saying:

    May every evil flee as I speak the words of conjuration. I call forth
    humility and strength that the Lord and Lady be with me to cast upon
    me their divine love, charity, prosperity, and harmony.

    The High Priest makes the second circle at breast level with his athame or finger, saying:

May the keepers of peace assist and defend this circle.
May discord, discontent, and disorder disappear from it.

The High Priestess makes the third circle with incense at head level, swinging the censor from East to West thrice, then North to South thrice, then around the head deosil (if you don't own a censor, a stick of incense will do), saying:

Assist and magnify me. Bless my sabbat, esbat, working, and my
speech. Bless my entry into this, thy sacred circle.

Those assembled chant:

Earth my body; water my blood; air my breath;
and fire my Spirit. Blessed be!

The High Priestess stamps her foot on the ground, and says:

This circle is sealed!

The Drummer and Quarters stop. The Drummer says:

We have cast the three circles for the purpose of
(state intent of ritual). *So mote it be!*

All: *So mote it be!*

7. **Calling the Quarters.** The High Priest says:

Prepare to raise the powers of your elements, ye keepers of the
Quarters, and open their gifts as the Maiden sets these gifts at your
feet. She will hold high their symbols as you access their energies.

The Drummer begins a steady, even beat. The Quarters do not join in, as they will be busy with their own parts in this section of the ritual.

Beginning at the North, the Maiden sets the salt bowl from the altar or a crystal at the feet of the North, then moves to the East, South, and West, setting the remaining symbols at their feet. The Maiden moves back to the North. The North Quarter faces the outside of the Quarter (with back to the center of the circle) with arms crossed. The Maiden picks up the Quarter gift and holds it high above her head. She stands directly behind the Quarter person with her back to the center as well. The Quarter person opens his or her arms slowly as he or she says the Quarter call.

All turn toward the North, raising one arm in a salute.

North Quarter:

> *Ye guardians of the North, element of earth, and all ye in the realm*
> *of fairy, I* (your name) *do summon the elemental energies,*
> *stir the ancestral dead, and call Artios forth. Bear, sacred to our Clan,*
> *bring your energies forth to witness this rite and*
> *guard our sacred space. So mote it be!*

All: *So mote it be!*

Then turn toward the East, raising one arm in a salute.

The Maiden puts the North gift down, then moves to the East. She picks up the East gift. East turns and faces outward with arms crossed over the chest. East slowly opens his or her arms, saying:

> *Ye guardians of the East, element of air, and all ye in the realm of*
> *fairy, I* (your name) *do summon the elemental energies, stir the*
> *ancestral dead, and call Herne forth. Stag, sacred to our Clan,*
> *bring your energies forth to witness this rite and guard*
> *this sacred space. So mote it be!*

All: *So mote it be!*

Then turn toward the South, raising one arm in a salute.

The Maiden puts the East gift down, then moves to the South. She picks up the South gift. South turns and faces outward with arms crossed over the chest. South slowly opens his or her arms, saying:

> *Ye guardians of the South, element of fire, and all ye in the realm*
> *of fairy, I* (your name) *do summon the elemental energies, stir the*
> *ancestral dead, and call Tarvos forth. Bull, sacred to our Clan,*
> *bring your energies forth to witness this rite and guard this*
> *sacred space. So mote it be!*

All: *So mote it be!*

Then turn toward the West, raising one arm in a salute.

The Maiden puts the South gift down, then moves to the West. She picks up the West gift. West turns and faces outward with arms crossed over the chest. West slowly opens his or her arms, saying:

Ye guardians of the West, element of water, and all ye in the realm of fairy, I (your name) *do summon the elemental energies, stir the ancestral dead, and call Epona forth. Horse, sacred to our Clan, bring your energies forth to witness this rite and guard this sacred space. So mote it be!*

All: *So mote it be!*

The Maiden returns to her original place. Note: Another way to open the Quarters is as follows. The Maiden keeps her place beside the altar. The High Priestess moves behind the Quarter person. The High Priest moves into place behind the High Priestess. The Quarter person opens the Quarter. The High Priestess holds the gift high above her head. The High Priest protects her back by saluting with the sword.

The Drummer stops, and says:

We have called the Quarters for the purpose of (state the intent of the ritual). *So mote it be!*

All: *So mote it be!*

8. **Anointing the Coveners.** The High Priest and High Priestess move to where the door will be cut, a previously specified area of the circle designated by group consensus.

The Drummer begins a slow, steady beat. The Quarters may join in with their rattles.

The High Priest cuts a door with his hands, the sword, or the athame. He stands to the right of the door. The High Priestess stands to the left of the door. As each individual enters the circle the High Priest blesses each Covener, saying:

Be thou cleansed, regenerated, and purified, so that evil will neither harm nor abide in thee.

The High Priestess sprinkles them with holy water and says:

Welcome into our circle. Join us in perfect love and perfect trust.

She gives each person a hug.

After the Covener receives purification, he or she walks to the altar (in a clockwise direction) and salutes the God and Goddess, then moves on to his or her place. There should be no gaps in the circle. If they have rattles or drums with them, these should be placed at their feet or behind them.

When the last person has passed through the door, the High Priest or the High Priestess seals the circle, feeling the energies move beneath his or her hands in a steady rhythm. Take your time here, don't rush just so you can get on with the ritual. Make sure the energy under your hands is smooth and seamless and your visualization strong before you turn away. Please note that some groups allow the Coveners in before the Quarters are called.

The Drummer and Quarters stop. The Drummer says:

> *All have been anointed for the purpose of*
> (state intent of ritual). *So mote it be!*

All: *So mote it be!*

9. **Becoming a Group Mind.** To get the circle energies moving and building power, the group recites the Verse of Power below. In a group working, this action allows the group to solidify the group mind. Everyone envisions the energy running in a clockwise direction around the circle.

The High Priest says:

> *Please join hands as we sing the coven chant.*

The Drummer begins with a beat to match the chant:

> *From the earth and from the sky, Energy, I call ye nigh.*
> *From the moon and from the sun, let the Holy Power run.*
> *Through my body and my mind, earth, sky, moon and sun be kind!*
> *Stag and bull, horse, bear, and raven, let my circle be your haven.*
> *Fill my tools and fill my hands with your might at my command.*
> *Till the circle is undone, let my life and yours be one;*
> *while your life beats in my breast, what I will, will manifest!*
> *Let what starts now in this sphere go on when I'm gone from here;*
> *let the rhythm of this verse be that of the universe.*
> *Let the power I now draw turn my wishes into law!*
> *Seven times three; wing! hoof! claw! paw!*

(Repeat last line several times as the Drummer speeds up the beat.)

If this chant is too long for you to process, don't fret. You may like to use a shorter one instead.

The Drummer stops, and says:

> *We have become one for the purpose of*
> (state intent of ritual). *So mote it be!*

All: *So mote it be!*

10. **Recognizing the energies of the Gods within the circle.** The High Priest stands in the North and performs the God Salute while facing the coven. The coven returns the salute.

    The High Priestess stands in the South and performs the Goddess Salute, facing the coven. The coven returns the salute.

11. **Invoking the God and Goddess.** The Drummer begins a slow, steady beat.

    All Coven Members whisper "Into the light" in repetitive fashion.

    The High Priest draws the Goddess into the High Priestess, then she, in turn, draws the God into the High Priest. Together, they become the conduit for divine energy. In some cases this procedure is done simultaneously, in others, the procedure is done one at a time. I'm going to give you a few different examples here for you to try.

(1) The High Priest may draw into the High Priestess with a kiss. Then she walks the circle in a clockwise direction, touching the aura of each female Covener. Sometimes she may kiss the Covener, simply touch her face, or not touch her physically at all. The High Priestess is possessed (yes, you got the word right—I'm tired of doing the politically correct jazz of using the word "channeling"—call a spade a spade) and is passing the Goddess' blessing on to each female coven member. After the High Priestess draws down the God in the same manner, he walks in a clockwise direction around the circle and does the same procedure to each male Covener. The High Priest may hug the male Covener, clap him on the shoulder, or clasp the Covener's hand to his chest. All of these acts are acceptable in circle.

(2) The very best drawing-down procedure I've seen with couples works this way: The High Priestess and High Priest face each other. The High Priestess takes her right hand and puts it on the central area of his chest. The High Priest takes his right hand and puts it on the center area of her chest (so you both can feel your hearts beating). The the High Priestess puts her left hand over his hand that is on her chest. The High Priest puts his left hand over her hand that is on his chest. Together, they draw down at the same time. Then the High Priestess leads off clockwise around the circle, touching the auras

of the women, and he follows, touching the auras of the men. It's a nice touch and a wallop of energy. At this point, Mom and Dad have entered the circle and Divine magick begins.

(3) Another drawing procedure for group work is as follows:

High Priest: Kneels before the High Priestess and gives the eightfold kiss upon her feet, knees, yoni (womb), breasts, and lips, saying:

> *Blessed are thy feet that walk the sacred paths of the Goddess.*
> *Blessed are thy knees that kneel at the sacred altar.*
> *Blessed is thy womb, that brings forth sacred life.*
> *Blessed are thy breasts formed in beauty and strength.*
> *Blessed are thy lips that speak the sacred words.*

Then he holds his arms up, imploring:

> *I invoke thee and call upon thee, O Mighty Mother of us all,*
> *bringer of all fruitfulness by seed and by root, by stem and by bud,*
> *by leaf and flower and fruit, by life and love, do I invoke thee*
> *to descend upon the body of this, thy Priestess. Hear with her ears,*
> *speak with her tongue, touch with her hands, kiss with her lips,*
> *that thy hidden children may be fulfilled. So mote it be!*[1]

All: *So mote it be!*

Then he makes the descending triangle matrix from the Priestess' yoni to her right breast, to her left breast, and back to her yoni with his wand or athame, then holds his arms up again and invokes the Mother through her.

The High Priestess stands in the Goddess position with her athame up to the heavens, saying:

> *Veiled Lady—I call thee forth from heavenly sky and underhill,*
> *bring thy holy essence divine, to answer now my call of nine:*
> *One, I stand before thy holy throne;*
> *Two, I invoke thy power alone.*
> *Three, I hold aloft my magick blade;*
> *Four, descend! your Spirit is made.*

---

1. Attributed to Doreen Valiente.

Five, Elements of Witchery. O Gracious Goddess now be with me.
Six, enchantment! your essence bright!
Seven, bring power! to give me light.
Eight, come now! the call is done.
Nine, your essence and I are one.
So mote it be!

All: *So mote it be!*

The High Priestess kneels before the High Priest and gives the eightfold kiss upon the High Priest's feet, knees, phallus, breasts, and lips, saying:

Blessed are thy feet that walk the sacred paths of the God.
Blessed are thy knees that kneel at the sacred altar.
Blessed is thy phallus, that brings forth sacred life.
Blessed are thy breasts formed in beauty and strength.
Blessed are thy lips that speak the sacred words.

Then she holds her arms up, imploring:

I invoke thee and call upon thee, O Mighty Father of us all,
bringer of all fruitfulness by seed and by root, by stem and by bud,
by leaf and flower and fruit, by life and love, do I invoke thee to
descend upon the body of this, thy Priest. Hear with his ears,
speak with his tongue, touch with his hands, kiss with his lips,
that thy hidden children may be fulfilled.
So mote it be!

All: *So mote it be!*

Then the High Priestess makes the descending triangle matrix from the Priest's phallus to his right breast, to his left breast, and back to his phallus with her wand or athame, then holds her arms up again and draws the deity down through him.

The High Priest stands in the God position with his athame up to the full moon, saying:

Hooded Lord—I call thee forth, from heavenly sky and underhill,
Bring thy holy essence divine, to answer now my call of nine:
One, I stand before thy holy throne;

Two, I invoke thy power alone.
Three, I hold aloft my magick blade;
Four, descend! your Spirit is made.
Five, Elements of Witchery. O Gracious God now be with me.
Six, enchantment! your essence bright!
Seven, bring power! to give me light.
Eight, come now! the call is done.
Nine, your essence and I are one.
So mote it be!

All: *So mote it be!*

The High Priestess stands with arms gracefully down by her sides and with legs together to start. Then she blossoms and gives the sign of the invoking Priestess by opening her legs farther apart and spreading her arms up in a lunar crescent and throwing her head back, thus forming a pentagram with her body, building power. When she is finished, she takes her athame or finger and places it in the bowl of holy water. This transfers the power of the Goddess into the water. At this point in the rite, the Coveners can transfer all this power with their athames into a bowl of holy water reflecting the Moon. Later, pour this charged astral fluid energy into bottles and distribute it to all. At home and throughout the month, the Coveners can then use this water for their own magickal purposes.

The Drummer stops. The chanting stops. The Drummer says:

We welcome our Mother and Father into the circle for
the purpose of (state intent of ritual). *So mote it be!*

All: *So mote it be!*

12. **The Working.** As this formal ritual functions as a master ritual (that which could be used for many purposes), here the working or reason for celebration begins. In this example, the High Priest and High Priestess will be dedicating a group shrine.

    The Drummer begins a soft, slow, steady beat. Everyone may use their rattles and follow the lead of the drummer.

    The High Priest holds the High Priestess' left hand. They put their free hands in the air, and say:

Silver RavenWolf

I invoke thee and call upon thee, O (name of deity),
bringer of all fruitfulness by seed and by root, by stem and by bud,
by leaf and flower and fruit, by life and love.
You, who protect the homes of the faithful,
who bring harmony to land, shelter, and family,
do I invoke thee to descend upon the statue of your likeness,
so that you may have the eyes to see, the ears to hear,
and the heart to hold sacred both myself and my family
that thy hidden children may be fulfilled.
So mote it be!

All: *So mote it be!*

Then both touch the statue, box, whatever, with their hands, and say:

(Name of divinity), *Holy Goddess—I call thee forth;*
from heavenly sky and underhill;
Bring thy holy essence divine,
to answer to this call of nine:
One, I stand before thy holy throne;
Two, I invoke thy power alone.
Three, I hold aloft my magick blade;
Four, descend! your Spirit is made.
Five, Elements of Witchery. O Gracious Goddess, be with me.
Six, enchantment! your essence bright!
Seven, bring power! to give it light.
Eight, come now! the call is done.
Nine, this statue and thee are one.

Now, both High Priest and High Priestess make the descending triangle matrix on the statue, then hold their arms over the statue, making the motions of drawing down the essence of the deity into the statue.

The Drummer speeds up the pace, then stops, and says:

We prepare to raise power for the purpose of
(state intent of ritual). *So mote it be!*

All: *So mote it be!*

13. **Raising Power.** The Maiden lights the thurible with the assistance of the Temple Summoner. (Be careful!)

Now the chanting and group drumming begins. You can use the following chant or choose one of your own.

> *We are the flow, We are the ebb,*
> *We are the weavers, We are the web.*

The Maiden throws the pumpkin spice into the thurible while the flame rises.

The Coveners, during the continued chant, beginning with the first Covener clockwise from the altar, walk up to the altar or shrine and give their offering and petition, one at a time. The High Priest and High Priestess offer their petitions last.

Group drumming stops.

The Drummer says:

> *We have raised power for the purpose of*
> (state intent of ritual). *So mote it be!*

All: *So mote it be!*

14. **Reaffirming Your Faith.** The Drummer begins a soft, slow beat.

The Maiden lights the fresh white pillar candle from the candle at the South Quarter, then carries the pillar candle clockwise through the circle to the shrine or altar. Each individual should concentrate on reaffirming his or her faith. The Maiden passes out a candle to each Covener. The High Priestess carries the affirmation candle to each Covener in a clockwise direction. When all the candles flame, together the Coveners step forward, humming to unite the candles and raise energy for the well-being of the coven. This is an act of rededicating themselves to the path of Wicca. Each regains their position and then, together, they snuff out their candles.

The Drummer stops, and says:

> *We have reaffirmed our faith in our Mother and Father*
> *for the purpose of* (state intent of ritual).
> *So mote it be!*

All: *So mote it be!*

15. **Communion.** The Maiden picks up the chalice. The Temple Summoner picks up the cakes. The Maiden hands the chalice to the High Priest, who kneels before the High Priestess, holding the chalice out before him. The High Priestess holds her hands over the chalice, and says:

> *From the rain to the root, from the root to the vine,*
> *from the vine to the berry, from the berry to the wine,*
> *from the wine to the cup, I instill the blessings of our Mother*
> *into this wine. So mote it be!*

All: *So mote it be!*

The High Priestess picks up the athame, lowering the blade slowly into the chalice, saying:

> *As the rod is to the God, so the chalice is to the Goddess,*
> *and together they are one!*

The High Priestess presents the cup to the High Priest, who drinks while she says:

> *May you never thirst.*

The Drummer begins a slow, steady beat.

The High Priest presents the cup to the High Priestess in the same manner. The High Priestess presents the cup to the Temple Summoner in the same manner, who presents the cup to the Maiden, who presents the cup to the first Covener clockwise in the circle. After the cup has returned to the Maiden, she pours a bit in the libation bowl at the foot of the altar or shrine, then puts the chalice back on the altar or shrine.

The Drummer stops.

The Temple Summoner gives the plate of cakes to the High Priestess, who kneels at the feet of the High Priest, holding up the tray. The High Priest holds his hand over the tray and says:

> *From the sun to the root, from the root to the stalk,*
> *from the stalk to the wheat, from the wheat to the flour,*
> *from the flour to the bread, I instill the blessings of our Father*
> *on these cakes. So mote it be!*

All: *So mote it be!*

The High Priest then presents a cake to the High Priestess, saying:

May you never hunger.

Then she, in turn, presents one to him.

The Drummer starts with a steady, even beat.

The High Priest presents a cake to the Maiden, who presents one to the Temple Summoner, who presents one to the first Covener in the clockwise direction of the circle.

When all have finished, the Temple Summoner takes the tray, puts a cake in the libation bowl at the foot of the altar or shrine, and places the tray back on the altar.

The Drummer stops, and says:

*We have celebrated communion in honor of our Mother and Father
for the intent of* (state purpose of ritual). *So mote it be!*

All: *So mote it be!*

16. **Group Breathing.** The High Priestess says:

*Join with me to ground and center yourselves
through group breathing.*

When she finishes conducting the breathing, she says:

So mote it be!

All: *So mote it be!*

17. **The Final Blessing.** Most traditional groups have the Elder perform the final blessing before the closure of the ritual. The Elder holds his or her hands up over the Coveners and says:

*We are a circle, within a circle, without an ending, with love
ascending. Go now, in peace, prosperity, and joy, and remember
to keep the energies of this ceremony safe in your heart. So mote it be!*

All: *So mote it be!*

18. **Closure.** The closure of the ritual involves the following three components:

   1. Thanking deity.
   2. Closing the Quarters.
   3. Opening the circle.

The Drummer begins a very slow beat, then works slowly into a faster one through the next few steps.

In group ritual, the High Priestess thanks the deity. The High Priest then says:

Prepare to release the Powers of your elements, ye keepers of the Quarters, and close their gifts as the Maiden returns these gifts to their appropriate places.

All turn toward the West.

The Maiden, walking in a widdershins fashion, removes the bowl of water from the feet of the West Quarter, then returns to the West and stands with her back to the circle. The West Quarter turns with his or her back to the center and, beginning with arms open and subsequently closing them, says:

Guardians of the West, element of water, and all ye in the realm of fairy. Epona, great horse, thank you for participating in this ceremony. Go if you must, stay if you like, hail and farewell!

All: *Hail and farewell!*

Then turn toward South.

The Maiden moves next to the South Quarter and removes the fire candle, continues to walk in a widdershins fashion back to the altar or shrine, and deposits the gift there. Again, walking in a widdershins fashion, she returns to the South Quarter. The South Quarter turns with his or her back to the center and, beginning with arms open, and subsequently closing them, says:

Guardians of the South, element of fire, and all ye in the realm of fairy. Tarvos, great bull, thank you for participating in this ceremony. Go if you must, stay if you like, hail and farewell!

All: *Hail and farewell!*

Then turn toward the East.

The Maiden moves to the East Quarter, removes the incense, continues to walk in a widdershins fashion back to the altar or shrine, and deposits the gift there. Again, walking in a widdershins fashion, she returns to the East Quarter. The East Quarter turns with his or her back to the center and, beginning with arms open and subsequently closing them, says:

Detailing the Ritual

Guardians of the East, element of air, and all ye in the realm of fairy.
Herne, great stag, thank you for participating in this ceremony.
Go if you must, stay if you like, hail and farewell!

All: *Hail and farewell!*

Then turn toward the North.

The Maiden moves to the North Quarter, removes the crystal, continuing to walk in a widdershins fashion back to the altar or shrine, and deposits the gift there. Again, walking in a widdershins fashion, she returns to the North Quarter. (She won't have to walk very far if the shrine or altar rests in the North). The North Quarter turns with his or her back to the center and, beginning with arms open and subsequently closing them, says:

Guardians of the North, element of earth, and all ye in the realm of
fairy. Artios, great bear, thank you for participating in this ceremony.
Go if you must, stay if you like, hail and farewell!

All: *Hail and farewell!*

The Maiden returns to her original place. **Note:** In some Craft groups this procedure is done clockwise (deosil).

The High Priestess steps forward and, beginning at the West, removes the inner circle (drawing the circle into her hand) by walking the circle widdershins. Again—some perform this deosil.

The High Priest steps forward and, beginning at the West, removes the second circle (drawing the circle into his hand) by walking the circle widdershins. Again—some perform this deosil.

The Temple Summoner steps forward and, beginning at the West, removes the outer circle (drawing the circle into his hand) by walking the circle widdershins. Again—some perform this deosil.

All three walk to the center and place the hand holding the circle one on top of the other. Together, the three release the circle.

The Maiden takes the libation bowl and places it out-of-doors, offering the contents to the Gods, while the group sings:

Now our work is done and the change has begun;
Let us go in joy and peace.

When the Maiden returns, the High Priestess pounds the ground and says:

This circle is open, but never broken. Merry meet and merry part,
until we merry meet again. We are the people, we are the power.
We are the change!

The group can continue to sing as they clean up the area.

Whew! How's that for a full script? It takes as long to write as it does to perform! Did you read the script visualizing actual people performing the parts? You might want to tape the script and play your tape back, visualizing the ritual as you listen. As you can see, the formal ritual has many, many steps and a great deal of choreography. If you ad-libbed any sections, such as the communion or the Quarter calls, then you would have a complex ritual. Notice again that we gave the Drummer the responsibility of stating and re-affirming the purpose of the ritual throughout the script. You can give this responsibility to anyone; however, by giving this task to the Drummer, you actually give him or her the responsibility of queuing the major players in the various portions of the ritual, thus allowing this person to set the pace of the ritual. In a Shamanic ritual, the Drummer is just as important as that of the High Priest and High Priestess.

Informal Ritual

An informal ritual holds some scripted information or memorized, generic passages, uses few tools, and usually takes anywhere from fifteen minutes to a half-hour to perform (depending upon the number of people involved). Many of the rituals in this book fall under the informal ritual heading. You'll find steps often combined in an informal ritual, but rarely deleted. For example, rather than blessing the cakes and beverage separately, you might bless them together. You can cast a circle with a hug, rather than practicing the circle casting we find familiar (single or triple). You might cleanse and consecrate everyone at the same time, rather than separately. The following two moon rituals, written by Breid FoxSong, give an example of the informal ritual format. Ad-libbing by all players in an informal ritual seems to come naturally.

An informal ritual, then, (1) combines steps; and (2) allows liberal deviation.

Informal Master Moon Rituals

Part of the mystique of the Craft lies in our companionship with the moon. Unlike the structured religions of our time, we celebrate most of our services in the dark, gaining strength from the soft light of the moon and our belief in this heavenly body's relationship with our Goddess. We use candles indoors to substitute for the delicate touch of moon. To us, the dark manifests as the endless possibility of the universe—where the act of lighting candles, working by firelight, or moving through the cool essence of moonlight represents our shining spirits traveling through the unknown, and the spirit of the All manifesting within our lives. We do not celebrate the dark as something dank and evil but rather as the birth of the soul from the void.

Although a Witch can design and perform a ritual at any time, moon rituals, whether full or new, provide auspicious timing for magickal work. In some traditions, the full moon represents a banishing time, where the new moon provides a time for growth; however, other traditions view the full moon as an "all-purpose" force of energy, where the new moon remains the primary representation of birth.

Breid FoxSong, my close friend and teacher, has graciously shared a master moon and new moon ritual for your use. Feel free to tailor these rituals to meet your needs.

Solitary Master Informal New Moon Ritual by Breid FoxSong[2]

Before the ritual, write on a piece of paper something that you want to start or change in the coming months, such as a project, a life decision, a new attitude, et cetera. Rub cinnamon on the paper. You will also need: Illuminator candles, a single altar candle, incense, salt, a cup or bowl of water, a candle for each Quarter (North—Green; East—Yellow; South—Red; West—Blue), simple food on a plate (such as bread, cookies, cake, or fruit); wine or juice in a cup or chalice; a separate cup placed at the foot of the altar for your libation to the Gods, a fireproof cauldron containing one teaspoon of alcohol and ¼ teaspoon of Epsom salts.

---

2. Breid FoxSong, having spent most of her life in Colorado and California, now resides near Buffalo, New York. A British Tradition Priestess, she has practiced for over twenty years, hoping that someday she'll be good enough for Carnegie Hall. A cornerstone of her faith is that you never stop learning, from all kinds of sources. Breid teaches a Wicca 101 class in Strange Brew, a Craft shop in Kenmore, and organizes four open circles a year on the Fire Festivals along with her husband and partner, Joe, and her coven, Balefyre. Their public ritual style is best described as "Southern Revivalist Wicca." Breid and Joe have performed rituals for groups of 100 or more (up to 500) people, and have written and performed several main rituals for festivals, including Dragonfest in Colorado and the Heartland Pagan festival in Kansas.

Step One: Set up your altar with your continuity for arrangement. (You'll find complete traditional and non-traditional altar set-ups in my book *To Stir A Magick Cauldron,* should you wish to study altar arrangement.) For this master ritual, we focus on the cauldron and altar candle, placed at the center of the altar. Of course, you could do this rite in your shrine area, making adjustments for placement of items.

Step Two: Begin the actual ritual after dark. Ground and center. Light the illuminator candles first, or if you have prepared Mother and Father candles, light them now. Breathe deeply and prepare your mind for magick. If you have a standard altar devotion, do that now, or light the altar candle and charcoal for the incense, saying:

> *Children of Light. I greet You with Light.*
> *Bless this space with your presence.*

Carry the altar candle and incense around the area you have designated to raise your circle, so that the light reaches all corners of the room.

Step Three: Mix a few grains of salt into the cup of water and stir, saying:

> *Children of the Earth and Sea, I greet You by your own.*
> *Bless this space with your presence.*

Carry the cup around the circle. You can sprinkle a little water to help cleanse the area if you desire.

Step Four: Notice in this particular ritual that the circle casting and Quarter calls combine into one function. As you call the Quarters, you build the circle, therefore, you need to keep this visualization in mind as you walk from one Quarter to the next. The same type of visualization occurs when you release the Quarters. This Quarter to Quarter circle casting builds and subsequently takes down, the circle in stages. Call the Guardians of the circle, beginning in the East. (If you prefer, you can begin at the North; remember the order of calling from East through North, or from North through West, rests as a matter of personal preference.) Stand at the Quarter and visualize the Guardian coming to join you. Open your arms slowly, saying:

> *I call the Guardians of the East, Keepers of Air. The wind blows*
> *mysteries to me at dawn, the scent of spring is carried on the breeze.*
> *Come! And be welcome in this circle!*

Detailing the Ritual

Stand at the South Quarter, open your arms slowly, saying:

I call the Guardians of the South, Keepers of Fire. The fire in my heart brings me strength and love. Summer's heat and solar blaze will keep me warm! Come! And be welcome in this circle!

Stand at the West Quarter, open your arms slowly, saying:

I call the Guardians of the West, Keepers of Water. Rivers running free; oceans, the womb of life, Autumn's harvest comes by your bounty! Come! And be welcome in this circle!

Go to the North Quarter, open your arms slowly, saying:

I call the Guardians of the North, Keepers of Earth. The winter is dark, holding its secrets! Mother Earth, your womb is creation. Come! And be welcome in this circle!

Walk to the center of the circle, and hold your hands, palm downward over the altar, and say:

I call the Guardians of the Center, Keepers of the Life Force. New Moon, the low tide begins to turn upward, as the moon waxes, so too will I grow and change. The Lady moves from Dark to Light, the Cycle of Life continues! Come! And be welcome in this circle!

Step Five: Hold the paper with your goal or change in your hands, and say softly:

This is the time of new beginnings, when the changes I make tonight will continue to help me to grow and become stronger in my faith.

Hold the altar candle out over the cauldron and light the paper with your wish or desire on it. Once it is burning, drop it in the cauldron or bowl, (be careful of your alcohol combination, the flame will flare) and say:

This is my goal, my direction, my beginning.

Step Six: Using one of the hocus-focus exercises I gave you in chapter three, concentrate on your desire. Then softly chant, *"As I will, so mote it be!"* over and over until you feel you've sufficiently given your mind that necessary kick-start to manifest the goal. You can substitute any chant, add drumming, the sound of the rattle, a singing bowl, et cetera.

Step Seven: When you have finished the chant put one hand over the food on the altar, and the other over the cup of wine or juice, and say:

Nourishment for the soul and body, nourishment for the mind and heart, when all find balance, I am whole. So mote it be!

Pour a bit of the wine or juice in the libation cup, saying: "For the Gods." From your own chalice and the food you placed on the altar, eat and drink, sharing thought with the Goddess until you wish to finish the circle.

Step Eight: Take down the circle, starting with the center, placing your hands over the altar, saying:

Oh Guardians of the Center, thank you for joining my worship this night. May you travel safely and well to your home. My thanks and farewell! Blessed be!

Extinguish the altar candle.

Go to the North and raise your hands, visualizing the Guardian leaving as you say:

O Guardians of the North, thank you for joining our worship this night. May you travel safely and well to your home. My thanks and farewell! Blessed be!

Extinguish the candle.

Go to the West and raise your hands, visualizing the Guardian leaving as you say:

O Guardians of the West, thank you for joining our worship this night. May you travel safely and well to your home. My thanks and farewell! Blessed be!

Extinguish the candle.

Go to the South and raise your hands, visualizing the Guardian leaving as you say:

O Guardians of the South, thank you for joining my worship this night. May you travel safely and well to your home. My thanks and farewell! Blessed be!

Extinguish the candle.

Go to the East and raise your hands, visualizing the Guardian leaving as you say:

O Guardians of the East, thank you for joining my worship this right.
May you travel safely and well to your home.
My thanks and farewell! Blessed be!

Extinguish the candle.

Return to the center and say:

My rite ends, but my love remains. The circle lifts and I return
to my everyday world. By the grace of the God, and the love
of the Goddess, we will join again!

Ground and center. Dispose of the contents of the libation bowl and the cauldron out-of-doors.

Solitary Master Informal Full Moon Ritual: Celtic Rendition by Breid FoxSong

You will need: Illuminator candles (or your Mother and Father candles), a single altar candle, incense, salt, a cup or bowl of water, a candle for each Quarter (North—Green; East—Yellow; South—Red; West—Blue), simple food on a plate (such as bread, cookies, cake, or fruit); wine or juice in a cup or chalice; a separate cup placed at the foot of the altar for your libation to the Gods. Have any other supplies ready that correspond to your working for this night.

Step One: Set up your altar with your continuity for arrangement

Step Two: Begin the actual ritual after dark. Ground and center. Light the illuminator candles first, or if you have made Mother and Father candles, light them now. Breathe deeply and prepare your mind for magick. If you have a standard altar devotion, do that now, or light the altar candle and charcoal for the incense, saying:

Children of Light. I greet You with Light.
Bless this space with your presence.

Carry the altar candle and incense around the area you have designated to raise your circle, so that the light reaches all corners of the room.

Step Three: Mix a few grains of salt into the cup of water and stir, saying:

Children of the Earth and Sea, I greet You by your own.
Bless this space with your presence.

Carry the cup around the circle. You can sprinkle a little water to help cleanse the area if you desire.

Step Four: Again, the circle casting and Quarter calls combine into one function. Call the Deities, beginning in the East. (If you prefer, you can begin at the North; remember the order of calling from East through North, or from North through West, rests as a matter of personal preference.) Stand at the Quarter and visualize the Deities coming to join you. Open your arms slowly, saying:

Arionhrod, Taranis, be with me this night; share with me
the powers of clarity and compassion.

Stand at the South Quarter, open your arms slowly, saying:

Brigid, Lugh, be with me this night; share with me
the powers of passion and forgiveness.

Stand at the West Quarter, open your arms slowly, saying:

Rhiannon, Manonnon, be with me this night; share with me
the powers of love and laughter."

Go to the North Quarter, open your arms slowly, saying:

Cerridwyn, Cernunnos, be with me this night; share with me
the powers of strength and understanding.

Walk to the center of the circle, and hold your hands, palm downward over the altar, and say:

Great Mother, Great Father, in all your aspects, be with me tonight;
share with me the power and the knowledge that you are me,
and that I am you.

Step Five: Do any magick you have come to do, or meditate on the season and the changes in your life. This is a good time to think about what the deities mean to you in daily life, or how you can help make the world a better place to be in. It is also a good time to relax and simply *be* . . . allowing the moment to last as long as you need. You can play music or you can dance . . . it is a time to be in contact with the Goddess and God within you.

Step Six: When you have finished put one hand over the food on the altar, and the other over the cup of wine or juice, and say:

> *Nourishment for the soul and body,*
> *nourishment for the mind and heart.*
> *When all find balance, I am whole. So mote it be!*

Pour a bit of the wine or juice in the libation cup, saying: *For the Gods.* From your own chalice and the food you placed on the altar, eat and drink, sharing thought with the Goddess until you wish to finish the circle.

Step Seven: Take down the circle, starting with the center, placing your hands over the altar, saying:

> *Great Mother, Great Father, in all your aspects, I ask this of you,*
> *guard me with Your blessings, help me to learn what is needful*
> *to live in Your ways. My thanks and farewell! Blessed be!*

Extinguish the altar candle.

Go to the North and raise your hands, visualizing the deities leaving as you say:

> *Cerridwyn, Cernunnos, and all the deities of the North, I ask this*
> *of you, guard me with your blessings, help me to grow stronger.*
> *My thanks and farewell! Blessed be!*

Extinguish the candle.

Go to the West and raise your hands, visualizing the Guardian leaving as you say:

> *Rhiannon, Manonnon, and all the deities of the West,*
> *I ask this of you, guard me with your blessings,*
> *help me to grow deeper.*
> *My thanks and farewell! Blessed be!*

Extinguish the candle.

Go to the South and raise your hands, visualizing the deities leaving as you say:

Brigid, Lugh, and all the deities of the South, I ask this of you,
guard me with your blessings, help me to be brighter.
My thanks and farewell. Blessed be!

Extinguish the candle.

Go to the East and raise your hands, visualizing the deities leaving as you say:

Arionhrod, Taranis, and all the deities of the East, I ask this of you,
guard me with your blessings, help me to be wiser.
My thanks and farewell. Blessed be!

Extinguish the candle.

Return to the center and say:

My rite ends, but my love remains. The circle lifts and I return to my
everyday world. By the grace of the God and the love of the Goddess,
I will walk in the light!

Ground and center. Dispose of the contents of the libation bowl out-of-doors.

The Basic Ritual

A basic ritual might carry some sort of script; however, this ritual does not contain all the steps or details found in a formal, complex, or informal ritual. Therefore, a basic ritual falls under the heading of a simple ritual. For example, there may not be a circle casting, Quarter calls, or communion. Basic rituals work better for two or three people, or solitary practice, rather than for group interaction, simply because groups of people use the various steps in formal and complex rituals as successive triggers. Let's face it, the more people in a room, the more data exists for the conscious mind to deliver to the brain. If you give the conscious mind lots to do, then it will stop worrying about whether or not your robe is as good as Sally's, the fact that James always acts like an idiot when he's supposed to meditate, and so forth. This is not to say you can't perform a basic ritual in a group format.

Let's try a sample basic ritual together. I don't know about you, but I have had periods in my life when I feel like nothing moves the way it should. I experience days, sometimes weeks, when I think, "If I just had this under control . . . ." To build order from chaos, I devised the following basic ritual. This ritual consists of the following steps:

Cleansing and consecrating the area where the ritual will be performed

Casting a magick circle dedicated to a higher power worded to reinforce the intent

Calling the chosen Quarters worded to reinforce the intent

Speaking an invocation to a higher power worded to reinforce the intent

Doing the actual working, which may be a spell, a meditation, or an act of honor strategically built around your intent (in this case, we are going to use a spell)

Thanking deity

Releasing Quarters, worded to reinforce the intent

Closing the circle

Grounding

Clean-up

Notice I've left out many of the steps found in the formal ritual, and have eliminated the communion. Let's do a basic ritual together, so you can see the difference between the formal, informal, and basic format.

Taking Control of Your Life

For this ritual you will need: A sage smudge stick, your Mother (or Father) candle, your choice of incense, and set of child's building blocks (Legos™ would be excellent).

Cleansing and consecrating the area where the ritual will be performed.

Let's assume you plan to use your shrine area for this working; however, if you feel more comfortable using your altar, that's okay too. Since you have already cleansed the shrine area, then subsequently consecrated and empowered the area, you don't need to follow that procedure now. Today, we will smudge the area with sage, using a generic phrase:

By this creature of smoke and fire, I purify this space.
May all impurities flee before its approach. May my hopes and
aspirations rise with this veil of smoke, carried by the element of air
to the Lady and Lord. With each step I take, I gain control over my
own life, and handle all situations with wisdom.

Casting a magick circle dedicated to a higher power worded to reinforce your intent. Begin at the North, and walk deosil (clockwise), and cast the circle with your palm outward and a bit down, saying:

I conjure thee, O world-hedge of power, so that you will be for me,
a boundary between the world of the human and mighty spirits.
A meeting place of perfect love, peace, trust, and joy, containing the
power I raise within thee. I call upon the powers of the North, the East,
the South, and the West to aid me in this consecration. In the name of
the Veiled Lady and Hooded Lord, thus do I conjure thee O great
world-hedge of power, to assist me in taking control of my own life,
and handle all situations with wisdom. So mote it be!

Stamp your foot on the ground and say:

This circle is sealed!

In some traditions, magickal practitioners begin to cast the circle at the Quarter that closest represents the time of day of the working. North would be midnight. East equates to dawn, South to noon, and West to twilight. For example, let's say it is three o'clock on July 25. If you decided to cast your circle at four in the afternoon, then you may choose South to begin, as that would be closest to noon during summer hours. If you were casting the circle at the same time in December, when the length of light is shorter in the Northern Hemisphere, you may wish to begin casting the circle in the West, at the twilight indicator. Other traditions have seasonal Quarters, where Spring equates to East, South to Summer, West to Fall, and North to Winter. If, on July 25, you decided to do this particular magickal working, then you would start at the South Quarter. The proverbial bottom line here says you should begin at the Quarter where you feel most comfortable. Not where I tell you to start. Not where someone else tells you to start, but where you feel the appropriate beginning energies should be for what you want to do.

Calling the chosen Quarters worded to reinforce your intent. Although I'll give you generic calls, you really should try to fashion Quarter calls for yourself that focus directly on your intent. I always begin at the North Quarter, but you can start wherever you feel most appropriate. I stand at the North Quarter, arms crossed over my chest. As I say the Quarter call, I open my arms slowly, envisioning a portal opening, and the element and totem animal of that Quarter coming through:

Detailing the Ritual

Guardians of the North, Element of Earth, home of the bear. I call ye forth. To witness this rite, and to help me take control of my life. And handle all situations with wisdom. May ye guard this sacred space.

I've alerted the ancestors of the North (so I've stirred them). I've summoned the element of Earth. I've called the bear. Next:

Guardians of the East, element of Air, home of the Stag.
I call ye forth to witness this rite, and to help me take control
of my life. And handle all situations with wisdom.
May ye guard this sacred space.

Guardians of the South, element of Fire, home of the Bull.
I call ye forth to witness this rite, and to help me take control
of my life. And handle all situations with wisdom.
May ye guard this sacred space.

Guardians of the West, element of Water, home of the Horse.
I call ye forth to witness this rite, and to help me take control
of my life. And handle all situations with wisdom.
May ye guard this sacred space.

Notice that for the third time, we have stated our intent—*to help me take control of my own life.* The repetitive nature of this ritual allows you to cement your desire firmly in your brain, as well as in the universe. Notice also that I didn't summon the elements this time, I called them, and I did not stir the ancestral dead.

Speaking an invocation to a higher power worded to reinforce your intent. Again, I suggest you write this yourself; but if you just can't seem to come up with something, feel free to use the following invocation:

Veiled Lady, She who walks through mists of time, whose power knows
no bounds, whose eternal love permeates the Universe. Descend upon
the body of thy Priest(ess) *and Witch so that I may be able to take*
control of my life and handle all situations with wisdom.

or

Hooded God, He who protects the Hidden Children, whose
tremendous strength cannot be matched, whose eternal love knows no

> *bounds. Descend upon the body of thy Priest*(ess) *and Witch*
> *so that I may be able to take control of my life*
> *and handle all situations with wisdom.*

or

> *I call upon thee, Ancient Mother, to enter this sacred space. Mother of*
> *Light; Mother of Love; Mother of Life; Grant me with the ability to*
> *control my life and handle all situations with wisdom.*

Invoke the God or Goddess by bringing this energy into the circle, or moving the energy into yourself. If you call divinity into your own body, you experience divine possession. Now, don't get your knickers in a twist. Divine possession will not hurt you. Christians practice divine possession when they say they have been "touched by the spirit" or blessed by the Holy Ghost. Some of the more fundamentalist factions speak in tongues, which they consider a manifestation of divinity. In the Voodoo and Santerian religions, divine possession is quite common. Today, we have pretty words, such as "channeling," "aspecting," and so on; however, we are talking about the same sort of experience—possession by deity to assist you in whatever goal you desire to manifest. In this case, we again affirm the purpose of this working: So that I may be able to take control of my life, and handle all situations with wisdom.

Doing the actual working, which might relate to a spell, a meditation, or an act of honor strategically built around your intent (in this case, we are going to use a spell). Cleanse, consecrate, and empower the building blocks. Set them in a pile in the middle of your altar. Pick up the first block, and say:

> *As I place this first block on my altar, I begin to build order from*
> *chaos. I gain control of my life. I handle all situations with wisdom.*

Spend time building something neat on your altar. Each time you add a block, say the same words. In between, you could chant or sing. When you have used all your blocks, hold your hands over your creation, and say:

> *I have brought order into chaos. I have gained control*
> *over my own life. From this moment forward I will handle*
> *all situations with wisdom.*

Draw energy up through the ground into your feet, on up through your hands. Feel the power of divinity spiral down into your head, then through your hands. Gather the energies of the elements, from each direction, into your body, and out through your hands. Visualize the type of person you want to be. When you finish, drop your hands and take a deep breath. Ground and center. Again, we have reaffirmed the purpose of the ritual.

Thanking deity. Don't forget your manners. Thank deity for assisting you, not only in the performance of this ritual, but in the asked for results as well.

Spontaneous Rituals

Spontaneous rituals contain a basic plan of action, and . . . you take it from there. Where formal ritual provides no room for error and complex rituals leave only slight room for error, informal, basic, and spontaneous rituals allow the participant greater freedom. Many of the spells in this book would lend themselves well to the spontaneous ritual, and many of the Pow-Wow applications in this book (and in *American Folk Magick*) function best in a spontaneous ritual format. Groups normally practice either formal, complex, or informal ritual. The group environment does not usually suit spontaneous ritual (especially large groups of twenty or more) due to the tendency of group chaos rather than aligned manifestation of the intent. It takes a strong willed High Priest and/or High Priestess to run a good spontaneous ritual. In a good spontaneous group ritual the control is there, you just don't see it.

Now, excuse me just a moment while I put on my asbestos cape and pointy hat. Wait . . . the hat is slipping over my eye . . . there, that's better. Thank you. Historically, complex and informal rituals work best for long-term group mental health, where formal and spontaneous rituals have a tendency either to smother creativity or allow too much of it. Formal rituals foster dictatorial relationships and the ebb of power, whereas spontaneous rituals leave too much room for error and uncontrolled energy. Remember, don't construe ritual as a game. You can make mistakes that will affect more than you may be aware of at the time. Of course I realize that exceptions always exist to almost any rule, and that some groups have managed to last for many years practicing nothing but formal or spontaneous rituals! The best rule of thumb for any group that wishes long-term involvement with each other, is to primarily practice complex and informal rituals, with a few well designed formal and spontaneous rituals to take the edge off of boredom.

As a solitary practitioner, whether you belong to a regular group or not, you can utilize all forms of ritual with ease. The type of format you choose depends upon the amount of time, preparation, and lifestyle you have available to you. Regardless of the format you use, remember that *the main purpose of ritual focuses on the attunement of your mind to the natural forces of the universe.* Ritual functions as a form of auto-suggestion in which your subconscious mind becomes receptive to various energy patterns of your choosing. Indeed, we use ritual to fascinate (or seduce) the conscious mind, so that the subconscious mind can let its proverbial hair down, and work real magick. In Craft ritual, the mask of day-to-day living dissolves, revealing the true nature of the practitioner. At the same time, Craft ritual allows you to touch the mysteries of the divine, pulling those beautiful, liquid pulses into yourself to manifest outward change.

All individuals can use ritual, regardless of race, religion, philosophy, theology, social standing, age, or sexual orientation. Regardless of what you may think, anyone can write a ritual. You don't need a 4.0 average in ritual writing to construct or perform a ritual for yourself. You do not need to run out and buy a book of spells and rituals in order to accomplish your most fervent desires. Ritual functions as a natural extension of human behavior, and should never be viewed as either unnatural or frightening. Indeed, the best rituals you perform on a solitary basis are those rituals you design yourself. Why? A ritual tailored to your specific needs will hold more power, because the words belong to you, therefore the symbolism and images remain specifically your own.

You can perform ritual with, or without physical objects. You don't need an entire room full of amazing tools to conduct a ritual. Each evening I perform a blessing ritual in my head, before I fall asleep. I mentally walk through the steps, visualize places, things, and desires, and then allow myself to drift off. In this way, I continually train my mind to go beyond physical props, strengthening my skills in the realm of mental magicks.

Although scripted rituals can have their place, I have encouraged my students to write their own rituals, and to reach out and touch their inner creativity through the use of complex, informal, basic, or spontaneous ritual. From this self-actualization comes security, an improved self-image, and the knowledge of one's personal power. Besides, I'll be the first one to tell you I make more mistakes in a formal, scripted ritual than anyone else. Also, there is nothing more irritating than standing around in a circle with twenty people, while three or four well meaning individuals rustle pages, drop clip boards, read long, boring passages, and look like cardboard stage props. I'm not saying all scripted rituals manifest like that, but I've attended enough of them to know that group interest dies when dogma takes over. In fairness, the absolute worst ritual I ever attended revolved around a young man giving a spontaneous, forty-five minute non-scripted, free-form dissertation that lost me in its meaning three minutes into the soliloquy. I was wishing then, let me tell you, that he had a script, so I could judge just how long I would experience boredom.

Detailing the Ritual

In WitchCraft, whether you work alone or in a group, all ritual performance unfolds either in a magick circle or sacred space. Briefly, sacred space consists of cleansing and consecrating the area, then calling the Quarters (or not calling them); where a magick circle consists of cleansing and consecrating the area, casting a magick circle dedicated to deity, and then calling (or not) the Quarters.[3] Your magick circle becomes an immensely powerful energy configuration. Whatever you draw into that image through mental and physical acts, evolves into a real force that will manifest itself in the outer world, once that magick circle dissolves. If you make a mistake in ritual, the error will manifest outside the circle, unless, of course, you remember to fix the error.

For example, a friend of mine tells the story of a wonderful group ritual done several years ago. The group had such a fantastic time in the ritual, that they forgot to close the Quarters. The next day, everyone who participated in the ritual stomped around the festival grounds in an irritable, bitchy, and downright grumpy mood. Finally, someone remembered that the group had forgotten to dismiss the Quarters, therefore the Quarter energies (I have no clue *what* they called) were still there, at the ritual site, tapping their little footsies, waiting for release by the stupid humans who originally called them. Once they ritually released the Quarters, everyone got back to acting like happy little Pagans.

In the life of a Witch, the magick circle constitutes the foundation of ritual work, where the Witch becomes the center of the magick, therefore we always dedicate the circle to a higher power. In the case of the Witch, we usually dedicate the circle to The Lord and the Lady, the God and the Goddess, the Mother, the Father, or archetypes (seen as extensions of the God and the Goddess). The invocations, symbols, triggers, salutes, chants, and psychic manifestations of the Witch act as deliveries of conscious thought that bridge to universal energies available to us all. By creating this bridge, our stated goals and desires will manifest. The more we state these goals during the ritual format, through the choreography of sight, sound, and movement in invocations, statement of intent, energy raising, and other ceremonial portions (such as communion or the Great Rite), the stronger the bridge. The more the Witch focuses his or her physical and mental senses on manifesting the desire, the less his or her conscious mind will fight to sabotage the entire ritual.

---

3. For complete instructions on sacred space, casting a magick circle, or calling Quarters, please refer to *To Stir A Magick Cauldron* (Llewellyn Publications, 1995).

The Black Forest Healing Ritual

I've received thousands of letters from individuals who have read my books, then subsequently found an interested friend or two, and are now looking for some sort of ritual or activity to employ their magickal techniques, help others, and heighten their own spirituality. Several years ago, a friend of mine and I began what are now known as our famous Black Forest Healing Circles. Any number of people can participate; however, with a group over thirteen, you will need to change a bit of the original structure.

I'll explain how our circles run, and then you can pick and choose what aspects you would like to keep, enhance, or drop for your own circles. The nice thing about healing circles centers on their informal approach to magick. We use a great deal of spontaneous dialogue, welcome humor, and information not bound by any Trad secrets. Anyone can participate, regardless of religious background. For those of you who have only experienced very structured rituals, hold on to your witchie hat, because we break almost *all* the rules of formal ritual content and *still* have an effective and successful ritual.

In the beginning, my friend and I set up a card table, put a candle and a fire-proof cauldron in the middle, and worked with only three to five people. Over time, our healing circle grew to almost thirty, sometimes more. When Mick and I began traveling and doing seminars, we learned to incorporate our techniques with a larger group, basically for instruction, so that they could take the ideas back with them and try the circles on a smaller scale. The largest group that has performed this Healing Circle numbered a bit over 700 people. However, in this example we use a minimum of players.

You don't need many supplies for a healing circle. A candle, a fire-proof cauldron, small pieces of paper and pens for everyone—and that's about it. We added incense, soft music, a sage stick, a big pot of coffee, munchies . . . and later on drums, rattles, and other musical thingies.

Here's how a healing circle runs at my house. Before 8:00 P.M. I clean the dining room (or the back porch if the weather is good) and cleanse the area with sage or other incense. If it's been a particularly bad week, I may cleanse the area with my drum, a rattle, or salt. I put on a pot of coffee (the big pot takes an hour to perk), pick the music for the evening and load it into the CD player, and put out a stack of slips of paper and a box of pens. I set the cauldron in the middle of the table, and, depending upon the season, put a decoration or two around the cauldron (flowers, a Goddess or God statue, et cetera). I use oil lamps for sufficient lighting during circle, so I make sure they are cleaned (usually, sometimes those chimneys escape me) and filled. I set them at strategic places in the room or hang them from nails in the ceiling of the back porch. I say strategic because when you get a lot of people crammed together in my tiny dining room, you've got to place things where they aren't going to get knocked over.

As the coffee pot perks, I make sure there are plenty of disposable cups, cream and sugar on the counter. Sometimes I make a separate pot of decaffeinated tea for those folks who can't stomach caffeine. Beside these two pots goes the donation box. Why the donation box? If you are seriously planning to do this kind of activity, then keep in mind you are going to lose things. For example, I've replaced my dining room table, chairs, a toilet, the bathroom vanity, two coffee pots, my kitchen floor, a picnic table, and I've had to repaint my dining room twice since I've begun inviting loads of people into my house. Lots of bodies put wear and tear on your house—there's just no doubt about it. Also, you will need the money to buy candles, oils, incense, paper, and pens. Of course, you can always ask that these items be donated.

Back to the healing circle. About fifteen minutes before 8:00 P.M., I go into my room and chill out. I usually just lie on my bed and relax, clear away all the junk in my head, and get myself mentally ready to play hostess as well as work magick. I have a very stern rule here. Nobody is to show up before 8:00 P.M. I have a family and I hate it when I've been working all day, have thrown together a late dinner, and people walk in a half hour early while we are sitting around the table still eating dinner. Sorry if this makes me crabby, but my kids are very important to me, and over the years, I've had to learn to separate group activities from the kids, allowing them to get their needed time with me, and with each other, without disruption.

Once everyone has gathered around the table, I give them a chance to chat, catch up on gossip, show each other things they've brought, or whatever. This is also the time for them to write their healing or other requests down on the pieces of paper. One request per paper. You can ask for a new job, help in any type of difficulty, etc. At the top of each piece of paper they write down one of these five categories: Love, Money, Protection, Healing, or Other. Close to 8:30 a pre-selected individual gathers up the papers and separates them into piles, according to the keyword written at the top of the paper. You don't have to sign your name to the paper if you don't want to, but when you are working with a small group, you can figure out who the request belongs to anyway. Around 8:30 P.M., we get down to business. There is no smoking or eating during a healing circle, but they do drink coffee, water, and tea. We put on the music, turn down the lights, get situated in our chairs, and begin.

First, we pass a bowl with a candle or lit sage clockwise from one person to another. Each individual does a mental cleansing, then offers the light up to the universe before passing the bowl along. As the bowl moves from person to person, regular conversation ceases. When the bowl reaches full circle, the first person will do the cleansing again, and say something like:

"We have gathered here together to work as one in the combined effort of helping ourselves and helping others. We call upon the Lord and Lady to assist us in our workings here tonight. We ask for their blessings, their power, and their love. So mote it be!"

If only a few of you plan to participate in a healing ritual, then you can do each request separately. If you have a large group, then sticking to the categories of Love, Money, Protection, Healing, and Other might be a good idea, or separate the categories into groups of two each. The idea is to get everyone to participate, so separate the papers accordingly.

Let's go through some of the categories to show you how you can diversify the healing circle. Let's pretend we have five individuals at the table—Sam, Harold, Jenny, Alicia, and Ruth. And, for clarity's sake, let's say that the house belongs to Ruth, so she's the pseudo leader (because there is really no leader in a healing circle.) Ruth has the papers in front of her. She lights the tea candle in the cauldron and says, "Is everybody ready?" After the establishment of mutual consent (Sam had to go to the bathroom quick), Ruth might say, "Let's do the healing category first. Who feels like they'd like to do that one?"

"I'll do it," says Harold eagerly, "I feel pretty darned good tonight!"

Ruth passes the papers to Harold, who sets them out in front of him so he can read each one. Everyone holds hands.

"Which way are we going?" asks Alicia.

"Well," Harold answers, "we'll do the banishing illness requests first, so we'll want to send the energy widdershins, so that means we push from our right hands around the circle."

"Sounds good to me," remarks Sam, shaking Alicia's right hand in the air and grinning.

"You only like to do these healing circles so you can hold my hand," remarks Alicia.

Ruth sniffs reprovingly, but smiles. "Let's get on with it, shall we?"

Harold closes his eyes and says, "There is one power, which is the God and Goddess, which is perfect in truth, order, clarity and mutual good. We hereby call on the

Universal energies of healing to assist the following individuals."[4] Harold takes a deep breath, opens his eyes and begins to read the papers in front of him. "For Ruth's mother who is currently in the hospital with the flu, may the disease be banished from her quickly. For Alicia's sister, who has a benign tumor in her right side, may it continue to shrink in size . . ."

"Here, here!" whispers Alicia.

"For Janice Doppelfinger, who is making a valiant effort to lose weight because of her heart condition, and for Bruce Haffer, who is trying to banish depression from his life," continues Harold. "We ask for the assistance of divinity in these matters, and may all astrological correspondences be correct for this working."

The group begins to raise energy. Alicia rocks back and forth. Ruth begins to hum, Sam joins in, then Jenny, followed by Alicia and Harold. As their humming increases they begin to raise their hands. At the apex, when Harold feels they have raised enough energy, he shouts, "Release!" and all allow the energy to travel into the Universe. It's Harold's job to direct that energy. Then he says, "With harm to none, may this spell not reverse or place upon us any curse!"

"Yes!" shouts Jenny, clapping her hands. "That was a good one! I could really feel the energy!" She reaches over and takes the papers, then one by one, burns them in the cauldron. Each individual watches as the flames in the cauldron consume the slips of paper. As they watch the papers burn, they chant the word "change" or they may say together:

Paper will give way to flame
The essence of the word remains
Fire destroy and fire create
Let what's written be their fate
Fly to the Mother, fiery bird
Bring back the fact behind the word—
Change!

"That felt great!" says Sam, reluctantly letting go of Alicia's hand.

"For Pete's sakes," says Alicia, looking at Sam. "We've been married for over two months! You can hold my hand all you want to at home!"

Sam grins and gives her a kiss on the cheek. "Can't fault a fellow for trying." Alicia slaps him playfully. "What's next?"

---

4. Opening attributed to Marion Weinstein, author of *Earth Power* and *Positive Magick*.

Harold scratches his head. "The rest of the healing papers. These are for increasing healing, so we would move the energy deosil." Harold goes through the same process again, except this time, after he's read the papers, he begins to chant softly, "She changes everything She touches; everything She touches, changes!" The chant builds to a loud, foot-stomping crescendo, and the energy given to the Universe.

"Awesome!" says Jenny.

"Way cool!" remarks Sam, as he burns the papers.

"Quite nice," says Ruth. "Now, we have love, money, protection, and the other category left. "Who feels like doing love?"

Alicia elbows Sam. "Let Sam do it. That's all he thinks about."

"Okay, Sam. It appears that Alicia has volunteered your services . . . ." There is a resounding snicker about the table. "How about you do love?"

Sam grins. "Sure. Why not? Hand me those papers and you'll really see some magick fly now."

"Oh, big man on campus," remarks Harold.

"Hey, I'm a pro here," says Sam, patting Alicia's arm. Alicia rolls her eyes.

Sam sets out the papers in front of him. "We don't need to hold hands for this one."

"Oh no," says Ruth. "Not one of these . . . ."

Sam squares his shoulders. "I call upon Venus, she whose lovely face far outshines the most brilliant star in the heavens. She who brings the essence of Universal love into our lives. Come to us, oh Divine Princess, and bestow your gifts upon the following individuals: For Jenny, who is having trouble communicating with her parents right now . . . ."

"Oh yes, please do," mutters Jenny.

"For Amanda Parker, who is going through a terrible divorce. May her psychological wounds be healed, and may the love of the Lord and Lady touch her heart, and for Richard Devon, who recently lost his mother, may he feel the love and caring of the Lord and Lady about him." Sam begins to bang the table, chanting, "Love, Venus, Love, Venus . . . ." and the others join in until the table shakes and the room vibrates. "Release!" yells Sam. Alicia burns the papers.

"You know," says Jenny, "when you were reading my request? I felt like someone put their arms around me and held me real tight, like my guardian angel was giving me love or something. It was nice."

Ruth smiles. "Yes, I thought I saw your aura build, as if there was someone with you."

"Me too," said Alicia. "That was great, Sam!"

"Just ask me to play it again tonight," he says.

"Oh please . . . ." Harold replies.

"What's next?" asks Jenny.

Ruth looks over the remaining papers. "How about money? Who hasn't done one yet? Alicia! Why don't you do money?"

Alicia holds up her hand and shakes her head. "Not me. I've been feeling pretty depressed about my finances lately. Pass it to someone else."

Ruth looks at Jenny. "You're always good with money, how about you do it?"

Jenny steals a look at the bag at her feet. "Okay, if we can use my stuff."

"Oh no," grumbles Harold good naturedly, "she brought THE STUFF."

Jenny nods emphatically, and opens the bag. There is a great deal of banging and clanging as she passes out rattles and tambourines.

"Where's your drum?" asks Alicia.

"I was so anxious to get here, I forgot it," shrugs Jenny.

"I want the big rattle, "says Harold. "Did you remember to bring the big rattle?"

Jenny grins and with a grand shake, produces a large gourd wrapped with a loose netting of dried beans from the bag.

"Decent!" says Harold, snatching at it like a baby coveting a favorite rattle.

Ruth shakes her tambourine delicately. "I always liked the sound of this one."

"Let's stand up," says Jenny. Amid quiet, occasional tings and rattles, Jenny calls on Rosemerta, Goddess of abundance and plenty, then reads off the requests on the money papers. The group slowly moves around the table in a clockwise direction, shaking their instruments and chanting, "More money, more money, more money . . . " They move faster and faster. Harold trips over a chair, but saves himself. Sam recklessly bumps into Alicia more than he has to. Among much laughing, rattling, and giggling, the group raises power, then releases that power to the Universe, collapsing into their chairs.

And so the healing circle continues, each individual contributing in his or her own special way. You can call any God or Goddess, any element, or natural energy, as long as it is positive in nature. You can sit in a chair, stand in the circle, or sit on the floor. It doesn't matter, the work will still get done. You can laugh, giggle, make amusing remarks, or be deadly serious. Still, the work will get done. You can be human . . . and the work will get done. No formal ritual. No script of Shakespearean quality—just words from the heart, joy from the group, and laughter from the soul.

At the end of the requests, Ruth has the members of the circle join hands. Together, they thank the Lord and Lady for assisting them in their work that night, and release any excess energy into the Universe, so that the Gods can handle it appropriately. When they finish, the group wanders out to the coffee pot, while Ruth clears away the magickal tools used. She gives the ashes of the cauldron to the winds, then puts out the food for the hungry circle members.

That's the work.

Why Rituals Bomb

The easiest way to blow up your carefully prepared ritual bridge, is by succumbing to the doubt-bomb. You know, those sneaky, little thoughts, that slither around in the back of our brains while we go about the choreography of our ritual? There are several ways to disarm the doubt-bomb (which is really your conscious mind that hasn't the sense to let go):

- Begin your ritual by doing Hewitt's 3-2-1 pattern. This pattern gives a green light to the subconscious mind and a red-light to the conscious mind. If you participate in a group ritual and you feel that doubt-bomb pulsating beneath the surface, practice Hewitt's 3-2-1 exercise to assist in bringing you back into focus.

- Ground and center, then restate your intent.

- Try using generic Quarter calls, circle castings, or invocations as the need arises. These short, memorized passages will serve you well when the doubt-bomb sizzles close to the exploding point. You'll find generic passages useful when you work in a group environment, and haven't a clue what to say. If you feel embarrassed in ritual because nothing will come out of your mouth (often called a brain-fart), then your energy will go spastic, affecting all the participants (real or imagined on your part).

- Use triggering mechanisms you have used before, such as a favorite salute, air drawn sigils, the lighting of a candle, et cetera.[5]

- Hum, say, or sing a chant, or use your drum or rattle. Of course, if you find yourself in a group-facilitated ritual, you might not have the opportunity to do this; however, keep this technique in mind for your solitary rituals.

- Physical movement will keep your conscious mind busy, so that you can get on with business at hand. Again, you may not be able to move in the group environment, but you can certainly move in a private ritual. Walk the circle

---

5. Check out my book *To Stir A Magick Cauldron* for complete information on salutes and triggers.

deosil (clockwise) to build power, and Widdershins (to dissipate power). If you must stand still, no one will usually say anything if you sway or rock side-to-side, especially if the ritual has a musical background.

Granted, you have less chance of bombing in a solitary ritual, than in a group one, merely due to the head-count-factor. The more people you have participating in a ritual, the more chance you have of something going wrong. Over the years, I've learned to laugh off mistakes, fix them if I can, shrug them off if I can't. I truly believe I make errors in ritual so that I can remember the lesson of humility. Just last week I ran a group full moon ritual and forgot to call the Quarters. Sheesh. I turned around to someone near the end of the ceremony and said, "Oh well, I guess the Quarters weren't supposed to be in this one," and let the situation go a that.

One of the biggest problems in group ritual revolves around the time factor. To have each person participate in an individual manner (such as saying the words "may you never thirst" and passing the chalice to the next person) takes at least five seconds per person. If you have twenty people, then that short time frame expands to approximately two minutes out of the whole ritual. If each individual steps forward, lights a candle, then says a short speech honoring their ancestors, then puts the candle in a cauldron (beside other candles that want to fall down) you may be talking two minutes per person. If your group consists of twenty people, then you are talking forty minutes on just this section of the ritual.

Uh-oh. What should everyone do for those other thirty-eight minutes? I'll tell you what they do. They shuffle their feet, pick at their robe, scratch . . . well, you know, talk to their neighbor, and so on. They are not concentrating on that portion of the ritual and guess what? Not only have you lost their attention, you have debilitated the power of the ritual. Better to hand out rattles and other noise makers, slap on a CD, or focus on a chant, than to have everyone playing in their own mental world. Several years ago I participated in a fantastic ritual that had one, major malfunction. We were to walk along a wooded path to a large, open group circle. There were 140 people at this ritual. Without other people, the walk on the path took four minutes. Needless to say, the average person spent over an hour on the path, or waiting at the circle site (if you were one of the first people to get there). If you have taken on the momentous task of a large group ritual, you may want to plan for "dead-time," or consider ways to avoid the boredom bug.

An easy way to get people involved when you do plan for "individual pieces," such as our earlier example in which each individual speaks about an ancestor, is to have the group pass a candle slowly, clockwise around the circle, while someone is doing their thing. At least the focus is on the candle, which in turn, helps to build power, rather than having a bunch of people picking their noses or talking to their neighbors. You could pass around a rattle, or something else, but there is nothing like a moving candle flame in circle.

Now, typically, your brain should float in the alpha state concentrating on that portion of the ritual when everyone else does his or her thing. This means you are to be focused, patient and, above all, quiet. For new people in circle, all three of these things are hard to do (sometimes for experienced people, too). If you get invited to a circle, and there are individual moments, or long boring passages, it is acceptable to close your eyes, do your 3-2-1 deepest, psychic and magickal level exercise, and focus on the intent of the ritual. You can even hold your palms to the circle, if you want to; or palms at your sides, turned slightly up. Sometimes, though, your mind will simply not cooperate. Old thoughts, like sticky candy stuck to the floor, will wad in your mind, gathering clutter and distracting emotions, or the boredom bug repeatedly bites you, and you just can't focus, no matter how hard you try. No problem, even famous Pagans and popular Pagans zone in circle when they're bored. Trust me. Just don't let anyone catch you snoring.

Simple Sacred Space

If you feel uncomfortable repeating a specific Quarter call to create sacred space, you may wish to try chanting at each Quarter. This works particularly well if you must do a ritual for over fifty people, and you would like to make the working interactive. Simply stand at each Quarter and begin to chant. For example, at the North Quarter, you would say: Earth, I am. Repeat thirteen times. If many individuals are in attendance, the group standing near the North and repeat the chant, giving everyone a chance to participate. You can do the Quarters separately, or you can begin at North, move to the East, to the South, and so forth. You will have a round of sound, then, to cast call the Quarters, AND this round of chanting will form your magick circle. The last to finish (which would be you, since you are running this great ritual, right?) uses the chant:

Spirit, I am.

Another popular chant for sacred space can function in the same manner:

The earth, the air, the water, the fire;
return, return, return, return.

I like to use this one on a solitary basis, walking the circle as I chant.

Ritual Openings and Closings

Although I've taken you through the various kinds of ritual, and pulled apart the steps of ritual so that you can better understand the inner workings of this magickal act, I've said nothing about ritual openings and closings. Sometimes done in poetry, and in other cases done with simple words from the heart, ritual openings and closings set the stage and close the curtain of your ritual act. Although you'll see ritual openings and closings in most group work, magickal texts rarely cover the subject because we take these sections of ritual for granted.

The ritual opening takes place before anything begins. Sometimes we use this period to give instructions to key participants in the ritual. Other times, we incorporate this time to explain to non-Wiccan guests what will, and will not happen in the coming ritual. If you are working with a mixed group, such as in a funeral or wedding, then you must explain certain aspects of the ritual for the edification of the participants. For example, "The circle is our holy area. Please do not leave the ritual circle for any reason. If you are ill, or feel you must leave the circle for any reason, please raise your hand, and the Maiden or Temple Summoner will escort you from the proceedings." Finally, you can formulate the opening into a very short poem or statement of purpose. This gives your mind the signal that you are ready to begin the entire procedure. Often, the ritual opening contains mention of the season, the deity of focus, and the purpose of the ritual. From the ritual opening, we move to the altar devotion, and then, finally, to the ritual itself.

A closing acts much like the benediction you often hear in a church service. The closing functions as the final blessing extended upon the participants by the High Priest, High Priestess, or both. Sometimes, the Elder performs the closing. This closing serves as a finishing touch of divinely driven energy. You can create the closing for a solitary ritual as well, said after the release of the circle, wherein you ask for the blessings of the universe to travel with you as you go about your daily life.

Pantheons

In *To Ride* and *To Stir*, I talk minimally about choosing your own pantheon. I don't get into too much discussion on archetype choices because I feel that they should be your own; however, I've received many letters from individuals who don't exactly understand the concept of how to choose a pantheon, and where, once they have made the choice, to find the information. A pantheon represents a set of cultural deities or a religious system of a particular area or era. For example, you'll find

Wiccans and Pagans following various pantheons, including Norse, Germanic (which is almost the same), Heathen (which is close to Wiccan Norse and Wiccan Germanic, but not exactly the same), Roman (Strega Witches and many Pagans and Neo-Pagans), Egyptian (mostly ceremonial practitioners and a few Wiccans), Grecian, and Celtic. The preponderance of Wiccans today use a Celtic pantheon (we're talking about fifty percent here, the other fifty percent split among numerous pantheons). A few Wiccans use Native American pantheons; but a strong warning here—the indigenous Native Americans don't appreciate the practice and will inform you of their feelings if you chance to have them in that type of a circle. The only place where I have seen this type of pantheon use appropriate is: Indigenous Americans who also practice Wicca, or where a Wiccan owns or practices on land that was at one time sacred to a particular tribe, is no longer used by that tribe, yet the energies are still extremely evident. Then the Wiccan is most welcome to honor that deity system. Please don't write me letters on this issue. I'm only relating what I have seen and heard, nothing more.

When choosing a pantheon take two things into consideration:

1. What appeals to you in the gut.
2. What your personal lineage includes.

You may find more power in Germanic Wicca or Pow-Wow magicks if your heritage is primarily German. The Celtic deity system (split remember, into those from Wales, those from Ireland, and those from Britain, although the Celts were also in Spain, Germany, and France) may appeal to you if your ancestors came from that part of the globe. Never ignore your roots. There is power there. If you are a human mutt, then go with what feels right; however, the rule still stands that you shouldn't mix pantheons, and if you do, design the ritual so that you know the energies you have chosen will work well together. This will require experimentation on your part.

Does one work with an entire pantheon? Probably not. In circle you don't want to call hundreds or even twenty deities into your "church" service, especially when choosing deities who have distinct personalities. As Breid FoxSong says, "You wouldn't call a plumber if you needed to fix your television." Most traditional groups choose a total of six or eight deities for regular use, then employ other deities of the same pantheon when the need arises. In the Black Forest Tradition we work with eight standard deities: One for each Quarter, two for center summer, and two for center winter.

We have a specific circle casting that involves these energies that we use for initiations, dedications, sabbats, handfastings, wiccanings, and crossings. For our moons (or esbats) we use a free-for-all system where all pantheons are fair game, as long as you stick within that pantheon.

When we work with the Germanic system, we have a different circle casting, keep the same totem animals, but do not use the same deity correspondences. Here, we use only the Veiled Lady and Hooded Lord, or we employ Dame Holda. When the ladies of the group choose to work a Dianic system, they work with the concept that all Goddesses are representations of the face of The Goddess, yet they are careful which archetypes they choose, and match the energies accordingly to the ceremony.

How do you find out about deity and archetype energies? You research historical and archeological texts. Most magickal books with deity information will give you a good kick-start, but you still need to do plenty of research and experimentation yourself.

More Master Rituals

I learned about master rituals from Nigel Jackson when we wrote *Witches Runes* together, and I've provided several for you throughout this book. Where North American Traditional Witches tend to formulate a separate ritual for each Sabbat, Esbat, or working, European Witches often use a Master Ritual, where the basic outline remains the same, but specific areas change to correspond with a particular subject. There are a few Gardnerian and Alexandrian Traditions that use Master Rituals, but you need to know that not all of them incorporate Master Rituals. Some Master Rituals wax long; others tend to be much shorter. Carefully review any ritual before attempting to perform it. Be sure you know why you are doing each section of the ritual, before doing any section.

Rituals—good rituals, take time to learn and time to learn how to perform. One doesn't normally do fantastically at every ritual, whether you've been doing them for years or this is one of your first few. We always make mistakes.

What if you are of that unfortunate percentage of our population who, because of family or roommate constraints, cannot drag out the proverbial kitchen stove, sink, and magickal cabinet to perform a long ritual. What do you do then? My theology has always been where there is a Wiccan will, there is a Wiccan way. Do most of the ritual in your head if you have to. Yes, read it to yourself. Whose to know what you are reading, anyhow? You got this book, didn't you—and you are reading it, right? Then just sit quietly and read the ritual, visualizing the steps in your mind. Close your eyes, take your time, and visualize each step after you read it. Of course the ritual isn't going to be like the "real thing," but then, if you could do the real thing, then you certainly would. The deity you choose for your ritual will understand that. Now, if you can do the full ritual and are just too lazy and would rather read the book and not bother with the activities, then don't expect the ritual to work. Most Gods and Goddesses abhor laziness. Sloth, as far as I am aware of, is not a Wiccan character trait.

An Angel Magick Master Ritual

Due to the necessity for ecumenical work in many of my healings and seminars, you'll find that I often employ angelic energies. Here, Jack Veasey has provided an informal Master Angelic Ritual for solitary use. Why do we call this an informal ritual? Jack combines some of the key procedures. See if you can determine which steps he combined.

Altar Layout/Supplies: Place white illuminator candles on both corners of the North end of the altar. Choose incense appropriate to your purpose and place at the East corner of the altar. Find a reasonably large, white feather. Place the feather in the East as well. Put a red candle on the South portion of your altar or shrine. Place a chalice or bowl of water in the West corner. Put a statue or the representation of the Goddess (Queen of Angels) in the North with a dish of salt at her feet. In the center of the altar, place an angel-shaped candle holder with an object candle (your color of choice—see Appendix for additional information) properly anointed with an oil of your choosing.

First, purify yourself with a ritual bath and perform the Lesser Banishing Ritual. Cleanse the area with the elements. Perform an altar devotion. Ground and center. Light the illuminator candles, raise them momentarily above your head, and say:

May the light of Heaven's Queen banish all ill shadows from this place, and from the souls of all who enter here.

As you consecrate the incense, fire candle, water and salt, visualize them being imbued with energy. First, light the incense in the East and say:

May Raphael's wings freshen and cleanse the air I breathe.

Light the fire candle in the South, and say:

May Michael's wings fan the cleansing fire that fills and purifies my heart.

Detailing the Ritual

Add a pinch of salt to the water in the West, and say:

May Gabriel's wings scatter moondust to make pure this holy water.

Take a pinch of salt from the North, and scatter it at your feet, and say:

May Uriel's feet hallow the earth on which I stand.

Take the feather in your right hand, and swirl it in a clockwise spiral over the altar, starting in the North, ending at the center. Chant, visualizing the elemental energies swirling together:

In the vibration of wings, energy sings.

When you feel the energies have mixed together, hold the image of them swirling together in your mind, lay the feather before the object candle in the center, extend your hands over the altar, and say:

May all bright energies that swirl upon this altar now be
safely sealed within. So mote it be.

Clap your hands loudly to seal the altar. Visualize the energies sinking into the altar.

Circle Casting. Take up the feather in your right hand. Starting in the East, draw the circle with it three times, going from East to South to West to North, as you say these words. Visualize white fire flowing from the feather, forming the circle. Say:

O Circle of Fire, I conjure you. Between the worlds of flesh and spirit,
you shall be a common ground; of the power raised within your
boundary, you shall be a lens to shape and focus; of the mortal flesh
that stands within you, you shall be a mighty shield, I call upon you,
Raphael, Michael, Gabriel and Uriel, to aid me in the kindling of this
flame. In the name of the Queen of the Angels, the circle is now cast
and sealed. So mote it be.

Quarter Calls. Call each Quarter facing the appropriate direction, drawing invoking pentagrams of blue fire with the feather in your right hand, going clockwise from East to North. Visualize the Angels arriving as you call them:

(Name Angel), Guardian of (Element), hear my cry.
I call you forth from the angelic realm to grace this circle

with your presence and your power, with your gifts and
your protection. Hail and welcome. So mote it be.

Invocation to the Queen of Heaven. Lay the feather back in the East. Stand in the center of the circle (you will be facing North, but see yourself as at the center). Raise your hands above your head and look up. As you say the following words, slowly lower your hands and eyes, drawing the Goddess down into the circle. Feel and visualize her arrival, coming down from above you:

Some call you Mary; some, the Shekinah; Some call you Cerridwyn;
some say Rosemerta. Some call you the Morrigan; some, Hecate;
Some call you Breid, some, the Lady. Some call you Isis; some, Kuan
Yin. I call you now, enter, come in. Whatever name or face you wear,
you are the Source of all. You are the Moon that tugs at the sea, and
the tides that respond, and the earth that the waves wear away, and
the heavens that watch. Stars are the sequins on your endless cloak;
from your womb's blood flows all creation. Mother of All you are,
and mine, as well. Hear now the cry of your child, born fresh again
now at the center of your circle. Many are my needs of you, yet tonight,
I ask but one: that you be here with me, that you grace this pure space
with your presence, and your blessings on my work. Let all the Angels
called herein know you are watching, sovereign of the universe.

Invocation of the Angel for the Working's Purpose. Light the object candle, thinking of your goal or request. If the Angel chosen does not function as the guardian of a Quarter already called, raise your hands at the beginning of this invocation and lower them slowly toward the level of the flame, as with the invocation of the Goddess. If have called this same angel for Quarter representation, simply hold your hands, palms inward, to either side of the candle, beginning at some distance, then slowly moving them closer to the flame. If you call more than one angel, and the first angel has been called, the second one not, use the first procedure, raising and lowering your hands. Stare into the flame, seeing a kernel of the angel's energy glowing at the heart of it. Say:

Angel I now name, ruler of (planet), let the sound of that word which
carries your essence reach you now, whether in Heaven's realm or here.

Detailing the Ritual

I call upon you to bring to bear your might upon this task, within this circle, that my wish at last find form—first in your world, and then in mine. May the sound of your name feed my magickal flame.

Chant the angel's name, or names, rhythmically over and over, visualizing the kernel of energy and the flame around it growing larger and larger, brighter and brighter. You may use your drum or rattle to assist you in raising this energy. Build the power with your chant. When you feel you have built up enough power, sharply clap out the candle, visualizing the energy sucked down into it, imbuing it with power, and cry:

In the Lady's name, so mote it be!

Keep the candle if your wish is to attract something; bury the candle off your property or throw the candle into a body of water if your work involves banishing something. If you keep the candle, deactivate and burn or bury when your wish has manifested, and give thanks in your own way.

(Include communion here, if you so desire.)

Communion. Hold your hands over the chalice, and say:

From the rain to the vine, from the vine to the berry, from the berry to the wine, from the wine to the cup, we celebrate life and bless this wine.

Pick up your athame and hold the tool over the chalice. As you slowly lower the blade into the chalice, say:

As the chalice is to the Goddess, so the rod is to the God.
And together, they are one!

Drink the juice, and then pour a little in the libation bowl beside the altar or shrine. Hold your hands over the cakes, and say:

From the sun to the ground, from the ground to the wheat,
from the wheat to the flour, from the flour to the bread,
we celebrate life and bless these cakes.

Eat a cake, then crumble some of the cake into the libation bowl beside the altar or shrine.

License to Depart. As you say this, slowly raise your hands from your sides to above your head, feeling the Lady and Angels rising out of the circle:

Now in this space, but always in my heart, O mighty friends, I give you
license to depart. Dear angels who have hastened to my prayer;
Dear Mother, who's now here, but always there; with gratitude and
love, called from within, around, above you may return from whence
you came—great be your fame. Hail and farewell.

To open the circle, clap your hands sharply, visualizing its flame going out counterclockwise. Say:

This circle is open, but never broken.
In the name of Heaven's Queen, so mote it be.

Notice in Jack's ritual he combined the release of the Quarters with the release of deity and any assistants (angels, spirits, et cetera) that he called during the ritual. You can separate these functions (a complex ritual), or leave them together as Jack has (an informal ritual). Since this format constitutes a master ritual, you can use the overall work for moons, sabbats, or general work.

March Basic Indoor Planting Ritual

You don't have to incorporate rituals to just the esbats and sabbats. In spell-work, we can flesh out our desire by performing a full ritual. Seasonal activities can also function to bring ritual into our everyday lives, such as in the following two rituals.

Supplies: You will need illuminator candles (or your Mother and Father candles) packages of seeds, dirt, pots, fertilizer, water small bowls for each type of seed, and several ice pop sticks. Draw the rune Birca with a green marker on each ice pop stick. Place your supplies on your working altar. If you don't have a working altar, you can use a large, flat stone for your preparations.

Step One: Begin in the dark, as you will ask the Mother to bring forth seeds of light from the darkness of the warm earth. Light your illuminator candles (or the Mother and Father candles). Devote the altar, or use Breid's "Children of Light" sequence. Cast the magick circle by walking clockwise, with index finger pointing out and down, saying:

Creation flows from the arms of our Mother Goddess.
Creation flows from the strength and light of our God.
Creation is the mission of the Human Spirit.

Detailing the Ritual

From my lips the oath was sworn, from my hand a circle is born.
The earth, the air, the fire, the water return, return, return.
(Whisper these two lines as often as you desire, then continue.)
And the gifts of the land return. Behold, the circle is cast!

Step Three: Cleanse and consecrate all tools and the seeds.

Step Four: Although you've already called the Quarters with the circle casting, we want to ask for special blessings from each Quarter. You can use your own words, or you can use the following:

Elements of the North; rich earth, comforting soil, bless this ritual with your gifts. (Light the candle in this Quarter.) *Elements of the East; sweet breath, carrier of gentle, spring rain, bless this ritual with your gifts.* (Light the candle in this Quarter.) *Elements of the South; caressing sun, warming creation, bless this ritual with your gifts.* (Light the candle in this Quarter.) *Elements of the West; pure water, transformation energy, Bless this ritual with your gifts.* (Light the candle in this Quarter.)

Step Five: Return to the center. Open the seed packets and place them in the bowls. Hold your hands over the bowls, and say:

Great Mother, bless these seeds. May they grow into beautiful and glorious plants as a testament to your purity and love.
Great Father, bless these seeds. May they grow strong, protected by your loving energy as a testament to our virility and courage.

Step Six: While chanting, humming, or whispering, plant the seeds in the pots. Add appropriate fertilizer and water. You may like to try the Mill of Magick chant, or choose another that you feel matches the ritual. When finished, put one ice pop stick with the Birca rune in each pot. This rune will protect the plant and help it to grow.

Step Seven: Thank the Mother and Father for their blessings, as well as the Quarters. You may wish to put your pots on a tray, and carry them to each Quarter, asking that the energy of the Quarter be placed within the seeds. Close the Quarters, then take up the circle.

When the time comes to plant your green babies out of doors, perform the ritual again, this time in the light. Then plant your flowers or vegetables.

Don't forget to bless the land before you plant. Place the ice pop sticks at strategic sections in the flower beds and vegetable garden.

First Harvest Ritual (Basic Ritual)

Although we have Sabbats that entail the honor of harvest, in several areas of the country we may begin harvesting our vegetables before the Sabbat date. This simple ritual follows the same format as the Planting Ritual, providing sacred energies for the first of many harvests throughout the fall season. You will need illuminator candles (or your Mother and Father candles) an empty basket, and some of the tools you may use to harvest. Place your supplies on your working altar. If you don't have a working altar, you can use a large, flat stone for your preparations.

Step One: Begin in the light, as we will thank the Mother for Her birth children of the land. Light your illuminator candles (or the Mother and Father candles). Devote the altar, or use Breid's "Children of Light" sequence. Cast the magick circle by walking clockwise, with index finger pointing out and down, saying:

> *Creation flows from the arms of our Mother Goddess.*
> *Creation flows from the strength and light of our God.*
> *Creation is the mission of the human Spirit.*
> *From my lips the oath was sworn; from my hand a circle is born.*
> *The earth, the air, the fire, the water.*
> *Return, return, return.*
> (Whisper these two lines as often as you desire, then continue.)
> *And the gifts of the land return. Behold, the circle is cast!*

Step Three: Cleanse and consecrate all tools and the empty basket.

Step Four: Although you've already called the Quarters with the circle casting, we want to ask for special blessings from each Quarter. You can use your own words, or you can use the following:

> *Elements of the North, the harvest has begun.*
> (Hold the empty basket out to the North.)
> *Bless this harvest ritual with your gifts.*
> (Light the candle in this Quarter.)

Detailing the Ritual

> *Elements of the East, the harvest has begun.*
> (Hold the empty basket out to the East.)
> *Bless this harvest ritual with your gifts.*
> (Light the candle in this Quarter.)
> *Elements of the South, the harvest has begun.*
> (Hold the empty basket out to the South.)
> *Bless this harvest ritual with your gifts.*
> (Light the candle in this Quarter.)
> *Elements of the West, the harvest has begun.*
> (Hold the empty basket out to the West.)
> *Bless this harvest ritual with your gifts.*
> (Light the candle in this Quarter.)

Step Five: Return to the center. Place the empty basket on the altar. Hold your hands over the basket and tools, and say:

> *Great Mother, bless the harvest I am about to perform.*
> *May this harvest act as a testament to your purity and love.*
> *Great Father, bless the harvest I am about to perform.*
> *May we have food and beauty through the winter months, protected*
> *by your loving energy as a testament to your virility and courage.*

Step Six: Cut a door and gather a small sampling of your first harvest, enough to fill the basket. Remember to close the door after you. While chanting, humming, or whispering, gather some of your harvest. Again, you may like to try the Mill of Magick chant, or choose another that you feel matches the ritual. When finished, cut the door and enter the circle. (Don't forget to close the door.) Put the harvest basket on the altar.

Step Seven: Thank the Mother and Father for their blessings of the harvest, as well as the Quarters. You may wish to carry the basket to each Quarter, asking for continued blessings throughout the descent of the season. Close the Quarters, then take up the circle.

When you have made your final harvest of the season, you may wish to repeat the harvest ritual, this time in the dark, to symbolize the death of the season. Don't forget to bless the land as you remove the last vegetable from the ground. Place the last vegetable on the altar as an offering for the Gods.

Let's look over a spontaneous ritual. Do you see how the Tree Planting Ritual differs from Jack's Master Angel Ritual?

Tree Planting Ritual (Spontaneous Ritual)
by Breid FoxSong

This ritual refers to the act of planting a new tree. Dig an area deep enough to plant the new tree properly. Make sure that the soil contains the right nutrients for this type of tree. Once you set the tree in the ground and the soil has all settled, bring the family around the tree (or simply stand in front of the tree) for the blessing.

Pour diluted fertilizer around the tree, carefully covering the root ball, and say:

> *We* (I) *give this tree the gift of Earth, that its roots may be deep*
> *and its limbs may be strong.*

Tie a ribbon loosely onto a lower branch of the tree. Replace the ribbon later with wind chimes, once the limb is strong enough, and say:

> *We* (I) *give this tree the gifts of Air, that its beauty will grow*
> *and the birds will nest in its branches.*

Carry a lit candle around the tree (about three feet from the bark and branches) then pinch out the flame, saying:

> *We* (I) *give this tree the protection of fire, that it may be safe*
> *from the threat of burning.*

Pour water on the roots, soaking in the fertilizer, and say:

> *We* (I) *give this tree the gift of water,*
> *that it may live long and never thirst.*

Hug the tree gently, allowing your energy to go into the tree and strengthen it, saying:

> *We* (I) *give this tree the gift of our* (my) *selves, as a representative*
> *of all nature and the love we bear for the earth.*

Sing or chant over the tree, letting the spirit of the tree understand that you have welcomed the tree in its new home.

Family Rituals

Certain occasions relate only to families, such as a wiccaning (saining) or a hand-fasting. Feel free to rewrite the following rituals to suit your purposes. Remember, if you have a limited cast of characters at your disposal, double-up on the parts they play; likewise, if you have several participants and the ritual only calls for two or three, expand the parts so that each person can contribute.

The Shamanic Wiccaning (or Saining)

The guts of this ritual belong to Breid FoxSong, which she generously shared with us. I did some changing and rearranging, but the words and choreography are primarily hers.

Participants: The parent(s) or guardian(s), herein called Adult 1 and Adult 2; the baby; the Drummer

Supplies: Illuminator candles, water, salt, incense, anointing oil. Any gifts for the baby should be placed under the altar. Before the ceremony an Elder (or someone of your choice) should bless the gifts before they are received by the parents. This can be done in one blessing.

Step One. Preparing the Space and Devoting the Altar. Drummer begins with a soft, steady beat. Adults 1 and 2 stand by the altar. One of the adults holds the baby. If you have a Maiden, she can hold the baby.

Adult 1 lights the illuminator candles, saying:

> *Children of Light, I greet you with light.*
> *Bless this circle with your presence.*

Adult 1 carries the lit candle in a clockwise direction around the circle.

Adult 1 returns to the altar and performs the altar devotion. (See the formal ritual earlier in this chapter, or invent one of your own.)

Drummer stops, and says:

> *We have cleansed the area and completed the altar devotion*
> *for the purpose of saining this child.*
> *So mote it be.*

All: *So mote it be.*

Step Two: Casting the Circle. Drummer begins at a soft, steady beat.

Adult 2 casts the circle, walking clockwise, finger pointing down and out, saying:

> *I cast the circle-hedge between the worlds. Be thou the girdle*
> *of the Goddess, and a protection against all negative energies.*
> *I call upon the positive spirits of the North, the East, the South, and*
> *the West to aid me in this consecration. I weave the hedge.*
> *I create a tapestry of power. I call forth our birthright*
> *to sain this child. So mote it be!*

Adult 2 taps the floor or ground with his or her hand or foot, and says:

> *This circle is sealed. So mote it be!*

All: *So mote it be.*

Drummer stops drumming, and says:

> *We have cast the circle between the worlds to provide a safe haven*
> *for the saining of this child. So mote it be!*

All: *So mote it be.*

Step Three: Calling the Quarters. Drummer begins drumming softly.

Adult 1: Goes to the East and says:

> *I call the guardians of the East, keepers of air and new beginnings.*
> *Come! And be welcome in our circle! So mote it be!*

All: *So mote it be.*

Adult 2: Goes to the South, and says:

> *I call the guardians of the South, keepers of fire and future. Come! And*
> *be welcome in our circle! So mote it be!*

All: *So mote it be.*

Adult 1: Goes to the West, and says:

> *I call the guardians of the West, keepers of water and womb. Come!*
> *And be welcome in our circle. So mote it be!*

All: *So mote it be.*

Adult 2: Goes to the North, and says:

I call the guardians of the North, keepers of earth and growth. Come!
And be welcome in our circle. So mote it be!

All: *So mote it be.*

Drummer stops, and says:

We have called the Quarters to bless this child. So mote it be!

All: *So mote it be.*

Step Four: Saining the Baby. Drummer begins playing softly.

Adults 1 and 2: Hold the baby together, and say:

Our joy is one with the Lady and Lord.
We celebrate our creation of life in this form.
Lord and Lady, we present to you our daughter/son (child's name).

Both Adults 1 and 2 hold the baby up towards the moon, or toward the figures of the God and Goddess on the altar.

Adult 2: Returns the baby to the Maiden.

Adult 1: Picks up the holy water, anoints the baby on the lips, and says:

Blessed be your mouth, dimpled with laughter. So mote it be!

All: *So mote it be.*

Adult 1 hands the water to Adult 2.

Adult 2: Anoints the baby's hands, and says:

Blessed be your hands that you may be creative and skilled.
So mote it be!

Adult 2 hands the water back to Adult 1.

All: *So mote it be.*

Adult 1: Anoints the baby's chest, and says:

Blessed be your heart that you are generous and giving.

Adult 1 hands the water back to Adult 2.

All: *So mote it be.*

Adult 2: Anoints the baby's feet, and says:

> *Blessed be your feet which will walk the path of beauty.*
> *So mote it be!*

Adult 2 puts the water back on the altar.

All: *So mote it be.*

Drummer stops, and says:

> *We have sained the baby to the honor of our Lord and Lady.*
> *So mote it be!*

All: *So mote it be.*

Step Five: Declaring the Goddess-parents. (If you have any). Drummer begins beating softly. (We do not want to upset the baby.)

The Goddess parents step up to the altar. Both of them should touch the baby lightly.

Adult 1 says:

> *Lord and Lady, before you we bring one who has promised to be a*
> *Goddess-parent to our child.*

Adult 1 turns to the goddess-parent, and says:

> *Will you,* (their name), *promise before the Gods to care for our child if*
> *we can no longer do so, and do you accept responsibility to help him*
> (her) *understand the Wheel of Creation and the Ways of the Craft?*

Goddess parent answers. Drummer stops drumming, and says:

> (Name) *has declared him/herself as Goddess-parent, and has promised*
> *to help this child understand our ways. So mote it be.*

All: *So mote it be.*

Goddess-parent(s) steps to the side of the altar.

Step Six. Presenting the child to the Quarters, and releasing the Quarters.
Note: Although we've not written in the Goddess-parent's movements in this portion, the Goddess-parent(s) would stand behind Adults 1 and 2, at each Quarter, moving with them as they proceed through the Quarters.

Drummer: Begins drumming in a soft, steady beat.

Adults 1 and 2 take the baby to the North Quarter. Adult 1 holds the child up to the Quarter while Adult 2 says:

> *Guardians of the North, thank you for coming. We present to thee* (child's name). *Bless him/her as you go. Hail and farewell.*

All bow, and say: *Hail and farewell.*

Adults 1 and 2 take the baby to the West Quarter. Adult 2 holds the child up to the Quarter while Adult 1, says:

> *Guardians of the West, thank you for coming. We present to thee* (child's name). *Bless him/her as you go. Hail and farewell.*

All bow, and say: *Hail and farewell.*

Adults 1 and 2 take the baby to the South Quarter. Adult 1 holds the child up to the Quarter while Adult 2, says:

> *Guardians of the South, thank you for coming. We present to thee* (child's name). *Bless him/her as you go. Hail and farewell.*

All: Bow, and say: *Hail and farewell.*

Adults 1 and 2 take the baby to the East Quarter. Adult 2 holds the child up to the Quarter while Adult 1, says:

> *Guardians of the East, thank you for coming. We present to thee* (child's name). *Bless him/her as you go. Hail and farewell.*

All: All bow, and say: *Hail and farewell.*

Drummer stops drumming, and says:

> *We have presented the child to the Quarters and they have blessed him/her. So mote it be.*

All: *So mote it be.*

Step Seven: Parent's blessing. Drummer begins drumming softly.

Goddess-parent: Draws an invoking pentagram on the baby's forehead with anointing oil, and says:

> *Lord and Lady bless you and keep you as dear to Them as you are to me.*

Adult 1: Draws an invoking pentagram on the baby's forehead with salt, and says:

> *Lord and Lady bless you and keep you as dear to Them*
> *as you are to me.*

Adult 2: Draws an invoking pentagram on the baby's forehead with holy water, and says:

> *Lord and Lady bless you and keep you as dear to Them*
> *as you are to me.*

All together: *So mote it be.*

Drummer stops drumming, and says:

> *The baby has been blessed by our Lord and Lady. So mote it be!*

All: *So mote it be.*

Step Eight: Closing the Circle. Drummer begins drumming softly.

Adult 1: Thanks deity for attending the saining and granting blessings.

The Elder: Blesses the Baby and presents the gifts, and gives the parting group blessing.

Those present: Step forward and give a verbal blessing to the baby.

Adult 2: Takes up the circle, walking widdershins. Then says:

> *This circle is open, but never broken. Merry meet, and merry part,*
> *until we merry meet again!*

Drummer stops drumming.

Shamanic Handfasting

In Wicca we have three types of handfasting:

Ceremonial: A ceremony performed for a year and a day.

Legal: A legal ceremony performed for life under the rules and regulations of state law.

Spiritual: A ceremony performed for this lifetime and beyond.

You can use the following ceremony for the ceremonial (year and a day), legal marriage, or spiritual marriage. Our major players in this drama are: The Bride, The Groom, The High Priest, The High Priestess, The Maiden

(Maid of Honor), The Temple Summoner (Best Man), The Quarters, and the Drummer. Remember, you can double-up parts (just not the bride and groom, of course) for a smaller ceremony.

Supplies: General Altar Set-up, Cauldron, Tier candle holder (three candles: gold, silver, and black), Salt and Water bowls, Flower centerpiece, Chalice, Bread plate and Bread, Drink for Bride and Groom, Quarter Lanterns, Wand, Cord (black, white and red), Decorated Broom, Crystal, Need-Fire, Incense, Anointing Oil, the Rings or Tokens. The Tokens are held by the Maiden and the Temple Summoner, respectively.

All gifts to the Bride and Groom should be placed under the altar before the handfasting begins. The High Priestess or the Elder blesses the gifts before the ceremony begins.

1. The Elder walks the proposed ritual site. The Drummer takes his or her place, and begins to drum softly. The Maiden, High Priest, High Priestess, Temple Summoner, Quarters and Elder take their respective places.

2. The Summoner checks the altar to make sure all supplies are ready. He or she also checks to make sure the lanterns are at the Quarters and ready.

3. The Maiden prepares the circle site.

Prepare the Need Fire. Indoors you could use a small cauldron with a little candle. Out-of-doors you can build a fire circled by stones, or use a fire pit.

Cleanse and consecrate the area with salt and water and bell.

Drummer stops drumming, and says:

> ***The ritual site has been properly prepared for the rite of handfasting.***
> ***So mote it be.***

All: *So mote it be!*

4. **Altar Devotion and Circle Casting.** Drummer begins to drum softly. Quarters can rattle, if they desire.

   High Priestess Performs the Altar Devotion.

   The High Priest and High Priestess Cast the Circle together.

   The Drummer stops drumming, and says:

> ***Our altar has been devoted and the circle between the worlds has been***
> ***cast in preparation for the rite of handfasting. So mote it be.***

All: *So mote it be!*

5. **Calling the Quarters.** The Drummer: Begins to drum softly.

High Priest says:

> *Quarters, prepare to call the sacred energies.*
> *The Maiden will deposit the gifts at your feet.*

The Maiden puts the incense, a bowl of grain, a bowl of water, and a large crystal on the tray. She stops at each Quarter, depositing the respective gifts. She makes sure that each Quarter person has a lighter, then returns to her place and puts the tray under or beside the altar.

The Quarters—Begin at the North. Do not recite. Each Quarter individual should speak from the heart, and what they say should apply to the event. Only one rule—no mixtures. If one calls totem animals, all call totem animals. If one calls angels, all call angels, et cetera. As they speak, they light the Quarter lantern.

The Drummer stops drumming, and says:

> *The Quarters have been called to protect and*
> *bless this rite of marriage. So mote it be!*

All: *So mote it be!*

6. **Anointing the People.** The Drummer begins to drum softly.

The High Priest and High Priestess anoint each other, then the High Priest anoints the Maiden, who then anoints the Quarters, the Elder, and the Drummer. She gives the oil back to the High Priest.

The High Priest and High Priestess move to where the door will be cut. The High Priest cuts the door.

The People assemble outside of circle.

One at a time the High Priest and High Priestess anoint those who enter the circle, and welcome the guests. The Maiden and the Temple Summoner act as traffic control. You can follow the script given earlier in the formal ritual, or you can ad-lib. When all have entered the circle, the Maiden rings the bell to summon the wedding couple, or you can play music on a stereo, or you can have a band play music. The Groom enters, and moves to the West, the Bride follows, and takes her place in the East. High Priestess or the High Priest closes the door.

The Maiden says:

Welcome sisters and brothers to the handfasting of (state the couple's names). *To our guests, we welcome you and thank you for making this gathering possible. I realize that when your loved ones disappear on Sabbats and Esbats to join together, you have been excluded. Tonight, you will experience what it is like to join in a Wiccan Circle. This evening, we choose to honor the Goddess with the Charge to begin the ceremony. For those of you have never been in a Wiccan circle we extend the courtesy of a few explanations.* (Do this now.) *While you are in circle please do not move from your place. If for any reason you feel ill, or wish to leave, quietly walk clock-wise around the Circle and leave at the gate from whence you came. The Temple Summoner will guide you.* (Point out the Temple Summoner.) *As this is a holy ceremony, we ask that you do not speak during the proceedings. Thank you, and once again, welcome.*

The Drummer stops drumming, and says:

> *All who enter here come in perfect peace and perfect trust.*
> *Let the handfasting begin!*

All: *Let the handfasting begin!*

The Temple Summoner: (Ring bells)

7. **The Opening Ceremony.** High Priestess says:

> (Man's name) *and* (Woman's name) *will you please walk to the center of the circle, join hands, and step before me.*

The Bride and Groom walk to the center of the circle, join hands, then walk up to the altar.

High Priest:

We are gathered here today at this very special place to celebrate the handfasting vows between (Woman) *and* (Man)*, both of whom wish to unite their bodies and spirits in perfect love and perfect trust. As we stand between the worlds, they wish to acknowledge their undying love and share in the extension of the great mystery.*

The High Priestess says:

> *Holy Mother, descend upon your people*
> *in this sacred ritual of handfasting.*

The High Priest says:

> *Holy Father, descend upon your people*
> *in this sacred ritual of handfasting.*

The High Priestess says:

> *So mote it be!*

All:　　　　　　　　*So mote it be!*

Temple Summoner: Rings bells.

8. **The Vows.** The High Priestess says:

> *Who stands before me?*

The Bride and Groom answer by giving their full names.

The High Priestess says:

> *And why do you come here?*

The Bride and Groom must give appropriate answer.

The High Priestess says:

> *And what sacred words do you offer each other?*

The Bride and Groom must answer:

> *Perfect Love and Perfect Trust.*

The High Priestess says:

> *All who bring such are doubly welcome!*

Temple Summoner: Rings bells.

The High Priestess says:

Remember, above all, you are spirit. Equal in all things. Neither better
than the other. Each the support of the other. So mote it be!

All:　　　　　　　　*So mote it be!*

Temple Summoner: Rings bells.

Detailing the Ritual

The High Priestess says to the Bride and Groom:

Please kneel. (couple kneels)

High Priest (anoints Bride with oil) and says:

You are our Lady with many faces.
Our love, our nurturing, our growth.

High Priestess (anoints Groom with oil) and says:

You are our Lord through the ages.
Our strength, our protection, our passion.

The Drummer begins softly.

The High Priestess says:

Will the couple please rise and prepare to take their vows.
Place your right hand on this wand and repeat after me.

(Couple rises.) The High Priestess begins with the Groom. The Groom should tell, in his own words, why he wants to marry this woman.

The token is handed to the Bride or Groom:

With this token I give to you a reminder of our love and our vision for the future, a symbol of our union together. Will you join with me?

Bride/Groom answers:

I will.

The Bride now says why she wants to marry this man. The High Priestess now wraps the cords around the hands of the couple, leaving the ends to dangle.

The High Priest says:

These cords are a symbol of your union within this magick circle today. It is our custom that the elements bless your union. At each Quarter, a knot will be tied to signify this blessing. When the ceremony has ended and you stand in the receiving line, we ask that each adult guest also tie a knot of blessing as they congratulate these blessed children of the Goddess. Go now (man's name) *and* (woman's name) *on this first of your many journeys together.*

243

The Bride and Groom walk to each Quarter, beginning at the North.

Each Quarter blesses the Bride and Groom, and ties a knot in the cords.

The Bride and Groom return to face the altar.

The Drummer stops, and says:

> *The vows have been taken and the Quarters have*
> *blessed this handfasting. So mote it be!*

All: *So mote it be!*

9. **The Communion.** The High Priestess unwraps the cords and ties one end to the Bride's wrist and one end to the Groom's wrist.

Maiden: Gives the chalice to the bride, and says:

> *Please bless the contents of this chalice.*

Bride:

> *As the moon kisses the rain, which waters the soil, which grows the*
> *vine, which yields the berry into this cup, I ask for the blessings of Our*
> *Lord and Lady in our handfasting ritual.*

Bride holds her hands over the cup.

Groom holds the chalice and kneels, while Bride takes the athame and lowers it slowly into the chalice.

High Priestess says:

> *As the rod is to the God, so the Chalice is to the Goddess,*
> *and Together they are One!*

The Bride offers the cup to the Groom, saying:

> *May you never thirst.*

The Groom offers the cup to the Bride, saying:

> *May you never thirst.*

The Groom hands the chalice back to the Maiden.

Temple Summoner: Gives the bread to Groom, and says:

> *Please bless the bread.*

Groom says:

> *As the sun warms the ground, which nurtures the soil,*
> *which grows the wheat, which yields the flour to make this bread,*
> *so I ask for the blessings of the Holy Lord and Lady*
> *on this day of our handfasting.*

Groom holds his hands over the bread.

Groom offers the bread to the Bride, saying:

> *May you never hunger.*

Bride offers the bread to the Groom, saying:

> *May you never hunger.*

The Bride gives the bread back to the Temple Summoner.

The Drummer says:

> *The holy communion is ended. So mote it be!*

All: *So mote it be!*

10. **Raising energy.** The Drummer begins fast drumming.

The Maiden moves to the center of the circle with the decorated broom.

The High Priestess holds the hands of the Bride and Groom, and turns them to face the members of the circle. She holds her hands high, palms to the sky, and says:

> *In the name of the God and the Goddess* (Woman's name)
> *and* (Man's name) *are bonded as one. By the power invested in me,*
> *I now declare you wife and husband. You may now kiss the bride!*
> *So mote it be!*

All: *So mote it be!*

Drummer slows the beat.

Once the kiss has been completed, the Elder blesses them and the assemblage.

The Drummer begins with a fast beat.

The High Priestess says:

> *You may now jump the broom!*

Bride and Groom make a running jump over the broom as circle members clap.

High Priestess says:

> *May the blessings of the Old Ones, the Shining Ones,*
> *be with you now and always. Blessed be!*

11. **The Closing.** The Temple Summoner cuts a door, allowing the Bride and Groom to leave first, followed by the guests. The High Priestess, High Priest, Elder, Quarters, Maiden, and Temple Summoner remain.

    The Bride and Groom form a receiving line far enough away from the site so that the major players of the ritual can complete the closure.

    The High Priestess thanks the Lord and Lady for their blessings on the rite.

    The Maiden retrieves the Quarter gifts, then returns to her place.

    The Quarters release the energy, widdershins beginning at the West Quarter.

    High Priestess winds up circle, then deposits the energy in the gifts.

    The High Priest declares the circle open.

Summary

In this chapter I've given you an assortment of the various types of rituals. We covered formal, complex, informal and basic. Now it's time for you to take all the information I've given you in the book and begin applying the new things you've learned to your life!

Much love and luck to you!

Epilogue

Within every person's life there is usually one individual who, by his or her love, touches one to the very core. This person may not be the best or the brightest, but they reached within themselves and handed you their most precious gift—love.

The following is in honor of that love.

Let's say you, Mick (my husband) and I are sitting around my dining room table. We're doing the Goddess caffina thing, kicking back, enjoying a pleasant conversation. We've got Enya on the CD player, or perhaps Gypsy (met her in Peabody, Massachusetts—nice lady). We're talking politics, movies, and then, maybe, we move into Craft theologies and practices.

"Oh, wait a minute," I say. "There's something I want you to hear."

Mick refills your coffee while I mess around with the CD player. While we wait for the music to begin, I light a candle and place it in the middle of the dining room table. The tape starts, and you are a bit taken aback, because instead of music, you hear the deep, mellow voice of man, saying the following:

"The Craft is about love. This recording, *The Coven Grows,* is about our dream of the Craft. It's made of love. The love of friends of family. The love of people working together. The love that we can only express by working together. This is our hope for the community, expressed in the way that we can only hope that we can touch you and make you feel the love that was here when we did this. Love is the law. So mote it be."

At this point, you may look at Mick and me a bit strangely. Mick nods his head and smiles. I'm a bit misty, and I tell you that you just heard the voice of my Craft Father, Lord Serphant (Wil Martin). And then I tell you that he passed away on September 21, 1996. "Listen to the next song," I say, "called 'Pagan Saturday Night.'"

By now, you think I'm nuts because I'm banging the table and singing along with Shain as he belts out a country hoedown, Pagan style. Perhaps we will listen to the whole tape, but if you don't have time, I'll say, "Just a moment. There's more that you should hear." Mick checks your coffee and I bop over to the stereo again, fast forward and put on a song called "The Coven Grows."

Epilogue

As the first strains of a song filter through the house, my children meander in from various rooms, singing the lyrics to the song. My father descends the stairs from our second floor, and in a few minutes, the whole family is around you at the table, most of them singing this:

As the old order dies and the raven takes the skies
And you feel no longer threatened by the death of the Israelites
As the Mother holds us to Her breast and magick is on the rise
Those who have the eyes to see recognize the Coven grows.

Through the witch hunts and the inquisition the spark was kept alive
Through the long night burning bright yet hidden from hostile eyes
They stood against the darkness waiting for the Eastern glow
Now we stand revealed in the morning light and we know
The Coven Grows.
And it's growing.

Well the wind carries the melody and the earth joins in the song
And the moon the stars the oceans can try to sing along
And the universe it vibrates in the power that it stores
And those who have the heart to feel it simply can't ignore us
as we grow, and grow.

The wheel it has been turning and the old fires they are burning
And what was once diminished now it is returning
The ancient power advances all The earth in her spiral dances
She sings with a newfound light that she sows
And we in harmony with her we know
The coven grows.
And it's growing.

Do you feel the Mother's presence as the Nazarine cult dies?
Fresh and new like the light that flew from between the Mother's skies
Do you see the magick glisten in birthwaters of our eyes?
Do you have the ears to listen and will you recognize us as we grow?

Epilogue

As the old order dies and the raven takes the skies
And you feel no longer threatened by the death of the Israelites
As the Mother holds us to Her breast and magick is on the rise
Those who have the eyes to see recognize the Coven grows.

And then the family smiles at you, and I say, "Just a moment. Listen . . ." Once again you hear Lord Serphant's voice, saying: "There it is. We sang the songs, gave you our love. Take the songs and dance the dance the Mother gives you in the place you need. Take the love. Share it. Give it to everyone you touch. Everyone you meet. Let the love flow. That's how we stay alive. Let it grow. Let it swell. Love the love. Sing the songs. Dance the dance. The magick is alive and love is real . . . walk with it. Blessed Be."

Sniffing (this always gets to me no matter how many times I hear it) I turn off the stereo. There is a moment of silence as you digest what you've seen and heard. The family slowly disperses, and in a moment, the room contains only you, Mick, and myself.

That's the work. Taking the love and sharing it. Giving that love to everyone you touch, everyone you meet. The work is learning to let the love flow from you and into the lives of those around you.

So, love the love.

Sing the songs.

Dance the dance.

and . . .

Make the magick.

Yeah, you hear him—Walk with it.[1]

---

1. To order a copy of the wonderful tape, *The Coven Grows*, send $15.00 to Shain Stewart, P.O. Box 293, La France, SC 29656.

Acknowledgments

All great books usually have extended bibliographies; however, this book encompasses my work, my life, my research through verbal means, and my travels. Most of the information herein found its creation in the minds of Black Forest members (where annotated throughout the text) and from individuals who have been mentors to me, or who have impressed their wisdom on me in some manner. I would like to acknowledge the following individuals who gave me access to information either not found in books, or not in any books I've ever seen or heard of. By freely explaining procedures, giving thoughtful commentary, or just being themselves, these people have provided you with a record of the Craft in the 1990s.

Lord Serphant (Wil Martin)
Ray Malbrough (Baton Rouge, LA)
Breid FoxSong (Kenmore, NY)
David Norris (MI)
Lady Brigit (Columbus, OH)
Lady Phoebe (Wilkes-Barre, PA)
DawnRaven (Nashville, TN)
Solitare (Nashville, TN)
Michael Ragan (GrandFather)
Ray Buckland (OH)
Donald Michael Kraig (CA)
Laurie Cabot (Salem, MA)
Shain and Nancy Stewart (SC)
Lady Ariel (Atlanta, GA)
Lady Galadrial (Atlanta, GA)
Jessica Thoreson (MN)
The Members of the Black Forest Clan
The Family of Serphant Stone

Acknowledgments

My husband Mick, and my children: Angelique, Falynn, Nickolas, and Jamieson.

All the staff at Llewellyn Worldwide, especially: Nancy Mostad, Cynthia Ahlquist, Jim Garrison, Becky Zins, and, of course, Carl and Sandra Weschcke, owners of Llewellyn Worldwide.

Thanks for being "family."

Appendices

For Your Book of Shadows

Appendix I
General Candle Colors and Correspondences

The Black Forest Clan teaches students to use the colors that resonate with your personal energy. This will take some experimentation on your part. Use this list when in doubt; but don't view this information as "the last word on candle colors."

Color	Purpose	Deity
Black	Returning to sender; divination; negative work; protection	Scatha
Blue-Black	For wounded pride; broken bones; angelic protection	Diantach
Dark Purple	Used for calling up the power of the Ancient Ones; sigils/runes; government	Magog
Lavender	To invoke righteous spirit within thyself when doing good works	Brigid
Dark Green	Invoking the Goddess of Regeneration; agriculture; financial	Bomba
Mint Green	Financial gains (used with gold and/or silver)	Pridderi
Green	Healing or health; North Cardinal Point	Argante
Avocado Green	New beginnings	Cernunnos
Light Green	Improve the weather	Tyrannis
Indigo Blue	To reveal deep secrets; protection on the astral levels; defenses	Nansuelto
Dark Blue	Confusion—to create (must be used with white or you will confuse yourself)	Dwyn
Blue	Protection	Angus
Royal Blue	Power and protection	Arianhod
Pale/Light Blue	Protection of home; buildings; young, etc; young males	Hertha
Ruby Red	Love or anger of a passionate nature; sex magick	Fand
Red	Love; romantic atmosphere; energy; South Cardinal Point	Branwyn
Light Red	Deep affection of a non-sexual nature	Britiannia
Deep Pink	Harmony and friendship in the home	Danu, Hertha
Pink	Harmony and friendship with people; binding magick	Aeval
Pale Pink	Friendship; young females	Epona
Yellow	Healing; can also represent East Cardinal Point	Diantach
Deep Gold	Prosperity; sun magick	Lugh
Gold	Attraction	Pwyll
Pale Gold	Prosperity in health	Balor
Burnt Orange	Love bondage; opportunity	Queen Maub
Orange	Material gain; and to seal a spell; attraction	Gubba
Dark Brown	Invoking earth for benefits	Gaia
Brown	Peace in the home; herb magick	Dagda
Pale Brown	Material benefits in the home	Danu

Silver	Quick money; gambling; invocation of the Moon; Moon magick	Tyrian
Off-White	Peace of mind	Sulis
Lily White	"Mother Candle" (burned for 30 minutes at each moon phase)	Brigantina
White	Righteousness; purity, used for East Cardinal Point; Devotional magick	Drygdyn
Grey	Glamouries	Cerridwyn

Use White if none are available.

Appendix II
Herbal Correspondences

Herbs of Healing

Allspice	Angelica	Asafoetida	Bay	Boneset
Buckeye	Calamus	Carnation	Cedar	Chamomile
Cinnamon	Citron	Coxcomb	Cinquefoil	Eucalyptus
Fennel	Gardenia	Garlic	Heliotrope	Horehound
Laurel (Bay)	Lemon Balm	Lime	Mint	Mistletoe
Mugwort	Myrrh	Nettle	Pepper	Peppermint
Pine	Rose	Rosemary	Rue	Sage
Sandalwood	Spearmint	Solomon's Seal	Thyme	Vervain
Violet	Willow	Yerba Santa		

Herbs of Love

Apple	Apricot	Basil	Cardamom	Catnip
Chamomile	Chickweed	Cinnamon	Cinquefoil	Clove
Copal	Coltsfoot	Cowslip	Coriander	Dill
Dragon's Blood	Gardenia	Geranium	Ginger	Hibiscus Ivy
Jasmine	Juniper	Lavender	Lemon	Lemon Balm
Lemon Verbena	Lime	Lotus	Marjoram	Mastic
Mimosa	Mistletoe	Moonflower	Myrtle	Orange
Orchid	Pansy	Pennyroyal	Peppermint	Pulmeria
Rose	Rosemary	Sarsaparilla	Spearmint	Thyme
Tonka	Vanilla	Vervain	Vetivert	Yarrow

Herbs of Protection

Angelica	Asafoetida	Basil	Boneset	Cinnamon
Cloves	Comfrey	Coxcomb	Fennel	Garlic
Holly	Horehound	Hound's Tongue	Ivy	Laurel (Bay)
Mandrake	Marigold	Mistletoe	Nettle	Rosemary
Rue	Sage	St. John's Grass	Slippery Elm	Solomon's
Sunflower	Vervain	Yarrow		Seal

Herbs of Wealth and Success

Allspice	Almond	Basil	Bergamot	Boneset
Buckeye	Calamus	Cedar	Chamomile	Celandine
Cinnamon	Cinquefoil	Comfrey	Clove	Clover
Dill	Elder	Fenugreek	Gag Root	Galangal
Ginger	Heliotrope	Honeysuckle	Jasmine	Mandrake
Meadow Cabbage	Mint	Myrtle	Nutmeg	Oak
Orange	Parsley	Pine	Sage	Sassafras
Tonka	Vervain	Vetivert	Woodruff	

Herbs of Breaking Hexes

Angelica	Hemlock	Henbane	Horehound	Nettle
Nightshade	Rue	Solomon's Seal	Yew	Yarrow

Herbs of Consecration and Purification

Angelica	Anise	Arborvitae	Asafoetida	Avens
Basil	Bay	Bergamot	Calamus	Cedar
Chamomile	Cinnamon	Cinquefoil	Clove	Clover
Dill	Elder	Frankincense	Galangal	Ginger
Heliotrope	Honeysuckle	Hyssop	Jasmine	Juniper
Mandrake	Mint	Mistletoe	Myrtle	Nutmeg
Oak	Orange	Pine	Rosemary	Rowan
Sage	Sandalwood	Sassafras	Tansy	Thistle
Tonka	Valerian	Vervain	Vetivert	Woodruff

Herbs of House Blessing

Angelica	Basil	Bay Laurel	Camphor	Cinquefoil
Cowslip	Elderflower	Figwort	Garlic	Lavender
Mandrake	Orris	Orange Peel	Pine	Plantain
Rosemary	Rowan	Rue		

Herbs of Marriage (Handfasting)

Aconite	Apple	Basil	Broom	Caraway
Coriander	Elderflower	Ginger	Holly	Ivy
Jasmine	Lavender	Lemon Verbena	Licorice	Lotus
Maple	Marjoram	Mistletoe	Orchid	Rose
Rosemary	Skullcap	Yarrow		

Herbs of Funerals (Crossings)

Aconite	Basil	Bean	Bluebell	Elder
Hawthorn	Lotus	Mandrake	Marjoram	Myrrh
Parsley	Pennyroyal	Periwinkle	Pine	Poplar
Rosemary	Rue	Star Anise	Tansy	Thyme
Violet	Willow	Yew		

Herbs of Exorcism

Angelic	Basil	Clove	Cumin	Dragon's Blood
Frankincense	Fumitory	Garlic	Heliotrope	Horehound
Juniper	Lilac	Mallow	Mint	Mistletoe
Myrrh	Pepper	Pine	Rosemary	Rue
Sagebrush	Sandalwood	Snapdragon	Thistle	Yarrow

Appendix III
Moon Magick

New Moon

- Moon is 0-45 degrees directly ahead of the sun
- Moon rises at dawn, sets at sunset; for full use of these energies, stick between this time period
- Moon is from exact new moon to 3½ days after
- Purpose: Beginnings
- Workings for: Beauty, health, self-improvement, farms and gardens, job hunting, love and romance, networking, creative ventures
- Pagan Holiday: Winter Solstice (December 22)
- Goddess Name: Rosemerta's Moon
- Goddess Energy: Goddesses of Growth
- Offering: Milk and honey
- Theme: Abundance
- Rune: Feoh for abundance; Cen for openings; Gyfu for love
- Tarot Trump: The Fool

Appendix III

Crescent

- Moon is 45-90 degrees ahead of the sun
- Moon rises at mid-morning, sets after sunset; for full use of these energies, stick between this time period
- Moon is from 3½ to 7 days after the new moon
- Purpose: The movement of the thing
- Workings: Animals, business, change, emotions, matriarchal strength
- Pagan Holiday: Imbolc
- Goddess Name: Brigid's Moon
- Goddess Energy: Water Goddesses
- Offering: Candles
- Theme: Manifestation
- Rune: Birca for Beginnings; Ing for focus
- Tarot Trump: The Magician

First Quarter

- Moon is 90-135 degrees ahead of the sun
- Moon rises at noon, sets at midnight; for full use of these energies, stick between this time period
- Moon is from 7 to 10½ days after the new moon
- Purpose: The shape of the thing
- Workings: Courage, elemental magicks, friends, luck, and motivation
- Pagan Holiday: Spring Equinox, March 21
- Goddess Name: Persephone's Moon
- Goddess Energy: Air Goddesses
- Offering: Feathers
- Theme: Luck
- Rune: Algiz for luck; Jera for improvement; Ur for strength
- Tarot Card: Strength or The Star

Gibbous

- Moon is 135-180 degrees ahead of the sun
- Moon rises in mid-afternoon, sets around 3 A.M.; for full use of these energies, stick between this time period
- Moon is between 10½ to 14 days after the new moon
- Purpose: Details
- Workings: Courage, patience, peace, harmony
- Pagan Holiday: Beltaine

- Goddess Name: Nuit's Moon
- Goddess Energy: Star Goddesses
- Offering: Ribbons
- Theme: Perfection
- Rune: Asa for eloquence; Wyn for success; Dag for enlightenment
- Tarot Trump: The World

Full Moon

- Moon is 180-225 degrees ahead of the sun
- Moon rises at sunset, sets at dawn; for full use of these energies, stick between this time period
- Moon is from 14 to 17½ days after the new moon
- Purpose: Completion of a project
- Workings: Artistic endeavors, beauty, health, fitness, change, decisions, children, competition, dreams, families, health, knowledge, legal undertakings, love, romance, money, motivation, protection, psychic power, self-improvement
- Pagan Holiday: Summer Solstice
- Goddess Name: Sekhmet's Moon
- Goddess Energy: Fire Goddesses
- Offering: Flowers
- Theme: Power
- Rune: Sol
- Tarot Card: The Sun

Disseminating

- Moon is 225-270 degrees ahead of the sun
- Moon rises at mid-evening, sets at mid-morning; for full use of these energies, stick between this time frame
- Moon is 3½ to 7 days after the moon
- Purpose: Initial destruction
- Working: Addiction, decisions, divorce, emotions, stress, protection
- Pagan Holiday: Lammas
- Goddess Name: Hecate's Moon
- Goddess Energy: Earth Goddesses
- Offering: Grain or rice
- Theme: Reassessment
- Rune: Thorn for destruction; Algiz for protection; Thorn for defense
- Tarot Trump: The Tower for destruction; Hope for protection

Appendix III

Last Quarter

- Moon is 270–315 degrees ahead of the sun
- Moon rises at midnight and sets at noon; for full use of these energies, stick between this time frame.
- Moon is 7 to 10½ days after the full moon
- Purpose: Absolute destruction
- Working: Addictions, divorce, endings, health and healing (banishing), stress, protection, ancestors
- Pagan Holiday: Fall Equinox
- Goddess Name: The Morrigan's Moon
- Goddess Energy: Harvest Goddesses
- Offering: Incense
- Theme: Banishing
- Rune: Hagal; Ken for banishing; Nyd for turning; Isa for binding
- Tarot Trump: Judgement

Balsamic (Dark Moon)

- Moon is 315-360 degrees ahead of the sun
- Moon rises at 3 A.M. sets mid-afternoon; for full use of these energies, stick between this time frame
- Moon is 10½ to 14 days after the full moon
- Purpose: Rest
- Working: Addictions, change, divorce, enemies, justice, obstacles, quarrels, removal, separation, stopping stalkers and theft
- Pagan Holiday: Samhain
- Goddess Name: Kali's Moon
- Goddess Energy: Dark Goddesses
- Offering: Honesty
- Theme: Justice
- Rune: Tyr for justice; Ken for banishing
- Tarot Trump: Justice

Appendix IV
Runic Table

Feoh	ᚠ
Ur	ᚢ
Thorn	ᚦ
Asa	ᚨ
Rad	ᚱ
Cen	ᚲ
Gyfu	ᚷ
Wyn	ᚹ
Haegl	ᚺ
Nyd	ᚾ
Isa	ᛁ
Jera	ᛃ
Eoh	ᛇ
Peorth	ᛈ
Algiz	ᛉ
Sol	ᛋ
Tyr	ᛏ
Beorc	ᛒ
Eh	ᛖ
Man	ᛗ
Lagus	ᛚ
Ing	◇
Odal	ᛟ
Dag	ᛞ

Appendix V
Planetary Hours
Sunrise

Hour	Sunday	Monday	Tuesday	Wednesday	Thursday	Friday	Saturday
1	Sun	Moon	Mars	Mercury	Jupiter	Venus	Saturn
2	Venus	Saturn	Sun	Moon	Mars	Mercury	Jupiter
3	Mercury	Jupiter	Venus	Saturn	Sun	Moon	Mars
4	Moon	Mars	Mercury	Jupiter	Venus	Saturn	Sun
5	Saturn	Sun	Moon	Mars	Mercury	Jupiter	Venus
6	Jupiter	Venus	Saturn	Sun	Moon	Mars	Mercury
7	Mars	Mercury	Jupiter	Venus	Saturn	Sun	Moon
8	Sun	Moon	Mars	Mercury	Jupiter	Venus	Saturn
9	Venus	Saturn	Sun	Moon	Mars	Mercury	Jupiter
10	Mercury	Jupiter	Venus	Saturn	Sun	Moon	Mars
11	Moon	Mars	Mercury	Jupiter	Venus	Saturn	Sun
12	Saturn	Sun	Moon	Mars	Mercury	Jupiter	Venus

Planetary Hours
Sunset

Hour	Sunday	Monday	Tuesday	Wednesday	Thursday	Friday	Saturday
1	Jupiter	Venus	Saturn	Sun	Moon	Mars	Mercury
2	Mars	Mercury	Jupiter	Venus	Saturn	Sun	Moon
3	Sun	Moon	Mars	Mercury	Jupiter	Venus	Saturn
4	Venus	Saturn	Sun	Moon	Mars	Mercury	Jupiter
5	Mercury	Jupiter	Venus	Saturn	Sun	Moon	Mars
6	Moon	Mars	Mercury	Jupiter	Venus	Saturn	Sun
7	Saturn	Sun	Moon	Mars	Mercury	Jupiter	Venus
8	Jupiter	Venus	Saturn	Sun	Moon	Mars	Mercury
9	Mars	Mercury	Jupiter	Venus	Saturn	Sun	Moon
10	Sun	Moon	Mars	Mercury	Jupiter	Venus	Saturn
11	Venus	Saturn	Sun	Moon	Mars	Mercury	Jupiter
12	Mercury	Jupiter	Venus	Saturn	Sun	Moon	Mars

For Your Book of Shadows, Part I
Novelty Candles

Yes, you've seen them—Dispel Evil Candle, Prosperity Candle, Success Candle, Double Fast Luck Candle—are these candles better than the ones you pick up at the grocery store? Probably not. Any shop owner or business can give a candle a name. I've even been told there are RavenWolf candles. Can you believe it? I can't either. Trust me—I didn't make them. Named candles usually follow the connection between color and noted desire. Unless you know that during the making of the candle, specific herbals or oils were used, then these candles won't pack any more punch than those at your local supermarket. If you are on a tight budget, then skip the name candles and dress a plain candle with a favorite oil. You can even roll the candle in your hands, then roll it in your favorite magickal powder. In all fairness, some reputable dealers offer properly prepared candles according to their names. These candles usually have a piece of paper with them indicating the ingredients used to prepare it.

Let's take a moment and go over those shaped candles that march across the occult shop shelves. You know, there go the cats, followed by the people who stand beside those scary-looking devil candles, who crouch next to the skull candles, who look vacantly at the mummy candles, who are all tied up next to the snake candles, who slither to the . . . well, you get my meaning. We call these candles specialty or novelty candles.

The various shapes and depictions refer to universal consciousness symbols, or thoughtforms passed down from generation to generation, culture to culture. These novelty candles work in sympathy with your desire. Just as hex signs, dream catchers, and mandalas require activation to work, so too of the novelty candles, therefore these candles require the process of cleansing, blessing, and empowerment before use. Many practitioners use novelty candles in conjunction with petition and herbal magicks. Not all Wiccans or candle practitioners use these novelty candles, and their use appears to be more prevalent around ingrained folk traditions and practices, especially where vast numbers of a particular race, culture, or religious mythos have migrated in the larger metropolitan areas. In the seventies one would always be able to find novelty candles in occult shops, but today, with a definite division between occult, new age, or spiritual shops, you may have difficulty finding them, unless you live near an area where ethnic magicks prevail. From a business standpoint, novelty candles do not ship well and often arrive to the shop broken or damaged in some way. Finally, novelty candles carry a hefty price tag compared to a simple colored candle that will work in the same manner. Although candle shapes sometimes find association with Voodoo or the Black Arts, this isn't a fair assumption. Again, misinformation and the unfortunate practices of a very few (speaking in terms of Black Magick) have given novelty candles a bad rap. As with any type of magick, keep your intentions pure and your workings positive. Sometimes novelty candles (especially with mail order) come with directions, but more likely than not you'll find the candles perched in a row in an occult shop without information on what to do with them, their history, or what they mean. If you ever have a question about a novelty candle, make a special effort to ask the shop owner the full range of possibilities that each candle may represent, as he or she understands it. This will give you an idea of the energies represented by the entire shop, not just the candle in question. Remember, as with all candle magicks, the use of oils, herbals, and powders can intensify the novelty candle's intensity.

The Cat Candle.

Candles in the shape of animals relate to their totem energies. The cat candle is the most prevalent animal candle sold in occult shops. They come in a variety of colors and sizes. Many individuals equate the cat candle to mystery traditions, feminine energy, or the Egyptian Bast Goddess form. Cat candles basically fall into the prosperity category. Burn a black cat candle to reverse bad luck, break minor hexes, and bring good luck. The green cat candle relates to money and gambling magick or the healing of a sick pet or farm stock. Red cat candles function as love attraction or to heighten the energy during a romantic evening. Cat candles work well for spells involving workings of more than one day. Associate the numbers 3, 7, 9, and 11 with cat candles.

The Cross Candle or Calvary Candle.

These are used primarily by those individuals who practice Christianity or a folk religion that includes the trappings of Christianity, although the candle can be useful for anyone. Many Wiccans find the cross offensive, for as they understand this ancient symbol, which predates Christianity, it stands for attack. Cross candles come in a variety of colors, each candle sympathetically attuned to the meaning of the color. Also called the floral cross candle, the designs of embossed keys and the holy book equate to the act of unlocking wisdom and holy secrets as well as overall protection. Cross candles make nice gifts for your Christian friends, and will work well for them in angel magick.

The Devil or Satan Candle. This is rarely used by Wiccans or Witches simply because of their aversion to this evil entity. I've never quite understood the use for this candle, because burning an effigy of ultimate evil would, to me, bring ultimate evil upon you. However, some candle magick practitioners use this candle to break hexes, perform exorcism rites, remove jinxes, and destroy sinister forces. Since there are many other ways to do these same magicks without employing the satan candle, I've never worked with one.

Figure Candles. These have a variety of uses, depending on the color chosen. Red, black, brown, pink, and white figure candles each have their own assignation of energies. Red: To bring love. Black: To repel a negative individual. Brown: To find lost items and return them to their owners, or to help restore qualities in an individual which have weakened. Pink: Promote friendship. White: To bring spirituality. You can also employ figure candles as petition or astral candles, meaning you purchase the candle to represent yourself. Figure candles work well for workings of healing for an individual that will last several days. You can use the figure candle in place of a poppet by loading the bottom of the candle with herbs and something in sympathy (such as hair, nail clippings, et cetera) to facilitate healing (I have provided instructions for loading a candle later in this section).

With the permission of the other person involved, figure candles help to form a telepathic link between one person and another. If you are learning to send or receive information from a magickal partner, and wish to run several experiments, try them with and without the figure candles.

Double Action Candles. These contain two colors: a variety of colors on top, and black on the bottom. The upper color may be red, green, or white, though I have seen other colors employed. The combination of black and another color allows negative forces to repel and positive forces to take action. Black and white double action candles fall under the realms of more spiritual pursuits, house banishings, or other types of cleansing. Black and green candles work well for prosperity magicks, success spells, and overall abundance. You can also use the black and green double action candle to protect property or bring the appropriate property to you. Black and red double action candles help to relieve sexual dysfunctions, clear negative energy away from a marriage and bring a renewed sense of joy, or correct energy problems within the home.

Triple Action Candles. These work in the same manner as the double action candles, with an extra color for another type of magickal activation. Color symbology, as with most novelty candles, follows the standard interpretations.

Chakra Candles. Chakra candles, usually enclosed in glass, contain the seven colors of the energy vortexes of the body: red, orange, yellow, green, blue, violet, and white. Some candle makers pour the colors from red to white, where others may pour the colors from white to red. The chakra candles work great for meditation, cleansing of body and mind, house blessings, and other activities where you feel you need the full spectrum of color in the magickal activity.

Floating Candles. Floating candles do exactly what their title implies—they float in liquid. These candles work well for employing equal balance of water and fire elements in your working, and work wonderfully for scrying. Simply fill a bowl with water, light the candles, set them afloat in the bowl, turn out the lights, relax, let the candles settle, then gaze into the bowl.

Mummy Candles. Mummy candles usually fall under the heading of power or success; however, some practitioners use the candle to ward off negativity, catch stalkers, or keep mysterious and dark energies at bay, especially during times of sickness. One may use the mummy candle in ceremonies symbolizing death and rebirth.

Reversible candles. Reversible candles begin with a red body, then are dipped in black wax. The purpose hinges on burning away harmful energies and energizing the situation in a healthy way. Reversible candles can function as daily partners in magick if you are experiencing a rough patch or find yourself involved in negative circumstances.

Seven-knob or Wishing Candles. These particular candles have a variety of uses and are a favorite design among magickal practitioners due to their ease in timing. The seven knobs work for one wish or for seven separate wishes. Write each wish onto a knob with a heated nail or pin, or write each wish on a piece of paper and thumb-tack the paper to each knob. These candles come in a variety of colors and stand approximately seven inches high. As with other candles, energies associated with these candles correspond to their colors. Red for love, black for banishing, white for spirituality, green for prosperity, and so on. If you can't find a seven-knob candle, take a pillar candle and, with a knife, cut six notches equal distance from each other. Regardless of whether you buy a knob candle or make your own with the pillar candle, if you use the candle for a seven-day spell, don't skip any days, as you break the pattern and knock the foundation out of your magickal building.

Skull candles.

Available in a variety of colors, from white, black, green, to red, though I have seen skulls of other unusual colors. The skull candle's primary purpose falls in the realm of banishment, destruction of disease, or separation. Magickal applications involving white skull candles revolve around healing, protection, and peace, though I have used a white skull candle to separate an abusive husband from his wife when she was desperately in trouble. White was all I had, so that's what I used. If you work ancestral magicks or have an ancestral shrine, you can place a picture of your deceased loved one underneath a white skull candle, and burn the candle while praying for them. Early American Witches (Pow-Wow Doctors/Artists) fully believed that you could pray for a person any time, whether that person was alive or dead, to help them along their karmic path. With thought, I find this odd, as most Pow-Wow practitioners took on the Protestant religion (as that was the most prevalent in their areas), rather than the Catholic religion, which would have given them more freedom for candle magick. This is not to say that there weren't any Catholic Pow-Wows, simply very few in comparison to their Protestant compatriots.

The green skull candle has both positive and malefic uses. If someone owes you money, it's time to break out the green skull candle to get your money back or to receive what's owed to you. Green skull candles work well in magickal applications that require healing of the mind after bodily sickness or an emotional upset, memory retention for school students or endeavors where the focus entails good recall, or for individuals who suffer from more difficult mental disturbances. At its worst, the green candle separates someone from their fortune.

The red skull candle finds its use in jettisoning a love that is not good for you or for urging unpleasant neighbors to move away. Other uses of the red skull candle involve the saving of a marriage or relationship crossed by karmic circumstances, or where love is in trouble by miscommunication on behalf of one or both partners. If you've got a stray lover on your hands, the red skull candle works well to pull him or her back; however, as with all relationships, perhaps pulling this person back would not be the best for all.

"Skull Candles of the appropriate colors can be of great aid to activists who must deal with bureaucracies. The large entities can be equated to headless monsters that feed off the life energies of their employees. By using the Skull Candle to represent the thought form of the bureaucracy, you can tap this thought form's energy and thus control much of what happens to it. By making the thought form feed upon itself, you can destroy it or allow it to restructure."[1]

Snake Candles. Snake candles, sometimes called bust-away candles, take the shape of large, round candles about two inches in diameter and eight or nine inches tall, decorated with an embossed snake. Magickal applications involving these candles lean toward destruction of negativity and protection, and can be burned approximately once every twenty-eight days. Use the snake candle to awaken Kundalini energies, or pull the snake into your ritual circle as a totem energy.

Witch Candles. Witch candles, although not usually attractive (darn, they still can't get it right, can they?), provide the magickal practitioner with a multitude of uses, from practicing glamouries to representing the totality of our religion. Some practitioners see this candle as an extremely potent love catalyst, where others equate the energies to the Goddess or the lineage of those who have gone before us.

Heart Candles. Heart candles conjure a strong symbolism to romance. Burn red heart candles for luck in love, white heart candles for purity in love, and pink heart candles for strengthening a friendship.

Angel Candles. Angel candles come in a variety of colors. According to color, use for healing, higher learning, spirituality, creativity, and workings with angel magick or angel ritual.

Some magickal practitioners feel that novelty candles belong only to beginners, where other practitioners believe that specialty candles fall under the expertise of advanced magickal individuals. Go figure.

---

1. From page 197 of *The Candle Magick Workbook* by Kala & Ketz Pajeon (Citadel Publishing, 1995).

Flipping Candles

The practice of flipping a candle to repel negativity and to reduce erratic energy flow dates back to Gypsy practices and was prevalent during Early American Witchcraft. Gypsies would flip their candles to ensure they wouldn't get pinched when committing a crime, or that if unfortunate incarceration might occur, escape or release would manifest. To flip a candle, HexCraft practitioners took a white taper candle (later, in the mid-1900s, when the stigma of colors in candles died, red tapers were used) and cut the top off the candle. Then they cut the wax from around the bottom of the candle, leaving the wick exposed, and placed the candle in a safe holder (with bottom up and taper end in the holder). Light the exposed wick to repel and release any negativity. You can develop a chant or use a spell of release.

You can flip candles to repel an unwanted lover, someone who is interfering in your love life or your career, or whatever. Flipping three black, red, and brown candles will assist in repelling a stalker. Of course, you did do all the normal things someone would do when encountering such a situation. Don't ever rely on just flipping a candle for something so terribly serious. What happens when we flip those three colors? We repel evil (black), we repel the person's unwanted energy (red), and we repel that person's friendship (brown).

If you need to hurry, you can light a candle upside down and hold the candle that way for a few seconds to perform a "quickie" banishing of unwanted energies. Watch out for drips.

Loading Candles

Magickal practitioners often combine ground herbals or magickal powders with their candle magick. Loading the candle entails combining candles, herbs, and powders. For this purpose, you will need a candle with at least a one-inch base (it's better if it is two or three inches in diameter). Carefully carve out a hole in the bottom of the candle with a warmed knife or small spoon (this will help to eliminate breakage). Load your empowered herbs or magickal powder into the hole. Melt the wax shavings and pour over the packed mixture. Allow to cool. Scrape the bottom of the candle with a warmed knife to smooth the surface if necessary. Place in a candle holder for stability.

Suggested Reading

The Candle Magick Workbook by Kala & Ketz Pajeon. Citadel Press. 1995.

Charms, Spells, and Formulas by Ray Malbrough. Llewellyn Worldwide. 1994.

Advanced Candle Magick by Ray Buckland. Llewellyn Worldwide. 1996.

A Bard's Book of Pagan Songs by Hugin the Bard. Llewellyn Worldwide. 1996.

For Your Book of Shadows, Part II
Enchanted Powders

The use of magickal powders varies widely. You can blow powders into the air, sprinkle powders on the body, cast the powders on the altar or shrine, set under objects, blow around the room, load in a candle, use in a thurible or place in footprints. In the use of powders, the practitioner relies on his or her intuition. Herman Slater, in his book *Magickal Formulary*, indicates that your spontaneous action (being seized with Spirit) has great power, as belief indicates that the push for action comes not directly from yourself but from the spirit plane. I fully believe this line of thought. I've found when I give seminars that I'm drawn to those that the Goddess wants me to touch, talk to, laugh with, or use as an example for an exercise because he or she needs this interaction with me or with others in the group. Working with powders manifests in the same way. Powders connect your altar or shrine with the outside world, especially if, while a candle is burning at your altar or shrine, you are in another place, casting your powder for success. I don't always develop a powder to use in my magickal workings, but when I'm seized by the compulsion to make one, I do it. Many practitioners of magick feel that powders don't belong to the novice. More advanced practitioners start out with candle burning and work their way to more sophisticated and elaborate rituals and accessories, including the use of powders.

So what does a powder actually do? Good question. Basically, we use powders to bring about sudden change by incorporating two elements—that of earth and air. If you burn a magickal powder, then you are also incorporating the element of fire into your work. If you add a touch of oil, alcohol, or holy water, then you employ the element of water as well. When you make the powder you are activating the properties of each herb or ingredient in combination with the element of air.

To make a powder, you will need a mortar and pestle to start, and at least three to five different ingredients of equal proportions. As with oils, the more ingredients, the stronger the powder. Powders usually smell good; to retain that nice fragrance, add Orris Root powder.

To incorporate color in a powder, purchase a talc (in various hues) and add the talc in an equal portion to the herbs. I get mine from the Crossroads Spiritual Supply House. The colored talc brings in the psychological correspondences of color. Most measurements in powders are of an equal number. For example, if I use ⅛ teaspoon of lavender, ⅛ teaspoon of sandalwood, ⅛ teaspoon of angelica, ⅛ teaspoon of orange peel, and ⅛ teaspoon of frankincense to make angel powder, I would add ⅛ teaspoon of colored talc. The color of talc you use is entirely up to you. For my angel powder, I use ⅛ teaspoon of purple or blue talc.

I know you've seen on television where a magickal person walks up to another individual and blows a magickal powder in their face. Although I'm sure this has been done, I don't advise it. First, the other person will immediately know you are doing something weird, and secondly, blowing something into someone's eyes is rude and may hurt them. Don't get carried away with your powders—be a nice Witchie.

Powders rely on air magick. Therefore, you might like to develop a spoken charm to go along with the powder while you are mixing the concoction, depending on your magickal intent. You can say the charm again when you use the powder in a magickal application. Store your powders in a small plastic bag or dark glass bottle until ready for use. If you are afraid that you'll forget the charm you made up (which will happen on one occasion or another, trust me) you could write the charm on a piece of paper, roll the paper to conceal the words, and place it in the bag or storage jar.

Remember that powders are never, ever consumed; they ride the winds of change, not your intestinal tract. Don't forget that magickal powders function as a marvelous addition to your stationary thurible, or load the powders into pillar or votive candles. I always bless my magickal powders at my guardian shrine before taking them off the premises.

Powders, for whatever reason, carry an association with Voodoo practitioners, but I've found them used extensively in Early American Witchcraft by Pow-Wow Doctors/Artists. In Pennsylvania and West Virginia, practitioners sometimes used corn meal as a base ingredient to hide the essence of the powder. Where Voodoo practitioners want you to know they are cooking magick, Pow-Wow Doctors/Artists don't want you to know.

The first magickal powders a friend of mine and I made didn't work particularly well, and we almost decided that this simply wasn't a magick for us; however, we soon discovered that just as in other magickal pursuits, the blending of magickal powders takes practice. It is an application with nuances that will apply only to you, just as other magicks do, and it takes a while for those nuances to sink into the old brain cells.

The simple act of making a powder won't automatically pull the magickal essence into the mixture. Just as you activate other magickal tools, you must activate the powder through some sort of spellworking, chant or whispering magick, or ritual. Take into consideration the elements you used to create your powder. Earth and air are always present in a magickal powder, but if you add it to a liquid, then the water element gets equal billing. If you plan to burn the powder in a thurible, then you need to set the magickal stage for the fire element as well.

The Expense—O, the Availability!

What if you can't afford to buy some of the ingredients in a magickal powder formula? Learn to substitute. It won't hurt you, and it won't mess up your powder. Scott Cunningham's *Encyclopedia of Magical Herbs* (Llewellyn, 1985) is a tried and true must-have volume for any magickal person. In this book, Scott provides hundreds of substitutions.

What if you can't get your hands on tonka beans and you need them RIGHT NOW? Get to know your supermarket well. Sometimes, when I want to work a spell but haven't the faintest idea what ingredients I want to use, I'll browse through the supermarket aisles and purchase what feels right. You'll find yourself amazed at what you can come up with.

If you are really in a pinch, you can take standard boxed cone incense, grind it up, and use this powder along with your natural ingredients. I know, the purists are shuddering again, but it works.

Planning Your Magickal Powder

Although I've provided a list of magickal powders for your experimentation in this section, let's go through the actual creation of a powder. As in other magickal applications I've taught you, we need to get down to the one-two-three process. Before you purchase the ingredients, you need to answer some specific questions.

- What will this powder be used for?
- Is this a one-time situation, or will you want to make a larger batch of powder to use for several things (such as a spiritual cleansing powder)?
- Do you have time to order special ingredients, or do you need to make the powder right away? If so, what ingredients can you substitute for those you do not have?
- Do you want to add a "signature" ingredient? Some magickal practitioners add a signature ingredient, something that encompasses their essence and melds the powder to their energy field or vibration. For example, I always add a little ground silver to all my powders, as that is my signature ingredient.
- Depending on the use of the powder, what moon phase, day, or planetary hour would be appropriate to make the powder?

- Do you wish to add the particular energies of a deity, totem animal, or element to the essence of the powder? If so, what correspondences go well with that deity, totem animal, element, or Spirit?

- Do you want to employ the energies of a magickal alphabet or the powers of the rune symbols to the activation of your powder? If so, will the rune spirits be comfy with any other energies you may wish to use?

Along with these decisions, you might want to write a specific charm or ritual designed for your magickal powder development and subsequent application.

A Ritual for Blending Magickal Powders

1. Set out the supplies you will need, including herbs, talc, correct candle color, mortar and pestle, storage container, a token offering to the elements of air and earth, a large bowl of water, and a clean hand towel. Have a list of those properties and energies you wish to instill in the powder handy—a small slip of paper or a 3x5 card will do just fine.

2. Banish all impurities from the water, then consecrate the water in the name of your chosen God or Goddess, Spirit, or divinity. Dip your hands in the water, and say:

I purify myself in the holy dew of the Goddess. I wash away all unclean spirits and energies. I welcome the fire of divinity into my soul.
I cast off illusions and bask in the purity of Spirit. I hold about me, like a luxurious cloak, the protection of angels so that no harm will come to me or to those I love. I am pure of heart, pure of spirit, pure of mind. So mote it be!

Dry your hands on the towel.

3. Devote the altar. If you have chosen a rune or other magickal symbol, place this image on your altar. Cleanse and consecrate all supplies in the name of your chosen divinity.

4. Cast your magick circle and call the quarters. You may call only east (air) and north (earth); or you may choose to open all four quarters. This is your decision. Here are the circle casting and quarter calls I use. If you have any questions on the appropriate visualization that accompanies this circle casting and quarter call, please refer to my book *Witches Runes* (formerly *The Rune Mysteries*). Say:

I cast the circle-hedge between the worlds;
be thou the girdle of the Goddess and a protection
against all ill spirits and negative energies.
As above, so below; this circle is sealed.

For the quarter call, I stand at the appropriate quarter and use my hands to open the quarter, saying:

Holy element of earth (air, fire, water).
Hallow this hedge in (name of deity's) *name!*

5. At this point, we need to invoke divinity and any other energies you may wish to use. You can write an invocation yourself, as I've mentioned previously, or you can use the standard one given here:

Through the world-hedge power flows hither,
Great Goddess, Mother of all, feminine light,
grant me Your enchantment, Maiden, Mother, Crone.
Great Lord, Father of all, leader of the Wild Host,
purveyor of the forest, Green Man, Horned Man, Sage.
Grant me Your strength and skill.
Magick I kindle; power I gain!

6. It is now acceptable to formulate a prayer that will name each of the ingredients and any other energies you wish to employ in the blending of the powder. This is where you need to know what the magickal properties of each element are (which you should know because you're using them, right?). If you are reading a formulary out of a book, check Cunningham's *Encyclopedia of Magical Herbs* to get this information beforehand. Say:

Gracious Lady, lend your hand of magick and direction to these
supplies before me: (Example) *Angelica for protection, ginger for*
monetary reward, cinquefoil for monetary success, parsley for
exponential energy, green talc for sympathy of money, wealth,
and abundance. So mote it be!

Gracious Lord, lend your hand of power and growth to these supplies
before me: (Repeat list) *Angelica for protection, ginger for*

> *monetary reward, cinquefoil for monetary success, parsley for*
> *exponential energy, green talc for sympathy of money, wealth,*
> *and abundance. So mote it be!*

As you utter your prayer, pass both of your hands over your supplies, envisioning the power and magick of the Lord and Lady traveling through your body, into your hands, and into the supplies.

7. Next, you need to acknowledge any other energies:

> *Witches' lair and spirit-wolf night; Ancient Ones bring second sight;*
> *Blood and bones of those before; help me with this little chore.*
> *Herbs and talc and natural things; at my bidding, magick bring.*
> *North for earth, and east for air; I summon Spirit to help me here.*

Once again, pass your hands over your supplies.

8. Cleanse, consecrate and empower the candle color that matches the intent of your powder. You may inscribe a spell on it, your intention, a magickal alphabet, or runes. Light the candle, hold it aloft, and say:

> *Element of fire, work my will by my desire.*

Set the candle down. Now is the time to mix together the ingredients, first stating your purpose, then adding each ingredient slowly, stirring in a clockwise direction for growth (deosil); counterclockwise (widdershins) for banishing energy. If you have chosen a magickal chant, you can incorporate it here, singing or simply humming. If you choose to add a signature ingredient, leave this one for last, then as you add this ingredient visualize yourself connecting with the powder.

9. When you have finished making the powder, sit quietly and hold the mixture in your hands. Chant or hum, bringing the energies of the mixture together, and visualize the full extent of the purpose of the mixture. Do this for at least five minutes.

10. If you have chosen runic energy to assist you, here is where you call that energy. Check the appropriate rune spirit in the appendix to aid in your visualization, and so that you know what you are calling. Chant the name of the rune until you can feel its energies enter the circle; you may even see the rune wights (a rune wight is the spirit energy represented by the rune). through a misty veil. This process may take up to five minutes. Then say:

> *Ye hallowed powers and wights of the rune _____.*
> *My word echoes forth to the heights of Asgard, the deeps of Hel,*
> *Resounding through the nine kingdoms. To the roots and crown of the*
> *world-ash, bearing forth my spell from the realm of the becoming into*
> *the daytide of being. For this is my will _____.*
> *I direct your power into this magickal powder, and at the appropriate*
> *time, when powder flies through the air, go forth, Great Spirits*
> *of the rune _____. That the Web of Wyrd be turned*
> *in accordance with my wish and will.*

11. Take your magickal powder and present it to the north quarter. Ask the energies of the north to bless the powder and lend it stability. Leave an offering in the north quarter. Move to the east quarter. Ask the energies of the east to bless the powder and instill the strength and action of the air element into the powder. Leave an offering in the east quarter. If you have opened the other quarters, or used elements of the other two quarters, then you need to move to and acknowledge those quarters as well.

12. Put the powder in a storage container until you are ready to use it.

13. Thank all energies you have called. Close the quarters:

> *Holy element of the north* (east, south, west),
> *thank you for assisting me in this ritual.*
> *Go if you must, stay if you like. Hail and farewell!*

14. Walking widdershins, close the circle (remember, some Craft practitioners take up their circles deosil) and draw the energy into the open container of powder. Seal the container. Allow the colored candle to burn out. If this is a powder to bring something to you, cut an orange in half and put it in a brown paper bag along with the candle end and a bit of the powder. If the powder is to banish, cut a lemon in half, add the candle end and a little bit of the powder, and bury off your property.

Here's a list of powders and associated talc colors that you may find helpful in your magickal applications. I've marked each herb's focus, as many herbals serve various magickal intents. Use this list as a guideline and have fun inventing your own powders or expanding the powders listed.

Angel Powder

Silver or blue candle. Blue talc. Lavender (peace and purification); sandalwood (protection and spirituality); angelica (protection and visions); orange peel (love); frankincense (protection and spirituality). Holy water or spring water for spraying.

This powder brings forth the essence of the angels, protects from evil spirits, and overcomes curses. Sprinkle about the altar, the threshold of any portal, door, or window. Burn in a thurible for general good luck and waft about the room with a feather. Load into a candle for invoking love and spiritual aid. Use the powder with a pink candle to attract friendship. Use in conjunction with a silver candle for angel messages. Best day to make: Sunday in the hours of the sun, the moon, Venus, or Mercury.

Anger Powder

Brown candle. Black talc. Chili powder (protection and exorcism); black pepper (protection and exorcism); sulfur (exorcism); asafoetida (protection and exorcism).

Sprinkle around room to overcome feelings of irritation and anger. Helps to avert future fights and will cleanse the mind of all evil thoughts. If you are uncomfortable about using sulfur, then substitute basil. This powder helps clear the head when you are experiencing negative emotions. You can substitute angelica for Asafoetida (as this herb smells horribly). I don't suggest burning this mixture in a thurible if you are using sulfur or asafoetida—both will smell awful for quite some time. The same for loading into a candle. Should you wish to load that candle, choose the basil and angelica for the mixture. Best day to make: Saturday in the hour of Saturn.

Atlantic City Powder

Red candle. Red or green talc. Patchouli (money); lemon peel (longevity); jasmine (money).

Use to banish a streak of even the worst luck. Sprinkle on your chair before you sit down to play games of chance. Added to an oil base, the mixture is very good for anointing talismans, seals, conjuring bags, playing cards, and so on. Best day to make: Sunday in the hour of Jupiter or Thursday in the hour of the sun.

Banishing Incense or Powder

Black candle. Black talc. Bay leaves (protection and strength); cinnamon (power); red wine (strength); rose petals (protection); myrrh (protection); mint (protection); salt (protection).

Allow mixture to fully dry before use. Sprinkle to eliminate all bad spirit forces. Should be burned in a thurible at your shrine or altar during magickal applications or during circle. Also used for uncrossing.[2] Best day to make: Saturday in the hour of Saturn.

Beneficial Dream Incense and Powder

Blue or purple candle. Blue or purple talc. Bergamot (overall success); lemon (purification); frankincense (spirituality); orris (divination); thyme (psychic dreams).

Burn to make all dreams come true, especially those helpful to the dreamer. Also helps in clairvoyance. Rub powder on the forehead and sprinkle under the bed for ultimate effectiveness. Best day to make: Monday in the hour of the moon or Sunday in the hour of the sun.

Blended Trust Powder

Orange candle. Orange talc. Powdered nutmeg (fidelity); orris (love); rose (love); patchouli (lust); basil (to put in sympathy).

A special blend used only to create an atmosphere of trust and understanding. Best day to make: Friday in the hour of Venus.

Cleansing Spirit Oil

White candle. Sandalwood (spirituality and exorcism); musk (love); myrrh (protection and spirituality); allspice (healing). Pimiento oil base.

Will cleanse the soul before calling on the good spirits. Will also protect against hexes. Use for dressing candles, talismans, spell boxes, et cetera. Best day to make: Sunday in the hour of the moon.

Commanding/Controlling/Compelling Powder

Brown candle. Brown talc. Allspice (healing); orris (protection and divination); patchouli (lust); cinnamon (power); sandalwood (wishes); clove (exorcism).

Use when working with rune wights, elementals, or earth spirits. Good for sprinkling in the path of stalkers, abusers, or general evil. Load into black candles to keep attackers at bay. Best day to make: Tuesday in the hour of Mars.

---

2. Uncrossing: When a situation is adverse, then the circumstances are considered "crossed." Remember, however, that what got crossed over a period of time isn't going to get uncrossed right away. Early American Witches used to say, "You didn't get sick in a day, so you're not going to get well in a day." Use magickal applications that build or link together when working with severely crossed energies.

Concentration

Silver or white candle. Silver talc. Mastic (psychic powers and manifestation); cinnamon (power); myrrh (spirituality).

Anoint forehead with small amount to aid in solving a problem. Clears the mind, inspires sudden insights into problems. Sprinkle on divination tool or load into your meditation candle. Best day to make: Monday in the hour of the moon.

Confusion

Black candle. Black talc. Vetivert (curse-breaking and anti-theft); lavender (protection); galangal (protection and curse-breaking). A burnt knotted shoelace.

Confuses those who are trying to cast a spell on you. Breaks all forms of curses. Acts almost instantaneously. Works better when curse is new, but good idea to keep some on hand for emergencies. Best day to make: Saturday in the hour of Mars or Saturn.

Courage Powder

Purple candle. Blue talc. Blue bottle. Vanilla (mental powers); rose (protection and psychic powers); lilac (protection); lavender (protection).

Used to give great amounts of courage to those who are fearful or timid. With an oil base, used to anoint purple candles and wear the oil when confronting frightening or dangerous situations. Best day to make: Sunday in the hour of Mars.

Double Fast Luck Incense, Powder, or Floorwash

Green candle. Green talc (do not put talc in floor wash). Patchouli (money); rose (luck); juniper berries (anti-theft). A ground-up dollar bill.

Sprinkle at your business, on the doorway into your home, around any home business furniture, or in your wallet, purse, or pocket to increase luck and success. Load into candles or put in conjuring bags for money magick. Best day to make: Thursday in the hour of Jupiter.

Dove's Blood Ink

1 part dragon's blood; 2 drops cinnamon; 2 drops bay; 10 parts alcohol; 1 part gum arabic; 2 drops rose oil.

Write with this ink to bring forth wishes.

Dove's Eye Incense

Red candle. Red talc. Red carnation petals; frankincense; vanilla; cardamom; marjoram.

Write with this ink to bring peace of mind and happiness.

Dove's Heart Incense and Powder

Pink candle. Pink talc. Lavender (love and happiness); rose (love); wisteria (love); lilac (protection).

Will calm restless souls and solve all problems of the heart. Soothes love feelings. A good spell link for individuals who are trying to kick a habit, change mental patterns, or who are under psychiatric care. Burn in a thurible to cleanse an area after a fight. Load into candles when you are working for someone's mental health or for an individual who is dealing with the cycle of grief. Best day to make: Friday in the hour of Venus.

Dragon's Blood Ink

1 part dragon's blood; 15 parts alcohol; 1 part arabic.

Gives extra power to any spell.

Dragon's Blood Oil

Use same ingredients as in Dragon's Blood Ink, except use oil instead of alcohol. Use only for uncrossing a cursed friend. Anoint the person, not candles. Works best at midnight in a cemetery.

Drawing Powder

Blue candle. Blue talc. Jasmine (money); violet (luck & wishes); lavender (happiness).

Rub on your hands and sprinkle around the altar before calling the spirits. Helps attract good luck and assistance in important matters. Assists in quieting the nerves as well. Best day to make: Thursday in the hour of the sun.

Easy Street

Green candle. Green and gold talc. Allspice (protection); cinquefoil (money); clove (money); (dill) money; ginger (money). Cut-up pieces of a dollar bill.

Rub on hands, sprinkle around business and home, and place in purse or wallet to draw monetary abundance. Best day to make: Thursday in the hour of Jupiter.

Easy Wrath Powder

Blue candle. Blue talc. Ashes; red pepper (curse-breaking); rose (luck and protection); jasmine (love); sandalwood (protection and exorcism); salt (banishing).

Toss on or near any person who is angry over something you have done to eliminate all feelings of animosity. Also good for overcoming hatred. Write the person's name who is angry with you (or your family member) on a piece of paper. Sprinkle powder on the paper, roll into a tight cylinder, and put into a plastic bag. Put in the freezer. Best day to make: Saturn in the hour of Mars or Saturn.

Envy & Jealousy Powder

White candle. Blue talc. Bayberry (divine love); vetivert (curse-breaking); sassafras (health); yarrow (courage and exorcism).

Eases feelings of jealousy when placed on the door of anyone you wish to gain confidence of. Use sparingly. Load in candles to break a pattern of envy and jealousy. Best day to make: Friday in the hour of Venus.

Eliminate Money Stress Powder

Purple candle. Purple talc. Vanilla (mental powers); peppermint (purification); cinnamon (spirituality); patchouli (money).

Rub on the body to attract love and gambling luck. Make a floorwash to sprinkle about the house to remove bad influences hindering success. Best day to make: Thursday in the hour of the sun, Mars, or Jupiter.

Fates Powder

Black candle. Black and gold talc. Black pepper (protection); dragon's blood (power); rosemary (protection); patchouli (spirituality).

This is an uncrossing powder used to overcome the power of a strong ouanga or curse. Said to be a very dependable powder that works quickly. Best day to make: Saturday in the hour of Saturn.

Fiery Passion

Red candle. Red and gold talc. Patchouli (lust); mandrake (lust); musk (lust).

Increases your sexuality. Sprinkle under bed or in a pocket of your clothing. Best day to make: Friday in the hour of Venus.

Flying Without a Broom

Orange candle. Blue or purple talc. Lemon peel (purification); frankincense (protection); myrrh (protection).

Sprinkle under the bed before you attempt astral travel, to aid in travel during your dream cycle, or to assist in deep meditation. Best day to make: Monday in the hour of the moon.

Four Thieves Vinegar

White candle. High John (success); vetivert (breaking curses); Adam and Eve (love); Lo-John (success) or black pepper base (curse-breaking); red wine vinegar (curse-breaking).

A very popular mixture that has seen many, many cycles of the seasons in folk magick. Allegedly, this blend drives enemies from your door. Best day to make: Saturday in the hour of Saturn or Mars.

French Creole Powder

Purple candle. Purple and silver talc. Lilac (protection); musk (power); bay (psychic power); lime (protection).

A special powder designed to make your dreams come true. Helps to interpret dreams prophetically. Make into a dream sachet to put under your pillow before sleeping. Best day to make: Sunday in the hour of the moon.

Friendship Powder #1

Red candle. Red talc. Myrrh (healing and spirituality); rose (love); lilac (protection).

Attracts many new friends. Used in glamouries to help you appear appealing to others. Very good for potential lovers. Use in love charms or conjuring bags. Load in candles before you go to a new school, new job, or other new encounter. Best day to make: Friday in the hour of Venus.

Friendship Powder #2

Red candle. Red talc. Footprint in dirt; patchouli leaves (fertility); cinnamon (love and success).

Increases magnetism. Pulls others to you and facilitates friendships to develop. Sprinkle around home, business, or in your locker at school. Best day to make: Friday in the hour of Venus.

Good Business Powder

Green candle. Green talc. Frankincense (exorcism and protection); tonka beans (money and wishes).

Burn in a thurible whenever business is bad. Said to bring luck and financial gain. Helps business and luck. Best day to make: Thursday in the hour of the sun or Jupiter.

Great Rite Powder

Blue candle. Blue talc. Sandalwood (wishes); sage (wishes); rose (love); orange peel (love); jasmine (love).

Burn or scatter in room where lovers are to meet, to please the good spirits and to increase sexual awareness. Wonderful for lovers and the Great Rite ceremony. Best day to make: Friday in the hour of Venus.

Health Powder

Yellow, blue, or natural candle. Green and blue talc. Rose (love); carnation (healing); citron (healing); gardenia (healing).

Used to anoint candles, talismans, or anything pertinent to healing rituals. Best day to make: Sunday in the hour of the sun.

Hecate's Powder

Black candle. Black talc. Iron filings or tiny nails; nightshade (protection); pinch of black horsehair or black cat hair.

Protects you from all bad spells. Sprinkle on the altar before conducting Z. Budapest's "Send Him A Nightmare" spell. Also place a little on the floor. Excellent for use against stalkers, abusers, and criminals. Best made: Saturday in the hour of Saturn.

Herb Powder

Green candle. Green talc. Basil (sympathy); oregano (protection); sage (longevity); thyme (healing); lemon (longevity).

Brings good luck in gambling and will increase the memory of anyone who burns it. Also commonly used as health powder. Use in poppets or hollow out a small portion of a potato, pour in the powder, place in a slip of paper with the sick person's name, close the potato back up, and bury in the yard, saying:

As this potato rots, the disease will leave (name).

Best day to make: If used for banishing, Saturday in the hour of Saturn. If made for healing, Sunday in the hour of the sun.

High Conquering

Red candle. Green and red talc. Hi-John (money, love, success, and happiness); vetivert (love, luck and curse-breaking); bergamot (money).

A very powerful means of attracting wealth, prestige, love, and health. Use generously for desired change. Fast action mixture. One of the best oils or powders for good works. Best day to make: Thursday in the hour of Jupiter.

Holy Oil

Candle oil base; lily oil; rose oil; pentacle in a bottle.

A special oil used only for blessing candles before magickal ceremonies. Very attracting. Best day to make: Monday in the hour of Mercury.

Holy Spirit Powder

White candle. White talc. Lily of the Valley (happiness); lemon (spirituality); silver glitter.

Sprinkle on the altar, at the quarters, or during ritual. With oil, used only for dressing candles. Sprinkle liberally. Attracts good spirit forces. Brings out clairvoyant powers. Best day to make: Monday in the hour of Mercury.

Horned Lord Powder

Red candle. Red talc. Cinnamon (success); red sandalwood (male spirituality and protection); chili powder (protection); bayberry (strength).

Use to dust your hands carefully for temporarily blinding all opponents. Stops others from interfering in your personal business. Calls the hounds of the Wild Hunt in appropriate ritual setting. Best day to make: Tuesday in the hour of Mars.

House Blessing Mixture

White candle. Silver and green talc. Orange peel (love, luck, and money); vanilla (love and mental agility); strawberry (love and luck); basil (sympathy).

Sprinkle liberally around a room. Changes luck and reverses unfortunate circumstances. Good to eliminate poverty. Best day to make: Thursday in the hour of Jupiter.

House Protection Powder

Red candle. Dragon's blood (power); angelica (protection); salt; red glitter.

Sprinkle all around your home. No one will be able to cast a spell on you. Prevents hexing from ever taking place. Reverses the effect of evil things. Best day to make: Monday in the hour of the moon.

Job Protection Powder

Red candle. Red talc. Musk (power); chili powder (strength); tobacco (protection); pulverized newsprint.

Sprinkle around the boss' office at work and around your own area on the job. Forces your supervisor to leave you alone. Stops harassment. Also to be used in private life to cause one to receive kindness and consideration. Best day to make: Thursday in the hour of Jupiter.

Jungle Powder

Red candle. Red and gold talc. Cinnamon (success); Hi-John (protection); white sandalwood (protection).

Used to avert curses. Use sparingly. Load in candles to banish stalkers and avert negativity. Not for novices. Best day to make: Tuesday in the hour of Mars.

Ladies' Enchantment

Purple candle. Purple talc. Vanilla (love and mental agility); rose (love); jasmine (money); piece of coral; gold glitter.

A favorite among ladies to increase and ensure financial gain. Best day to make: Monday in the hour of the moon.

Legal Assistance Powder

Black candle. Black talc. Hi-John (protection); Lo-John (protection); clove (protection); sage (protection and wisdom); rosemary (protection); pipe tobacco (purification).

Very powerful in spellworking to burn in a thurible along with a black candle and salt. Sprinkle in your shoes before a court appearance. Use only to win court cases and to overcome legal entanglements. Best day to make: Tuesday in the hour of Mars.

Magnetism Powder

Blue candle. Blue talc. Sixteen parts wood base; 8 parts frankincense (protection); 4 parts sandalwood (wishes); 2 parts myrrh (healing); 4 parts cinnamon (power and success); 2 parts orris root (love).

Highly magnetic blend used to draw good spirits. Attracts love, power, luck, love, and money. Use before an important contract signing, interview, when buying a car, et cetera. Excellent for loading into success spell candles. Best day to make: Sunday in the hour of the sun.

Meditation Powder

Purple candle. Purple talc. Lavender (peace); cinnamon (spirituality).

Aids in developing concentration and creativity. Always use when preparing to meditate. Burn in thurible in the room before you meditate. Sprinkle in your meditation chair. Best day to make: Monday in the hour of the moon or Venus.

Money/Success Powder

White candle. Silver talc. Patchouli (money and fertility); cinnamon (success); vervain (money).

A good loading powder said to magnetize the candle. Added to an oil, use mixture to bless candles before a ceremony. Added to holy water and alcohol, use the mixture to wipe down an altar room. Sprinkle in your wallet. Best day to make: Thursday in the hour of Jupiter.

Pow-Wow Gretchyn

Orange candle. Rose; gardenia; large open safety pin; smaller safety pins; glass beads (optional).

Another popular blend. Added to a base oil, wonderful mixture to bring luck and good fortune to believers. Sprinkle powder liberally when feeling depressed. Mix safety pins and beads in powder. String small safety pins and beads on the large safety pin. Wear on your left shoulder to deflect harmful energies. Best day to make: Saturday in the hour of Saturn.

Protective Wall Powder

Red candle. Black talc. Dragon's blood (protection); frankincense (protection); myrrh (protection); salt (protection).

Helps to protect the user against any magickal attack or unexpected rebound. Restrains anyone from placing an evil curse on you. Sprinkle round a room to help ward off curses. Place by all windows and doors. Load in candles to use in protection spells. Load in a white candle and place outside of your house to keep people off of your property. Best day to make: Saturday in the hour of Saturn.

Psychic Awareness Powder

White candle. Silver or purple talc. Honeysuckle (psychic power); rose (psychic power); geranium (protection).

Helps to increase your natural clairvoyance. Some say that the use of this powder helps to open communication between yourself and Spirit, allowing positive vibrations to work with you. Sprinkle under your bed, put in a sachet under your pillow, or burn in thurible in your bedroom before you go to sleep or before you employ a divination tool. Sprinkle in the box or bag where you keep your divination tools. Place on your chair before reading for clients. Best day to make: Monday in the hour of the moon.

Psychic Dream Powder

White candle. Light blue talc. Musk (power); orris (divination); ambergris (psychic power); peppermint (psychic power); lavender (sleep).

Increases psychic powers and helps you to recall dreams in their entirety. Works very well in a loaded candle. Also, a pleasant side line: Exposes deceitful people who are working against you. Best day to make: Monday in the hour of the moon.

Return to Sender Powder

Yellow candle. Yellow talc. Rose (protection); frankincense (protection); vetivert (curse-breaking); honeysuckle (protection); angelica (curse-breaking); thistle (curse-breaking).

Used to break hexes or to order evil spirits to return to their sender. Load into candles when performing magick to catch criminals, to stop abuse, or return negative energies sent to you. Best day to make: Saturday during the hour of Saturn.

Sacred Ashes

White candle. Silver talc. White parchment paper; cinnamon; sandalwood; African Violet (all for spirituality).

Burn the white parchment paper in a bowl. Crush the ashes. Add the herbs. Mix well. Store in an airtight container. Use to anoint before a funeral, at Samhain, or on Ash Wednesday. Best day to make: Sunday in the hour of the moon.

Stalker Powder

Black Candle (with arrowhead on it). Black talc. Asafoetida (exorcism); chili powder (exorcism); nettle (to move away); mistletoe (hunting and exorcism); nightshade (exorcism); and a pinch of sulfur.

Sprinkle in the path of anyone you wish to stop bothering you. Also place on your window ledges and front doorstep. Turns people away on contact with the air. Best day to make: Saturday in the hour of Saturn.

Sweet Marriage Powder

Yellow candle. Yellow talc. Vanilla (love); wintergreen (healing, curse-breaking); vetivert (love, anti-theft, curse-breaking); narcissus (love); myrtle (love); basil (in sympathy); white sugar (harmony).

Brings harmony to a stormy marriage. Sprinkle under the bed or in any room where arguments take place often. Burn in a thurible in the bedroom at night when retiring. Gives peace of mind. Add to an oil to anoint white candles. Best day to make: Friday in the hour of the sun or Venus.

Sweet Spirit Powder

White candle. Purple talc. Cinnamon; tonka bean; patchouli; vanilla; lavender; gardenia; vetivert.

Designed to attract all good spirits to its user and assists in bringing forth psychic power. Use both on body (by adding a small amount of oil) and on altar. Add to incense or burn, as is, in a thurible to cleanse a room. Mix with holy water or oil to anoint candles. Place in a sachet and put among your ritual clothing. Best day to make: Sunday in the hour of the moon, Monday in the hour of the moon, or Wednesday in the hour of the moon.

Success Powder

Gold candle. Gold talc. Orris root (protectant of success and drawing power); frankincense (luck); vetivert (luck and money), sandalwood (wishes); gag root (career success); gold glitter.

Helps push aside those who hinder your rise upward to success. Stops gossip and evil talk. Load into a candle when casting a spell for a raise, better employment, or a better employment atmosphere. Works well in money spells. Best day to make: Thursday in the hour of Jupiter.

If you can't get some of the herbs listed, consider the grocery store for substitutions or make your own blends. Many supermarkets contain floral areas, too. If you wish to make magickal powders from fresh items, you'll have to cut very small pieces and let them dry. Work with a hand grater for many fruits and vegetables. Lay the pieces on paper towels and allow to dry. Change the towels as necessary. Tie items such as coriander, parsley, and other leafy plants together in small bunches and hang on a dowel rod attached to the kitchen wall with inexpensive ceramic cup holders. I did this for years. My father hangs his herbs from the rafters in the attic. Although some magickal individuals use a microwave to dry their herbs, I can't quite bring myself to do that, because I'm not sure if the waving process destroys the magickal properties of the herbs. I have used the microwave to banish the effects of an incident I did not create. I put the situation on a piece of paper, sprinkled herbs in the center, rolled the paper, and nuked it for 57 seconds (the number $57 = 5+7 = 12 = 1+2 = 3$). Poof! No more problems.

I'm sure you will find other substances that you may wish to combine with oils and powders, or use separately. I can think of four, including salt, brown sugar, refined sugar, and honey, as well as the famous Florida Waters. In Pow-Wow magick, one pours salt in the path of an enemy, in their footprints, or better yet, on their underwear (No kidding). Honey, brown and refined sugar make excellent ingredients for sweetening a situation. You can also mold brown sugar and various herbs together for a healing poppet.

Use floor washes, or Florida Waters, to banish unwanted energies in a house or place of business, and to dedicate any number of tools or objects to divinity; in essence, washes attract or dispel various energies. Many homes these days contain wall to wall carpet. Don't feel bashful about putting that Florida Water in a spray bottle to employ this useful magickal practice. Test a corner of your carpet just to be sure that your mixture won't stain the carpet.

Florida Water #1

1 gallon 90 proof alcohol; 1 dram lemon; 1 dram portugal; 2 drams lavender; 2 drams clove; ⅛ dram cinnamon; 1 pint water.

Florida Water #2

½ gallon 90 proof alcohol; 1 ounce lavender; 1 ounce bergamot; 1 dram lemon; 1 dram cloves; 1 gallon water.

Florida Water #3

1 gallon 75 proof alcohol, 3 ounces bergamot; 4 ounces cinnamon; 2 ounces benzoin.

Florida Water #4

2 drams lavender; 2 drams bergamot; 2 drams lemon; 1 dram tincture of turmeric; 20 drops Oil of Palm; 10 drops Oil of Rose; 1 dram naroli; 2 parts 75 proof alcohol.

Proportionally reduce these formulas to suit your needs and requirements. Here's a simple conversion chart for your formularies:

⅛ fluid ounce = 1 dram = ½ teaspoon + ⅛ teaspoon
¼ fluid ounce = 2 drams = ½ tablespoon
½ fluid ounce = 4 drams = 1 tablespoon

Bibliography

Andrews, Ted. *Animal Speak*. Llewellyn Publications, 1993.

Bogen, Nancy. *How To Write Poetry*. Macmillan, 1994.

Buckland, Ray. *Advanced Candle Magick*. Llewellyn Publications, 1996.

Cunningham, Scott. *Encyclopedia of Magickal Herbs*. Llewellyn Publications, 1985.

Davis, Audrey Craft. *Metaphysical Techniques That Really Work*. Sun Valley Publishing, 1996.

Denise Linn. *Sacred Space, Gathering and Enhancing the Energy of Your Home*. Ballantine Books, 1995.

Hadley, Josie. *Hypnosis For Change*. Self-Published, 1985.

Hansen, Daniel. *American Druidism*. Peanut Butter Publishing, 1995.

Hewitt, William W. *Hypnosis*. Llewellyn Publications, 1986.

Hugin The Bard. *A Bard's Book of Pagan Songs*. Llewellyn Publications, 1997.

Kraig, Donald Michael. *Modern Magick*. Llewellyn Publications, 1990.

Laurie, Erynn Rowan. *A Circle of Stones, Meditations for Modern Celts*. Eschaton, 1995.

Lip, Evelyn. *Feng Shui A Layman's Guide*. Heian International, 1987.

———. *Feng Shui For Business*. Heian International, 1990.

———. *Feng Shui for the Home*. Heian International, 1990.

Malbrough, Ray. *Charms, Spells, & Formulas*. Llewellyn Publications, 1986.

Matthews, Caitlin. *Celtic Devotional Daily Prayers & Blessings*. Harmony Books, 1996.

Obatala, El. *Creative Ritual*. Weiser, 1996.

Pajeon, Kala & Ketz. *The Candle Magick Workbook*. Citadel Press, 1995.

RavenWolf, Silver. *To Stir A Magick Cauldron*. Llewellyn Publications, 1995.

———. *To Ride A Silver Broomstick*. Llewellyn Publications, 1993.

Bibliography

Slater, Herman. *Magickal Formulary Spellbook*. Magickal Childe, Inc., (no date).

———. *The Magickal Formulary*. Magickal Childe, Inc., 1981.

Thompson, Janet. *Magical Hearth—Home for the Modern Pagan*. Weiser, 1995.

Valiente, Doreen. *Witchcraft For Tomorrow*. Phoenix, 1978.

Victor C. Klein. *New Orleans Ghosts*. Professional Press, 1993.

Webster, Richard. *Feng Shui for Beginners*. Llewellyn Publications, 1997.

Wood, Clement. *The Complete Rhyming Dictionary*. Laural/Dell, 1991.

Index

Index

Index

Index

Index

☽ REACH FOR THE MOON

To Ride a Silver Broomstick
New Generation WitchCraft

SILVER RAVENWOLF

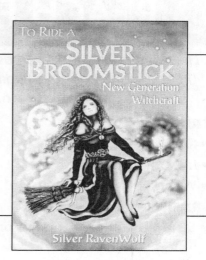

Throughout the world there is a new generation of Witches—people practicing or wishing to practice the craft on their own, without an in-the-flesh magickal support group. *To Ride a Silver Broomstick* speaks to those people, presenting them with both the science and religion of WitchCraft, allowing them to become active participants while growing at their own pace. It is ideal for anyone: male or female, young or old, those familiar with WitchCraft, and those totally new to the subject and unsure of how to get started.

Full of the author's warmth, humor and personal anecdotes, *To Ride a Silver Broomstick* leads you step-by-step through the various lessons with exercises and journal writing assignments. This is the complete WitchCraft 101, teaching you to celebrate the Sabbats, deal with coming out of the broom closet, choose a magickal name, visualize the Goddess and God, meditate, design a sacred space, acquire magickal tools, design and perform rituals, network, spell cast, perform color and candle magick, divination, healing, telepathy, psychometry, astral projection, and much, much more.

0-87542-791-X
320 pp., 7 x 10, illus., softcover $14.95

To Stir a Magick Cauldron
A Witch's Guide to Casting and Conjuring

Silver RavenWolf

The sequel to the enormously popular *To Ride a Silver Broomstick: New Generation Witchcraft*. This upbeat and down-to-earth guide to intermediate-level witchery was written for all Witches—solitaries, eclectics, and traditionalists. In her warm, straight-from-the-hip, eminently knowledgeable manner, Silver provides explanations, techniques, exercises, anecdotes, and guidance on traditional and modern aspects of the Craft, both as a science and as a religion.

Find out why you should practice daily devotions and how to create a sacred space. Learn six ways to cast a magick circle. Explore the complete art of spell-casting. Examine the hows and whys of Craft laws, oaths, degrees, lineage, traditions, and more. Explore the ten paths of power, and harness this wisdom for your own spell-craft. This book offers you dozens of techniques—some never before published—to help you uncover the benefits of natural magick and ritual and make them work for you—without spending a dime!

Silver is a "working Witch" who has successfully used each and every technique and spell in this book. By the time you have done the exercises in each chapter, you will be well-trained in the first level of initiate studies. Test your knowledge with the Wicca 101 test provided at the back of the book and become a certified Witch! Learn to live life to its fullest through this positive spiritual path.

1-56718-424-3

288 pp., 7 x 10, illus., softcover $16.95

American Folk Magick

Charms, Spells & Herbals
(formerly titled *HexCraft:*
Dutch Country Pow-Wow Magick)

SILVER RAVENWOLF

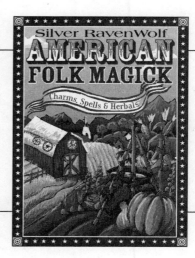

The roots of American Witchcraft can be found in a seventeenth century settler tradition comprising a variety of cultural and religious influences. Today Pennsylvania Dutch Country Pow-Wow Magick has virtually disappeared, but a few people remain to tell the real story of life in early America. Now, the history and growth of this tradition is brought to life. *American Folk Magick* revives the chants, charms, spells and healing methods of a vital heritage that offered New World inhabitants spiritual respite, magickal living, and political cover from reigning puritanical forces. For anyone interested in early America, magick, spirituality, or freedom of speech!

1-56718-720-X
320 pp., 7 x 10, softcover $14.95

Angels
Companions in Magick

SILVER RAVENWOLF

Angels do exist. These powerful forces of the Universe flow through human history, riding the currents of our pain and glory. You can call on these beings of the divine for increased knowledge, love, patience, health, wisdom, happiness and spiritual fulfillment. Always close to those in need, they bring peace and prosperity into our lives.

Here, in this complete text, you will find practical information on how to invite these angelic beings into your life. Build an angelic altar . . . meet the archangels in meditation . . . contact your guardian angel . . . create angel sigils and talismans . . . work magick with the Angelic Rosary . . . talk to the deceased. You will learn to work with angels to gain personal insights and assist in the healing of the planet as well as yourself.

Angels do not belong to any particular religious structure—they are universal and open their arms to humans of all faiths, bringing love and power into people's lives.

1–56718–724–2
288 pp., 7 x 10, illus., softcover $17.95

Teen Witch
Wicca for a New Generation

SILVER RAVENWOLF

Teenagers and young adults comprise a growing market for books on WitchCraft and magick, yet there has never been a book written specifically for the teen seeker. Now, Silver RavenWolf, one of the most well-known Wiccans today and the mother of four young Witches, gives teens their own handbook on what it takes and what it means to be a Witch. Humorous and compassionate, *Teen Witch* gives practical advice for dealing with everyday life in a magickal way. From homework and crabby teachers to parents and dating, this book guides teens through the ups and downs of life as they move into adulthood. Spells are provided that address their specific concerns, such as the "Call Me Spell" and "The Exam Spell."

Parents will also find this book informative and useful as a discussion tool with their children. Discover the beliefs of WitchCraft, Wiccan traditions, symbols, holidays, rituals and more.

1-56718-725-0
288 pp., 7 x 10, softcover $12.95

Beneath a Mountain Moon
A Novel by

SILVER RAVENWOLF

Welcome to Whiskey Springs, Pennsylvania, birthplace of magick, mayhem, and murder! The generations-old battle between two powerful occult families rages anew when young Elizabeyta Belladonna journeys from Oklahoma to the small town of Whiskey Springs—a place her family had left years before to escape the predatory Blackthorn family—to solve the mystery of her grandmother's death.

Endowed with her own magickal heritage of Scotch-Irish Witchcraft, Elizabeyta stands alone against the dark powers and twisted desires of Jason Blackthorn and his gang of Dark Men. But Elizabeyta isn't the only one pursued by unseen forces and the fallout from a past life. As Blackthorn manipulates the town's inhabitants through occult means, a great battle for mastery ensues between the forces of darkness and light—a battle that involves a crackpot preacher, a blue ghost, the town gossip, and an old country healer—and the local funeral parlor begins to overflow with victims. Is there anyone who can end the Blackthorns' reign of terror and right the cosmic balance?

1-56718-722-6
360 pp., 6 x 9, softcover

$15.95

Charms, Spells & Formulas

For the Making and Use of Gris Gris Bags, Herb Candles, Doll Magic, Incenses, Oils and Powders

RAY MALBROUGH

Hoodoo magick is a blend of European techniques and the magick brought to the New World by slaves from Africa. Now you can learn the methods which have been used successfully by Hoodoo practitioners for nearly 200 years.

By using the simple materials available in nature, you can bring about the necessary changes to greatly benefit your life and that of your friends. You are given detailed instructions for making and using the "gris-gris" (charm) bags only casually or mysteriously mentioned by other writers. Malbrough not only shows how to make gris-gris bags for health, money, luck, love and protection from evil and harm, but he also explains how these charms work. He also takes you into the world of doll magick to gain love, success, or prosperity. Complete instructions are given for making the dolls and setting up the ritual.

0-87542-501-1
192 pp., 5¼ x 8, illus., softcover $6.95

To order, call 1-800 THE MOON
Prices subject to change without notice